The
New
Complete
Great Pyrenees

"As you look in those eyes, the immense moral
value of the breed pierces your soul."

Ch. Quibbletown Boleros Ravel

Shafer photo

The
New
Complete
Great Pyrenees

PAUL STRANG

HOWELL
BOOK HOUSE

New York

Macmillan General Reference
A Simon & Schuster Macmillan Company
1633 Broadway
New York, NY 10019-6785

Library of Congress Cataloging-in-Publication Data

Strang, Paul D.
   The new complete great pyrenees / Paul Strang.
       p. cm.
   1. Great Pyrenees. I. Title.
SF429.G75S79   1991
636.7'3—dc20   91-11647   CIP
ISBN 0-87605-188-3

10 9 8 7 6

Printed in the United States of America

With love to my wife,
Edith Strang

In the Pyrenees—by Rosa Bonheur (1822–1899).

The Pyrenean Sheepdog, by Maude Earl, painted in 1901.

Courtesy, Mrs. C. Seaver Smith, Jr.

The Shepherd Dog of the Pyrenees

Ellen Murray

When day at last
Broke, and the grey fog lifted, there
I saw
On that ledge, against the dawning light,
My little one asleep, sitting so near
That edge that as I looked his red
barret
Fell from his nodding head down the
abyss.
And there, behind him, crouched Pierrot:
his teeth
His good, strong teeth, clenching the
jacket brown,
Holding the child in safety. With wild
bounds
Swift as the grey wolf's own I climbed
the steep
And as I reached them Pierrot beat his
tail,
And looked at me so utterly dis-
tressed,
With eyes that said: "Forgive, I could
not speak."
But never loosed his hold till my dear
rogue
Was safe within my arms.

Ch. Basquaerie Bibelot, owned by Mary W. A. Crane.

Contents

The Author   *xi*

Foreword   *xiii*

1   The Origin of the Great Pyrenees   *1*

2   Development of the Breed in France   *15*

3   Basquaerie Kennels—The Great Pyrenees Comes to America
    by Mary W. A. Crane   *31*

4   Early American Bloodlines   *47*

5   The Great Pyrenees Standards Now and Then   *57*

6   An In-Depth Look at the Standard   *73*

7   The Character of the Great Pyrenees   *85*

8   The Great Pyrenees: A Worker for All Reasons   *95*

9	The Modern Great Pyrenees in America	*115*
10	The Great Pyrenees in Canada	*157*
11	The Modern Pyrenean Mountain Dog in France	*171*
12	Pyrenean Mountain Dogs in Great Britain *by Joyce Stannard*	*179*
13	The Breed Around the World	*191*
14	Proper Care of the Great Pyrenees	*205*
15	Health Problems *by Robert Brown, D.V.M., and Patricia Princehouse*	*215*
16	Showing Your Great Pyrenees *by Mary W. A. Crane*	*223*
17	Breeding the Great Pyrenees	*233*
18	Spinning the Pyrenees Hair *by Zatha Hockridge and Constance Kousman*	*247*
19	The Great Pyrenees Club of America	*251*

The Author

PAUL D. STRANG'S intimate association with the Great Pyrenees spans more than sixty years. As a student in Paris after World War I, Paul became enchanted with the breed's nobility and breathtaking beauty. He bought his first Great Pyrenees from a mountaineer in the Pyrenees. His career as a linguist and correspondent led him to a life on the French Riviera where he found ample opportunity to add to his growing knowledge and expertise on weekend trips to dog shows and visits to breeders.

In the 1930s Paul and his wife, Edith, returned to the United States and occupied the family residence, High Windham, in Bluemont, Virginia. Here they bred Great Pyrenees under the prefix Castellan.

In 1972 Paul Strang and Sonya Larsen joined forces to edit and publish the popular magazine *the International Great Pyrenees Review*, widely read by Great Pyrenees fanciers in the United States and overseas. In 1977 he and James Giffin wrote the first edition of the award-winning book *The Complete Great Pyrenees*. Paul founded Medea Publishing in 1981. Medea now boasts a series of puppy and rare breed books. Four of the books concern the Chinese Shar-Pei. Mr. Strang studied the Shar-Pei in China and Macao in the 1970s, ultimately importing several top quality specimens of the breed.

Mr. Strang was one of the earliest members of the Great Pyrenees Club of America. He is the acknowledged English-speaking authority on the origin and development of the breed in France. He is a member of the Senior Conformation Judges Association, and has judged Great Pyrenees in many countries on four continents.

Mrs. Francis V. Crane with eight of Basquaerie's outstanding brood bitches. From left to right: Ch. Rhune du Pic du Jer, Ch. Pastoure d'Arros, Ch. Bigorre du Pic du Jer, Ch. Gerita, Ch. Basquaerie Nana, Ch. Arizes de Soum, Ch. Munia du Pic du Jer; and lying in front, Ch. Koranne of Basquaerie, CD. One of the most important arrays of brood bitches ever assembled.

Foreword

THE GREAT Pyrenees possesses breathtaking beauty, a marvelous disposition and a calm, stately bearing. An outstanding livestock guardian, the breed is also a wonderful companion for town or country.

Developed in France over millennia, today the breed flourishes there, in the United States, Canada, Great Britain, Australia, New Zealand, South Africa—indeed from Europe to Japan, from the South Seas to the Arctic Circle. It would be difficult to find any place on the seven continents where the Great Pyrenees is not known and loved. Great Pyrenees fans adore their big, gentle, white friends such that they overlook shedding, drooling, barking and the Pyr's tendency not to come when called.

Bernard Senac-Lagrange, founder of the original Pyrenees club at the turn of the century, valued expression as the breed's most defining characteristic. He wrote: "Only the true breed possesses this bewitching, almost indefinable expression in the eyes, both distant and caressing, contemplative and just a little sad. As you look in these eyes, the immense moral value of the breed pierces your soul."

Marjorie Butcher, whose Cote de Neige Pyrenees played such a vital role in establishing the breed in the United States, often spoke of her joy at hearing the deep sonorous bark: "That rumbling voice sounds like a lion's roar to the unwelcome stranger, but it turns to something more like a kitten's purr at the master's fireside."

Forty years ago, Mrs. Bruce Laymen of La Shan Kennels wrote, "No story of the Great Dog of the Mountains would be complete without a word about the puppyhood stage, for it is here that many of us make our first acquaintance with these dogs. As puppies, the Great Pyrenees are irresistible balls of white fluff, with small beady eyes that combine mischief with understanding, trust and adoration. They are loveable clowns and adorable in every way."

In the pages of this book, readers will be treated to an authentic and factual account of the Great Pyrenees—history, traditions and promise for the future. Perhaps you, the reader, are already a devoted fancier and need no further incentive to inspire your confidence and enthusiasm. In any case, it is hoped that these pages will give you something of the past and present glories of owning, or being owned by, one of these splendid creatures. And in so doing, pass it along to the next generation.

This book would not have been possible without the wonderful co-operation of many truly dedicated and unselfish Great Pyrenees fanciers. The late Mrs. Francis V. Crane enthusiastically supported the first edition of this book, and her contributions remain equally important to this, the second edition.

Devoted Great Pyrenees fanciers from around the world trusted us with irreplaceable photographs of great dogs of the past and present, and contributed their knowledge, expertise and advice to making this new edition of *The New Complete Great Pyrenees* a worthy and important addition to the Great Pyrenees literature.

A special expression of gratitude must go to Patricia Princehouse who contributed greatly to all aspects of this book, giving unsparingly of her time to assure that the second edition was as accurate and comprehensive as the first.

We are indebted to Robert Brown, D.V.M., for his chapter on special health problems, and to Mrs. Bridget Olerenshaw who drew the sketches for this book. We would also like to express our thanks to Jean Boyd, Judith Bankus Cooper, Michael Floyd, Lynne Gomm, Frances Princehouse, Anne Rappaport and Linda Weisser.

To these and the many other friends who have contributed through correspondence, pedigrees and pictures, we wish to express our sincere gratitude.

The
New
Complete
Great Pyrenees

Tibetan Mastiff, Ts'ang Ni Ch'uan, painted by Lang Shih-ning, circa 1740. National Palace Museum, Taipei, Taiwan, ROC.

1

The Origin of
the Great Pyrenees

THE GREAT PYRENEES takes its name from the Pyrenees Mountain range between France and Spain. Here for centuries the dog served not only as the shepherd's chief ally in defending the flocks from wolves and bears, but also as a valued sentry for the châteaux of the area—ever vigilant to sound the alarm in case of enemy attack.

In its native France it is known as *Le Grand Chien de Montagne*, the Great Mountain Dog of the Pyrenees. To say it is great is to refer not only to its size, but also to distinguish it from the other shepherd's dog of the Pyrenees, *Le Petit Berger*, or the little shepherd, that drives and herds the sheep. As the Petit Berger is becoming known outside its native haunts it is well to keep the difference between the two breeds in mind.

Most pedigrees of Pyreneans with a mountain background show a confusing number of dogs called Patou and bitches called Pastoure. These historic Gallo-Roman names, meaning the Shepherd and the Shepherdess, are part of the breed's ancestral heritage. To the mountain breeder they denote more fittingly than any other names the breed's unique supremacy for its age-old task. And so wherever Pyreneans are bred we find the names Patou and Pastoure often given in recognition of this link with the past.

In Great Britain and in other countries closely affiliated with the British Kennel Club such as Australia, New Zealand, and South Africa, our Pyrenean is called the *Pyrenean Mountain Dog*. The British Standard for the breed is quite similar to our American Standard, and neither differs, in essence, from the French Standard. So whether we call it the Great Pyrenees, the Pyrenean Mountain Dog or the Patou we are talking about the same majestic, white-furred aristocrat. An aristocrat that at the end of the nineteenth century was thought to have passed from the scene—but in the twentieth century has won the hearts of the canine world!

This increased popularity of the breed has sparked new interest and debate over its origins. Although its presence in the Pyrenees Mountains is documented as far back as Roman days, it is believed that its original home was elsewhere. Two theories have been developed. One is that the breed is a descendant of the Tibetan Mastiff. The other claims that his antecedents were the dogs of the ancient Sumerians.

THE TIBETAN MASTIFF AS POSSIBLE ANCESTOR

Robert Leighton in *The New Book of the Dog* (1911) points out that in spite of the fact that the Tibetan Mastiff is usually black, black-and-tan or red, while our Pyrenean is mainly white, the two breeds do have much in common. He writes, "But for the difference in color, the Pyrenean bears considerable resemblance to the Mastiff of Tibet. Somewhat higher on the leg and perhaps less muscular, it has the same massive body, the same character and texture of coat, and the same form of head. The shape of the skull is precisely similar; so is the carriage of the ear, the set of the eye, and the form of the muzzle." And, he concludes, both are used for protecting rather than herding the sheep.

D. H. Mut and von Stephanitz, both German authorities, and M. B. Senac-Lagrange, the French Pyrenean master, all subscribe to the thesis that this Tibetan dog was the ancestor not only of the Pyrenean but also of the other large, mostly white, pastoral guard dogs of Europe and the Near East.

According to this theory, as the nomadic tribesmen of distant Asia migrated westward thousands of years ago, they were accompanied by their flocks and their dogs. The more intrepid pushed on to the Atlantic Coast and some must have settled in the Pyrenees. Others stopped along the way. And in each region where these tribes put down their roots, a new breed of flock-guarding mastiffs developed—all fathered by the original dog from Asia.

With the passing of the years, this legend of the assumed Tibetan origin of our Pyrenean and the other sheep-guarding breeds came to be regarded as fact. A warning by von Stephanitz that the theory was based on assumptions and conjecture was nearly forgotten. But in some minds, nagging suspicions lingered. The question was, by what alchemy had the black dogs of Tibet been turned into the white shepherd dogs of Europe and the Near East?

2

Sir William Ingram's Tibetan Mastiff Bhotean, imported to England in 1906, as pictured by Robert Leighton in *The New Book of the Dog*.

Pyrenean Mountain Dog, painted by Nina Scott Langley for *Hutchinson's Dog Encyclopedia*.

La Chasse Aux Loups, depicting two Great Pyrenees fighting a wolf. Painted by Jean-Baptiste Oudrey, the famous French animal painter, 1686-1775.

Courtesy, Mrs. Francis V. Crane

4

One answer was given by C. Duconte and M. Sabouraud in *Les Chiens Pyrénéens* (1970). These French authors maintain that environmental and climatic changes may well have brought about the color paling over the years, a trend which they believe is still in operation. For evidence, they point to engravings at the Château de Lourdes, made at the end of the last century, which show specimens having brown heads and areas of dark coloring on the body. The fact that our dogs have less coloring today is offered as proof of a gradual whitening of the breed.

But Columella, the Roman agricultural historian, in a work entitled *De Re Rustica* published in the second century A.D., tells us that, "Sheep-herders insist on white guard dogs for their flocks, for otherwise a dog could be struck during an attack through being mistaken for a wolf." So it appears that white sheep-guarding dogs have been known for nearly two thousand years! Any theory of gradual paling is put to doubt, to say the least.

THE KU ASSA

Still another blow to the theory of the Tibetan Mastiff origin of our breed is to be found in the recent emergence of a new contender for the honor. This is the Ku Assa, a pastoral guard dog of the ancient Sumerians. The Sumerian civilization began in the fertile Mesopotamian basin between the Tigris and Euphrates rivers in Asia Minor.

"The Ku Assa Story," written by the Hungarian Dr. S. Palfalvy and translated by Dr. Edmond S. Bordeaux, appeared in the *Kuvasz Newsletter* in 1967. In 1974 Dr. Bordeaux published his book, *Messengers from Ancient Civilizations*, which gave further particulars. By deciphering cuneiform writing on clay tablets unearthed at Sumer in Southern Mesopotamia by British and French archeologists, Drs. Palfalvy and Bordeaux believe they have identified the Ku Assa as a pastoral guard dog employed by these agriculturists some thirty-five and forty centuries ago. And they maintain that the Ku Assa is the true ancestor of the European sheep-guarding mastiffs.

The Mesopotamian origin for this group is reinforced by the fact that today this region is the home of the Turkish Sheepdog, the Iranian Sheepdog and the South Russian Sheepdog.

Senac-Lagrange pointed out in his monograph on the Pyrenean in 1927 that the Turkish or Anatolian dog is astonishingly like the Great Pyrenees. It has, he says, the same powerful build and the same deep, but muted, voice. And it, too, was often equipped with an iron-spiked collar as protection against wolves.

But even more important, perhaps, is the claim by Palfalvy and Bordeaux that these ancient populations employed a small dog to herd the flocks. The big dog was the guardian and his little co-worker took care of the driving chores.

In Columella's time Asia Minor was part and parcel of the Roman Empire, and his familiarity with the great white dogs becomes much more understandable if indeed their homeland was on his very doorstep rather than in far-off Tibet. Descendants of Columella's wolf-fighters are still found today in Italy, where they are known as the Maremma. With the Maremma is a little dog that does the herding, called the Bergamese Shepherd.

Robert Leighton, in *The New Book of the Dog*, pointed out that the Romans were advanced in their knowledge of the dog and its uses. So much so, that a classification was drawn up. Three main divisions were recognized: (1) *Canes villaica*, or watchdogs; (2) *Canes pastorales*, or sheepdogs; and (3) *Canes venatici*, or hunting dogs. Of particular interest is Leighton's statement, "In their commerce with other countries the Romans acquired new breeds for particular purposes." British pugnaces, no doubt Mastiffs, were imported for the games at the Coliseum in Rome.

Another purpose for which the Romans needed exceptionally powerful and intelligent dogs was for use in the livestock provisioning camps which served as adjuncts to the numerous military posts set up throughout the far reaches of their Empire. And it is quite possible that, considering the evidence, the dogs from Asia Minor were selected.

Clockwise, round the countries of the Roman Empire, we find the following great white herd protectors: in Africa, the Atlas Mountain dog; in Spain, the Pyrenean Mastiff; in France, the Great Pyrenees; in Italy, the Maremma; in Germany, the old Pomeranian Sheepdog; in Hungary, the Kuvasz; in Czechoslovakia, the Chuvatch; in Poland, the Tatra Mountain dog; in Turkey, the Anatolian Sheepdog—and there are still others in the Balkans and the Near East.

And in many of these countries we also find, in company with the big dog, a little, shaggy, animated shepherd that leads and drives the sheep. Among them we can name the Pyrenean Shepherd in France; the Bergamese Shepherd in Italy; the Puli in Hungary; and the Valee or Nizinny Shepherd in Poland.

Does the presence of so many big white pastoral guard dogs and their little herding co-workers throughout so many of the areas of the Roman Empire really indicate a Roman connection? Or is it merely due to a strange coincidence? One thing is certain: whether its ancestors came from Tibet or Asia Minor, our Pyrenean Mountain Dog is definitely one of the oldest breeds in existence!

DEVELOPMENT OF THE BREED

The Great Pyrenees has achieved its present status by two different stages. During the first, which lasted for many centuries, its working qual-

A Tatra Mountain dog, photographed with Paul
Strang in the village of Zakopane in 1974.

The Historical Chateau De Foix — well guarded by Lanoux du Comte de Foix.

Anthony Miles Ltd.

7

ities were perfected by the mountain shepherds. The second stage is its recent emergence as a show dog.

Fanciers interested in our Pyrenean's show qualities tend to forget its past as a working dog. But we must recall the past to really understand the breed's essential character and special attributes.

Certainly the notion that mountain breeders in the old days were apt to breed anything to anything and hope for the best is in error. Actually, these peasant-shepherds usually imposed rigorous and severe standards of performance on their breeding stock. And only those dogs which met these stringent requirements were retained to produce the future generations.

As Columella pointed out nearly two thousand years ago, the first requirement was for a white dog that could easily be distinguished from wolves. Furthermore, the dog had to be big, strong, fearless and agile in order to cope with the enemy. Intelligence was required, not only to be able to act on its own initiative, but also to be able to understand and obey the shepherd's commands.

A rugged constitution and a weather-resistant coat were both essential—as the dog spent most of its life in the open. Excellent eyesight, an acute sense of hearing and a keen scenting ability were important. And a tremendous energy reserve was called for as the dogs had to stand duty around the clock—the hours of darkness being especially favored by the enemy predators.

J. Dhers, a breeder at the turn of the century who knew the dogs well, described the night scene in the following manner:

> As the evening shadows lengthen the sheep are assembled in the fold and the Patou, who may have drowsed a bit during the day, now becomes a protective demon. Head held high and tail wheeled over the back his keen nose bores into the darkness, first in one direction and then in another, as he circles the encampment. He listens intently for the slightest unwarranted rustling sound. At intervals he pauses to rest for a few moments and his deep bark sounds the signal that all is well.
>
> What controls his actions? Is it the shepherd's training or is it his atavistic hatred of the wolf and the bear? Does he know, or sense, that if either is allowed to approach, more sheep will be lost in a suicidal stampede than will ever be carried off by the attackers? In any case he will not sleep until, in the morning, the shepherd again takes charge of his flock.

We can be sure that such magnificent guard dogs were not produced by haphazard breeding, but rather through a centuries-old program of breeding only the best to the best. The shepherds have always prized their good dogs and parted with them only reluctantly.

The historian M. Doublet, in a work devoted to the highwaymen and cattle rustlers who infested the Pyrenean region in the Middle Ages, tells of the great lords and landowners who frequently purchased the Pyrenean dogs for sentry duty in their castles. They were trained to hunt down brigands and thieves with the same eagerness with which they would attack a wolf or a bear. Thus the citadels of Lourdes, Foix and Carcassonne all had their troupes of Pyrenean dogs to protect the holdings.

And, according to legend, the troubadours—those lyric poets and minstrels who traveled from castle to castle throughout Provence—were often accompanied by the big white dogs. Perhaps this was for the strictly utilitarian purpose of affording them protection from the highwaymen, but it seems more likely that the artistic temperaments of the troubadours were drawn to the dogs because of their beauty of form and nobleness of character.

M. W. Byasson, an early judge of our breed, published a booklet at the turn of the century in which he tells how Patou's beauty ensnared another set of admirers—members of the French royalty:

> Mme. de Maintenon visited Barrèges in 1675 accompanied by the young Dauphin, son of Louis XIV. In the countryside the boy made friends with a gorgeous male Patou about eight months old. The two became inseparable and eventually Patou and the Prince returned together to live at the Louvre.
>
> Two years later the Marquis de Louvois came to the Pyrenees and he, too, returned to Versailles with a magnificent male purchased at Betpouey. The dog became a great favorite at the court.
>
> From this time forward members of the nobility chose the Pyrenean above all other breeds.

After the French Revolution the Pyrenean retained his popularity and became, for the next century, one of the most sought after breeds on the large estates of France.

Turning briefly to the United States, we find that J. S. Skinner in *The Dog and the Sportsman* (1815) tells us that a Great Pyrenees was owned by a Mr. Beaudry of Delaware. The dog was pure white and stood thirty-two inches at the shoulder. Then in 1824 General Lafayette sent Skinner two other Pyreneans, both white with brown markings. Lafayette recommended them as being of inestimable value in all regions exposed to the depredations of wolves and sheep-killing dogs.

In the British Isles, Sir Walter Scott, in 1815, owned a cross-bred Pyrenean named Maida. Its father was a Patou that had come to Scotland with soldiers returning from the Napoleonic Wars. Its mother was a Scottish Deerhound of the famous Glengarry line. Robert Leighton's description of Maida is of considerable interest:

> He was a magnificent animal, partaking of his Deerhound dam, but having height and power from his sire. The cross was of benefit to the breed, and from Maida came many of our best Deerhounds. Washington Irving described him as a giant in iron grey. But Landseer's portrait shows him to have been a white dog with a grey saddle mingled with black, extending into patches on the thighs.

Mr. Dretzen's Pyrenean dog, Champion Porthos, purchased in the Pyrenees about 1907. Named the most beautiful dog in France.

Gazost the First. One of the dogs selected for the regeneration of the breed by the Argeles Club. Strong bone and arched toes. A typical mountain dog of excellent type.

Unfortunately, these early imports to America and Great Britain eventually disappeared without leaving a trace. Perhaps their size and strength were incorporated into other breeds, as happened in Scotland.

Two Pyreneans that came to Belgium in the late nineteenth century were destined to make a lasting contribution to our breed. A retired army officer by the name of M. L. Remy had visited the Pyrenees Mountains in the early 1890s. When he returned to Belgium, he brought with him two pure white pups named Neron and Diane. Diane was given to a Mme. Demaziere.

Organized dog shows, as opposed to informal expositions held in conjunction with country fairs, were just starting to get underway. Neron was entered in several European shows and his impact on the canine world was considerable. Dog fanciers fell in love with this "new" and magnificent breed.

The dogs thus came to the attention of the distinguished canine authority Count Henri de Bylandt, who was in the midst of writing a monumental encyclopedia on the races of dogs entitled *Les Races des Chiens* (Brussels, 1897). De Bylandt devoted several pages to the Pyreneans in his encyclopedia and included photographs of both Neron and Diane. He also drew up a standard for the breed, the first ever published, and included it in his text. All this publicity produced shock waves that reverberated throughout the canine world. Like lemmings heading out to sea, breeders from distant points headed for the Pyrenees to procure stock of these marvelous white-furred lords.

The effect of this sudden popularity was soon felt in the Pyrenees Mountains. In a few short years, most of the best breeding stock had been purchased by foreigners. This genetic drain placed the breed in perilous straits.

RECONSTITUTION

In 1907 M. Th. Dretzen, accompanied by Count de Bylandt, went to the Pyrenees to study the breed on the spot. Once in the mountains they secured the help of M. W. Byasson. Among 350 specimens they examined, Dretzen reported that he found isolated in different parts of the mountains only six specimens that could be regarded as presenting the characteristics of the true race. In an effort to reconstitute the breed, Dretzen purchased these six dogs and moved them to his Zailea Kennels at Bois-Colombes, near Paris.

M. Dretzen's most famous dog was French Champion Porthos. In the words of Robert Leighton, "Porthos was exhibited throughout Europe, and it was perhaps with justification that last year this splendid specimen of his kind was introduced to the President of the Republic as 'the most beautiful dog in France,' for he was a truly magnificent animal."

The Dretzen–de Bylandt–Byasson party had focused attention on the need for some kind of community action on the part of the mountaineers to preserve the breed from further depletion. At that time there was no official standard for the breed in France. Although de Bylandt's standard was written in French, he was himself a Hollander. Mountaineers were disturbed by this "outside interference."

In defense of what they considered the breed's best interest, as well as their own, the mountaineers banded together in an effort to reconstitute the breed and produce an official standard of their own. But rivalries soon broke out and, as a result, different clubs were formed.

One group calling itself the Pastoure Club was formed in 1907 at Lourdes. Among the principals in this venture were Senac-Lagrange, Dr. Moulguet, J. Camjou and the President of the Club, Baron A. de la Chevreliere.

A second club, formed in the same year at Argeles, called itself the Argeles Club. This one included Byasson, Dretzen and de Bylandt.

Each group, by dint of further diligent searching, located about fifty or sixty dogs considered to be purebred. The Pastoure Club organized the first Pyrenean Specialty show. Fifty-five dogs were entered in competition for the various prizes. Both groups made serious efforts to control the breeding and sale of nontypical dogs to eager buyers. And both fought to maintain the size, dignity and vitality of the breed.

At this late date it is difficult to understand why the rivalries were so intense. Two different standards were drawn up, but neither differed very much from the other, and both only slightly from the first by de Bylandt. But this general division into two separate camps may have marked the beginning of the misconception that a different type of Great Pyrenees, derived from the so-called mountain type, was developed for the show ring. In the Pyrenees, a good mountain dog has always been regarded as a good show dog—and vice versa.

Among the points of mutual agreement, those that have stood the test of time are: the use of the word "elegant" to distinguish the Pyrenees from the Saint Bernard and Leonberg; the addition of double dewclaws as a sign of racial purity; the addition of the color "gray" to the list of correct markings; and the statement that the tail is "carried over the back when the dog is going to attack."

Through the efforts of these two groups, the purity of the breed was restored and the Pyrenees appeared to be well on the way to future successes.

But World War I brought about an almost total collapse of the efforts of French breeders to revitalize the breed. Dretzen's Zailea Kennels at Bois-Colombes passed quietly from the scene. The two clubs ceased their

Champion Alba, one of the brood bitches at Zailea.

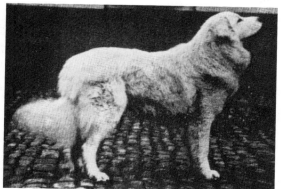

Neron, exhibited in the 1890s by his owner, Mr. Remy of Brussels, Belgium.

The Little Pyrenean Shepherds, co-workers of the Pyrenean Mountain Dogs. The big dogs were guardians of the flock, and the little dogs did the herding.

activities and were virtually disbanded. Many of the dogs they had assembled were put down due to lack of food; the few that did survive were malnourished and often proved to be, at the end of the hostilities, poor breeders.

After the war, registrations of Pyrenean Mountain Dogs in the *Livre Origines Français*, the Stud Book of the Société Centrale Canine in Paris, reflected the sad state of the breed. During ten years, only twenty Pyreneans were registered, all "without origins," i.e., of unknown ancestry and without pedigree.

An effort was made by a few mountaineers to restore size and substance by resorting to a cross with the Alpine Mastiff, but the results were disastrous. The specimens obtained totally lacked the majestic elegance so characteristic of the Pyrenean Mountain Dog. Heads were shorter and heavier; cheeks and stops too pronounced. Worse yet was the loss of the indefinable look which mountaineers called the "Pyrenean eye."

If it were not to be lost altogether, the cause of the Pyrenean Mountain Dog needed to be taken up seriously by a group of sincere fanciers. So it was at Lourdes, on the edge of the majestic region of Lebeda, cradle of the race, that a group of dedicated breeders met to consider the future of the breed. This was done, according to records of M. Senac-Lagrange, with very limited means and in the face of public indifference.

2

Development of the Breed in France

$\mathbf{B}$ERNARD SENAC-LAGRANGE, the man whose un-flagging devotion to the cause gave us the Great Pyrenees as we know it today, was born in 1880 at Cauterets, in the High Pyrenees, and died in 1954 at Bastens-de-Bigorre, only a few miles away.

As a young man Bernard entered the diplomatic service, but cut short this successful career as he felt unsuited to its restricted life. Returning to his paternal family home, near his place of birth, he devoted the rest of his life to hunting, writing, and breeding dogs and horses. He was one of the best-known all-around international judges, and officiated at field trials in France and elsewhere in Europe.

His efforts on behalf of the reclamation of many breeds were crowned with success. He was named President of the Gers-Pyrenees Kennel Club, of the Blue Ticked Gascony Hound Club, of the French Pointer Club and the Club for Shepherd Breeds. He was Vice-President of the Central French Kennel Club (S.C.C.).

But for Pyrenean Mountain Dog fanciers, the years from 1920 to 1930 were the high point in his career. Under his leadership a new club was formed—*La Réunion des Amateurs des Chiens Pyrénéens*, or Reunion of Pyrenean Dog Fanciers. This group, often referred to as the R.A.C.P., managed to combine in one club all the dissident factions which, in one way or another, were devoted to both the Mountain Patou and his little helper, the Petit Berger.

M. Bernard Senac-Lagrange at the judge's table, 1953.

Courtesy, Mrs. C. R. Prince

Toy de Soum. A beautiful bear-like head and superb Pyrenean expression — typical of his bloodline.

Aiding other breeders, particularly M. Cazaux-Moutou (de Soum) and Mme. Le Conte (de Langladure), he supervised their selection of breeding stock from the mountains and from the celebrated Betpouey Kennels of M. R. LaSalle, Lourdes, to aid in the establishment of France's foundation bloodlines.

As the work of reclamation continued, over a hundred fanciers joined Senac-Lagrange in his task. Named President of the Club, he immediately set about preparing an official standard for the Great Pyrenees. It was later published in the 1927 R.A.C.P. Yearbook. Here is the R.A.C.P. Standard:

THE FIRST STANDARD FOR THE GREAT PYRENEES IN FRANCE

General Appearance: A dog of large size, imposing and strongly built, but not devoid of a certain elegance.

Head: Not too large in proportion to the size. The sides of the head fairly flat, the crown of the head oval and not very rounded with a scarcely marked central furrow, the line of the head sloping gradually to a broad muzzle of good length and slightly more pointed at its extremity. The upper lips falling but little, only just enough to cover the lower jaw: they are black or very strongly marked with black; palate black and the nose black. In a word the head of a brown bear, with ears falling down.

Eyes: Rather small, intelligent and contemplative in expression, of an amber brown and placed a little obliquely in the head. The eyelids are close and bordered with black.

Ears: Placed at the height of the eye, rather small, triangular in form and rounded at their extremity, they fall flat against the head.

Neck: Strong, rather short with dewlaps but little developed.

Shoulders: Middling oblique, withers broad and muscular.

Body: The chest not very low but broad and extending well to the rear. Sides slightly rounded. Back a good length, wide and straight. The croup slightly oblique with haunches fairly prominent. Flanks dropping but little.

Members: Front legs straight, strong, well-fringed. Fringes also on hind legs. The thighs are rounded but not low. The hocks are often too straight—they have double spurs on the hind legs and sometimes on the front.

Feet: Not long, compact with toes a little arched.

Tail: Fairly long, thick and plumed. Carried low when in repose, just its extremity curled. When the dog is on the alert the tail is curled up above the back ("making the wheel," the mountaineers call it).

Hair: Thick, flat, fairly long and supple, longer near the tail and around the neck where it can be slightly undulated (wavy). The hair of the quarters finer, more woolly and very thick.

Coat: White or white with spots; colour of a badger or pale yellow or wolf grey on the head, the ears and at the base of the tail. Spots like the badger are esteemed most. One or two spots on the body are not considered as faults.

Size: Females from 65 to 72 cms. (25.59 to 28.34 inches). Males from 70 to 80 cms. (27.55 to 31.49 inches).

Weight: 45 to 55 kilos (99 to 121 lbs.).

Faults: Too heavy head, crown too much developed and front rounded; the stop of nose marked; bad dentition, unequal jaws; round eyes, too light or prominent; falling eyelids; light spots on nose and eyelids, insufficient pigmentation of mucous membranes; lips falling too low; long ears or with folds; tail not fully feathered or carried badly; short hair or curly; the hocks too straight (common fault); other colours than those mentioned above denoting crossing; height and weight below minimum.

To Be Eliminated: Absence of double spurs on hind legs.

Scale of Points:

Crown of head and muzzle (nose, lips, jaws)	15
Eyes	10
Ears	5
Neck, back rump	12
Shoulders, chest, sides	10
Legs and feet	10
Tail and carriage of tail	8
Coat, colour, pigmentation	15
General appearance (expression, height, movement)	15
	100

Commenting in *The Pyrenean Mountain Dog* (1927), Senac-Lagrange wrote:

The main preoccupation, then, of the members of La Réunion des Amateurs des Chiens Pyrénéens was to prepare a standard which would put clearly in relief the points of the breed which could be endangered through the use of untypical specimens, or through any admixture of foreign blood.

Breeding which produces the correct head, the proper coat, the typical expression and gait earns 60 points out of a hundred. Anatomical perfection, however important, cannot rate higher than the points which are the main indication of the purity of the race.

As regards the general appearance we insist the dog, while strongly built, should nevertheless give a distinct impression of elegance.

The carriage of the tail is very characteristic. As soon as the well-bred dog, in good health, goes on the alert, the tail wheels over the back. In the patois of the region this is referred to as *arroundera*.

Let us mention, concerning the coat, two rather common mistakes. Certain persons believe the all-white coat to be the only orthodox one. Others regard the all-white dogs as degenerate and insist the *blaireau* dogs are the correct type. Both opinions are equally wrong.

There is nothing wrong with an all-white dog providing the nose, eye-rims and mucous membranes are perfectly pigmented with black. As far as markings go, it is moreover certain that when they are present the dominant colour, the background, should be white. Most mountaineers prefer white dogs marked with badger on the head and perhaps a patch of the same colour at the base of the tail. In the dialect of Labeda this is *U ca pla p'apat*. This means a well-marked dog.

Though dewclaws are perhaps of doubtful use, they have always, within living memory, been considered by mountain breeders as a sign of racial purity. Under these circumstances we must therefore insist that their absence be considered a disqualification.

We will end these comments by adding that, at times, a Pyrenean dog adopts a gait like that described in literature on the horse and called not a "pace" but a "broken pace." In this gait the lateral bi-ped beat is in 4-time. As this gait may be observed in the little Pyrenean Shepherd Dog it must be considered as an adaptation to the mountain terrain.

As President of the French Club, Senac-Lagrange well knew that writing a description of a breed in dire straits was but the first step. Accordingly, he decided upon three further courses of action.

First, he persuaded other members of the Club to register their dogs with the S.C.C., and to breed only those specimens that met, in all respects, the requirements of the new standard.

Second, he drew up a list of judges he felt were competent to judge the breed. Uniform judging, he felt, would lead to uniform type. Only six judges in all of France were considered to have the proper background to judge the breed with competence. Members of the Club were advised to take into account, in their breeding programs, only those dogs that won under these judges.

His third effort was directed at stopping the genetic drain through which, in the past, so many good dogs had been sold off to nonbreeders and the public at large.

The importance of maintaining and controlling selected individuals

Merah de Langladure, owned by Mme. Le Conte. Merah was the dam of many splendid Langladure offspring, including American Champion Mitsou de Langladure. Pictured in 1936.

The outstanding head and expression of Pastoure de Langladure, born 1919. Foundation bitch at the kennels of Mme. Le Conte. Photo from *Les Chiens Pyreneens,* Senac-Lagrange, 1927.

Champion Mitsou de Langladure, a bitch of good type from one of France's best bloodlines, and an early Basquaerie import.

for the future good of the breed was vividly pointed out in a newspaper article by Senac-Lagrange in 1929. He wrote, "Out of two hundred Pyreneans I have examined in the show ring since the end of the war, only about fifty could be taken into serious consideration." To have squandered this capital would certainly have further endangered the breed.

GREAT PYRENEES BREED TYPE

Under the influence of Senac-Lagrange, a definite Pyrenean type was now emerging in the show rings and kennels of France and also in the mountains. It represented a significant advancement in the quality and consistency of the breed. Paul Strang wrote in the early thirties:

> Generally speaking, the show dogs are larger and more attractive than those found in the hands of the hard-working Pyrenean Mountain folk. Nevertheless, the latter do quite a business with tourists as these dogs never fail to command attention even though lacking some show points. On Fete days the peasants bring their best dogs to town to offer them for sale on the Esplanade or in the Grande Place. I remember seeing nine superior specimens thus offered one sunny morning in Bagneres de Bigorre. What with their glistening white coats contrasting so sharply with their black noses and dark eyes it was, to my mind, only natural that they should attract more attention than the official amusements.

With the publication of the French Standard in 1927, and its implementation by Senac-Lagrange and his associates, and the consequent emergence of Great Pyrenees type, the renaissance of the Great Pyrenees in France was well underway. At the same time, giant predators had been gradually disappearing from the Pyrenean Mountains and the dogs were no longer called upon to serve as they had in the past.

The Great Pyrenees, right arm of the lonely shepherd on the mountain steep, and chamberlain to the lords and ladies of the courts and châteaux of Medieval France, was now destined to become a show dog as well.

THE GREAT PYRENEES BECOMES A SHOW DOG

It was a bright morning in April. The year was 1933, and Pyrenean fanciers had turned out in force to witness the big event of the year—the judging at the prestigious Paris International. This year expectations ran high because the judge was the renowned Mme. Dretzen, who, with her husband, had founded the Zailea Kennels at Bois-Colombes, over thirty years before.

The exceptional quality of the entries plus the acknowledged expertise of the judge served to heighten the suspense. As Mme. Dretzen made her

When the original Standard was being drawn up at the turn of the century, fanciers disagreed as to whether the head should be described as "mastiff-like," for the breadth of skull, or "wolf-like," indicating the length of muzzle. The dissention was resolved by likening the head to that of the Pyrenean Brown Bear, a

relative of our grizzly. This resemblance is demonstrated by the grizzly "Old Scarface" above (photo: courtesy Linda Weisser); and Ch. Fanny de la Griffe d'Ours (photo: Rhett Feng). Note especially the tight eye and mouth, fill under the eye, length of muzzle and top line of skull with no apparent stop.

choices she, in turn, was being judged by the onlookers—not only the fanciers of the Paris region, but also the breeders from the High Pyrenees, men from Auch, Lourdes, Tarbes and Cauterets whose family ties with the breed went back through the centuries.

Perhaps the real importance of the event was not in the placings which were given that day, but in the fact here in one show ring were assembled all the famous bloodlines of the day. Bloodlines which history would later show were to be the power behind most of the later kennels of France, Belgium, England and America.

The males included Toy de Soum; the litter brothers Estat and Estagel d'Argeles; Athos de la Moriniare; Pastour d'Avron (of Careil bloodlines); Bastan de Soum; and Sancho de Langladure.

Among the females were to be found the litter sisters Luz and Monne de Langladure; "France" of du Givre breeding; Munia du Pic du Jer; Nive de Langladure; and the great Ariel de Soum.

Let us consider for a moment these great contenders and the kennels which produced them.

The stud dog, Toy de Soum, was well on his way to winning a French championship. He was out of Gazost de Betpouey, the most successful show winner of the previous decade. Gazost had won the Challenge Cup three times in five years, thus retiring the cup to his owner, M. Lasalle. The dam of Toy de Soum was Estom de Soum, who had won the Challenge Cup in 1926.

In the head and expression, Toy de Soum exemplified the perfection for which M. Cazaux-Moutou of Lourdes, in the Hautes-Pyrénées, had long been noted. Toy was the sire of America's first champion and producer, Urdos de Soum, the founder of Basquaerie Kennels.

Always a close personal friend of M. Senac-Lagrange, M. Cazaux-Moutou had been in 1907 one of the founders of the Pastoure Club, and later when it collapsed, the R.A.C.P. He showed extensively all over France in the early years. He bred with extreme wisdom and care, and he registered all his stock with the S.C.C. in Paris. In the 1930s he was taken with ill health, but managed to keep some of his dogs intact through World War II. Thus the career of this distinguished gentleman spanned nearly a half century.

Mme. Le Conte, owner of French Ch. Ariel de Soum, was the proprietress of the **Elevage de Langladure**. In 1933 this kennel was at its height, and almost no pedigree could be found in France that did not boast of de Langladure blood.

Ariel de Soum was of such a reputation that many described her as the best bitch France had ever bred. She was born in 1925 and won the Challenge Cup in 1929. She whelped her last litter at eleven years of age—

still a grand old matron with everything visible that one could ask for in an outstanding Great Pyrenees bitch—type, expression, coat, soundness and character.

De Langladure dogs were of mountain origin, heavy in Betpouey, and closely allied to de Soum. The foundation stock had been carefully selected by M. Senac-Lagrange. In addition to Ariel de Soum it included Merah de Langladure, another top producer for the kennel.

Among the kennel's offspring, Yel de Langladure went to Holland where he was the foundation stud at Van Euskara. I'Nethou de Langladure was sent to England and became a major factor at de Fontenay. Champions Maya and J'Nive de Langladure played important roles at Cote de Neige and Basquaerie in America.

Shown that day at the Paris International was the beautiful brood matron, French Champion Monne de Langladure, owned by Mme. Carel of the **Du Val d'Aure** Kennels. Monne was a bitch with an impressive pedigree: her dam was Ariel de Soum and her sire Toy de Soum.

A key mating between Monne de Langladure and Estat d'Argeles won fame for the Val d'Aure Kennels and made an important contribution to the bloodlines of France and America. This mating produced a remarkable litter of six puppies which were kept by the Carels and shown extensively throughout the Continent where they won innumerable prizes. One male, Hermes, later became Champion of France.

Hermes was bred to his litter sister Halia—thus doubling up on the blood of d'Argeles and de Soum. This led to the birth of Ch. Ibos du Val d'Aure of Basquaerie, imported by Mrs. Crane in 1935 in advance of his grandfather Estat d'Argeles. He was used extensively at stud in America, and thus left many progeny to carry on his bloodlines.

Perhaps the most famous Great Pyrenees to be shown that day— indeed one of the all-time great dogs—was the above-mentioned Tri-International Champion Estat d'Argeles (Belgian, French, Luxembourg). With his litter brother Estagel d'Argeles, he was exhibited all over Europe in 1935 and 1936. Acclaimed the most perfect pair in France, Estat and Estagel were both stud factors of great force and value in their native land, and their voyage to America was also to prove of lasting value to the breed in this country.

They were owned by the American-born Countess de Bertier de Sauvigny, who divided her stay between her Paris residence and her French home in the historic Château de Morsang-sur-Orge near Chartres, where the dogs were often seen taking the country air in her gardens.

Mme. la Comtesse had made an extensive search throughout France in seeking her original breeding pair, and selected as foundation matron Estaube de Soum, a beautiful specimen whom she mated to the great show winner of 1929–1930, Rip de la Noe (M. Zivi), a true "dog of the mountains."

These two brothers were actually all that existed at the **Chenil d'Argeles**. Mme. la Comtesse had raised but one litter. Two sisters, equally fine, unfortunately went to homes as pets and never were bred.

The **Elevage des Loubonnieres** was another successful kennel of the day. It distinguished itself by combining de Langladure blood with a mountain outcross. Located at Grasse in the Alpes Maritimes, it was owned by the two Crist sisters.

Mlles. Crist selected as their foundation matron l'Neige de Langladure, who was among the last born to Ch. Ariel de Soum, then eleven years of age, and Ch. Estagel d'Argeles.

I'Neige was bred twice to an outcross male, a famous and successful stud, Fram de la Moriniere, of mountain ancestry. The first mating of these two dogs produced Krici des Loubonnieres. At one year of age, he won at the Paris Exposition and was crowned Champion of France. The second mating produced Lisey des Loubonnieres (of Basquaerie), who became an American champion and carried on her bloodlines in the States.

Des Loubonnieres exported dogs to the Chenil du Mont Picry, thus contributing to the establishment of this famous kennel in Belgium.

One of the Crist sisters was tragically killed in a freak accident after World War II when a war balloon alighted near her home. She was inspecting the balloon when someone lit a match and the balloon exploded.

Many of the French kennels of those early postwar years were kept by hotel and restaurant owners, butchers and food concessionaires. Thus the dogs could be fed scraps from the tables, making it economically feasible to keep more than a handful. The **Chenile de Careil** was no exception. It was owned jointly by M. L. Janning and Mlle. Suzanne Luce.

Originally the Manoir de Careil was located in Brittany and it was here that the foundation of the bloodline was laid. The brood bitch was Mirka de la Noe. She was mated to the stud dog Rip de la Noe, owned by M. Zivi; the mating produced the dog Patou—the first to bear the kennel affix.

While vacationing in Brittany in 1929, Mme. Harper Trois-Fontaines had been drawn to the Manoir de Careil because of its famous cuisine. Here, for the first time, she saw the Great Pyrenees, and later wrote, "I fell in love with the noble creatures, who were as sweet as they were beautiful." She attempted to import a pair of pups but they both died in quarantine.

In 1933 M. L. Janning and Mlle. Luce moved their establishment to the Châteaux de Jacques-Coeur in Boisy. It was a typical and charming feudal castle, and after it was renovated it became a famous showplace and one of the top-flight inns of the day. During its career, it numbered among its guests both Mme. Harper and Mr. and Mrs. Crane.

The famous brothers. In the foreground, Tri-International and American Champion Estat d'Argeles of Basquaerie, and in the background American Champion Estagel d'Argeles of Basquaerie.

Two Young Soum Dogs.

Mme. Harper returned to the Chenile de Careil in 1933 and persuaded M. L. Janning to part with Kop de Careil, whom he had intended to retain as a stud dog. In the background of Kop de Careil was the blood of the mountains through his grandsire Rip de la Noe, who was also the sire of Estat and Estagel d'Argeles. Kop also combined, on his dam's side, Betpouey and de Soum. He became the foundation sire at de Fontenay.

It is interesting to note, therefore, that through the blood of de Soum and d'Argeles, admixed the same mountain outcrosses, the basic bloodlines in England and America were nearly identical.

With the onset of World War II, M. L. Janning and Mlle. Luce dispersed their remaining stock and moved their hostelry to the French Riviera—thus writing a finis to one of the most colorful chapters in Great Pyrenees kennel history in France.

We turn now to another famous kennel of the day. Located a few miles outside the city of Lourdes, the dogs of **Du Pic du Jer** gazed across the beautiful Lac Lourdes to the distant snow-capped mountains bordering Spain. No more picturesque setting ever existed for founding a kennel of Great Pyrenees. The proprietors were Mme. and M. Jos. Abadie-Toulet, who eked out a living tilling the soil and running a small refreshment concession for the summer tourists on the edge of the Lac. Litters were whelped in a barn, and the dogs were free to roam at will within the fenced boundaries of the yard, often going back into the mountainside with M. Abadie-Toulet on his chores. Brood bitches were farmed out to the surrounding mountaineers. If a client wanted a good dog, M. Abadie-Toulet would mysteriously disappear into the mountains and return in a few days with a good specimen.

The foundation sire was Roland du Pic du Jer, a badger-marked dog—sturdy, strong-boned and of mountain origin. The bitch was Fanchette. In all respects, du Pic du Jer was a typical mountain establishment.

The kennel prospered under the kindly supervision of the Toulets. By the late 1930s dogs had been exported to America, England, Belgium and Holland.

Bigorre, Rhune and Aspe du Pic du Jer were brought to Basquaerie, and Aspe distinguished herself by being the first female of the breed to win her American Championship. All left many descendants in the United States.

Baby du Pic du Jer became the foundation stud at De Mont Picry in Belgium, also winning a Tri-International Championship. Nethou du Pic du Jer was a popular stud and a champion in Holland.

Mme. Harper also bred heavily to the du Pic du Jer strain through the blood of her great stud, Labada du Mont Picry, son of Labeda du Pic du Jer. Thus the kennel had a far-reaching effect on the early bloodlines of many lands.

M. Abadie-Toulet reported that during World War II he was able to keep his collection of dogs intact, although at great expense to himself, and privation of food on his part. After the death of M. Abadie-Toulet, Madame was able to continue breeding for many years until, at the age of eighty-seven, in the year 1975, she too died and thus another great kennel passed into Pyrenean history.

At the **Chenil de Truchard**, outside of the small village of Ussen-En-Forez, Loire, Mme. and M. Charet maintained a small collection of Pyrenees. The old dog of the kennel was Roland de Soum, a magnificent specimen and son of a fine sire, Tiarko, of mountain origins. The brood bitch was Pastoure de Bagneres. These two had produced a number of puppies, which were dispersed throughout France and the Continent. One of these was Arlette de Truchard of Basquaerie, who became an American champion and left many descendants to carry on her blood. The death of Roland and Pastoure in 1938 ended the breeding of Pyreneans at de Truchard.

The role played by M. Charles Fasquelle, founder of **Du Givre**, was a brief one, but of considerable importance. This gentleman led a somewhat double life. On the one hand he was an ardent devotee of the theaters, cafes and boulevards of "Gay Paree," but he was also a serious and dedicated Pyrenees breeder.

Fasquelle had discovered the mountain dogs as a young man on vacation in the Pyrenees. He was especially impressed with the breed's size and strength and selected his breeding stock with these in mind. Many of his dogs were trained to pull wagons and sleds. Once, when taunted at a Paris dinner party for spending so much money on "good for nothing" dogs, he wagered his dogs could pull him from France to Spain. He won his bet by shipping dogs and a sled to the frontier and having his team pull him a hundred yards over the border.

The most renowned bitch of the Du Givre line was Blanchette, who was imported by Mrs. Crane and became the dam of the first litter born in America.

Also present at the Paris show was the stud dog Athos de la Moriniere, whose qualities were brought to America through the de Guerveur-bred dogs, Ch. H'Echez de Guerveur of Basquaerie and Ch. K'Eros de Guerveur of Basquaerie. The **Elevage de Guerveur** was, in those days, run jointly by three sisters, the Mlles. Leger, one of whom, Christine, lived with her father in an apartment on the outskirts of Paris and attended to the sales and correspondence. The other two sisters resided at the kennel on the Belle-Isle-En-Mer, located off the coast of Brittany.

One of its principal values lay in its rather remote location, which provided "cold" blood, not admixed with the strains of the late thirties. It therefore was considered a useful outcross for the de Soum and de Langladure strains.

Reports from de Guerveur in the late forties indicated that the kennel was still very much alive and going strong, sharing honors at the Paris shows with M. Delattre's Pontoise dogs. Today one still hears of dogs bearing the de Guerveur affix at shows in France. Therefore, this kennel ranks among the oldest in existence.

Perhaps every entry at the Paris International should have been a winner that day. But the dogs were not being judged by the historian. As Mme. Dretzen stood back to consider her final choices, it was to be the great stud dog Toy de Soum, six years of age and in the magnificent bloom of his male maturity, who was to be given the honors. And as the winning bitch, Mme. Dretzen chose the incomparable Ariel de Soum, then eight years old and every inch the Queen of France. Another Paris show had passed into history.

Thus the forces set in motion by B. Senac-Lagrange had unerringly brought together at Paris in 1933 a nucleus of bloodlines of such force and distinction that its influence on the breed in France would endure for years to come. With the founding of Basquaerie Kennels in the United States and de Fontenay in England, the type would blossom and propel the Pyrenean Mountain Dog around the world.

Urdos de Soum, the first Great Pyrenees champion in America, in 1934. His parentage: Toy de Soum — Lutour de Langladure.

From a painting by Edwin R. Megargee

Basquaerie Marsous, the first American-bred Great Pyrenees champion. His parentage: Ch. Patou — Ch. Mitsou de Langladure.

From a painting by Edwin R. Megargee

3

Basquaerie Kennels— The Great Pyrenees Comes to America

by Mary W. A. Crane

As our chapter title implies, the story of the Basquaerie Kennels of Mr. and Mrs. Francis V. Crane is also the story of how the Great Pyrenees came to America. During its long and distinguished career, Basquaerie accounted for over 150 Great Pyrenees champions, a record which has yet to be broken. Mrs. Crane's contributions to the growth and betterment of the breed have been incalculable. We are particularly pleased to have this important story in her own words.

UNTIL THE FALL of 1930, my husband Francis and I were happily living in our home in Massachusetts with two imported English Cocker Spaniels—Desmond and Towser of Ware—and one Field Spaniel bitch—Dinah—for pets, little dreaming of enlarging our doggy family, founding a kennel, or introducing a breed to make history for the canine world.

But who, when they are dog lovers to begin with, can resist the charms of two ten-week-old Great Pyrenees puppies, all white and cuddly, seen for the first time, as were the brothers Bazen and Nethou de Soum, brought home from a summer spent in France by the Misses Hedge of Massachusetts? The sisters had been visiting their aunt, Clara Perry, an American artist who lived part-time abroad, and who also happened to be a friend of our family. When Miss Perry next returned to France, it was with the instructions to buy a pair, suitable for breeding, to bring to the Cranes in the fall of 1931. And thus it was that Basquaerie was born!

An interesting side note, I think, was the fact that Miss Perry's interest in the breed stemmed from her enthusiasm for the "Seeing Eye" equivalent in France. Les Grands Chiens des Montagnes were in favor in France for this purpose, appreciated above all for their intelligence, keen eyesight and white color. The wetness of a long coat on stormy days did not seem to disturb the French people, as it has Americans.

Thus arrived Urdos and Anie de Soum from the de Soum kennels of the eminent French breeder and judge M. A. Cazaux-Moutou at Lourdes, Hautes-Pyrénées. Improper and inadequate vaccination in France and ignorance on the part of the Cranes tragically cost the life of Anie from distemper the first winter, and the serious illness of Urdos who, fortunately, was saved. A second bitch, Blanchette du Givre, was brought over a year later, and thus the Great Pyrenees was launched in the United States.

As preparations to register the breed with the American Kennel Club were carried on, the breed name had to be condensed from the long official breed designation in France. Hence, "Great Pyrenees," derived from "The Great Dogs of the Pyrenees Mountains," was chosen.

Also, a kennel name had to be selected for registration. Proper names were out, so to try to give the feeling of the high Pyrenees, "aerie" (for high home of the eagle) was combined with "Basque" (for the dogs' homeland in France). The designation **Basquaerie** was registered with the American Kennel Club on April 17, 1933, thereby becoming the first Great Pyrenees kennel to be registered in the U.S.A.

Contacts having been made in France with various breeders through exchanges of correspondence, photographs and personal contacts on the part of Miss Perry and myself, it was but a short time before other specimens were purchased and on their way to America. The next to come to Basquaerie were Patou (a real mountain dog) and Aspe du Pic du Jer, again from a peasant's farm, owned by M. Abadie-Toulet, up in the high mountains at Lac Lourdes. The third import was Mitsou de Langladure, from a well-known and long-established breeding kennel owned by M. and Mme. Georges Le Conte, Château de Villechenay, located in the château country at Millancay in the Province of Indre. From here on, others followed in rapid succession, some from the mountains and some from kennels. Included among them were dogs of such notable contribution to the breed as Champions H'Echez de Guerveur, Pastoure du Pic du Jer and Pastoure de Vieuzac.

From the start Basquaerie combined the strength and ruggedness of the true working type of peasant-owned and -reared dog, and the more refined, polished and genteel type to be found in the French breeding kennels. This combination, I feel, gave a balanced refinement to Basquaerie's American-bred dogs that produced dogs of good temperament: strong in body, bone and conformation; correct in type and expression; elegant in stance and appearance.

This combination was the result of a fortunate set of circumstances, because the true peasant-bred dog lacks (and always has) a three-generation pedigree suitable or acceptable for official registration with both the French Kennel Club and the American Kennel Club. The peasant breeders, being far removed from the shows, and especially the Paris Show at which a win is required to attain a French title, were neither able to attend nor sufficiently interested in showing to make the effort to meet the expense. At best, they kept very sketchy records of the ancestry of their dogs. Furthermore, they distrusted those in authority in the registering organizations in Paris. They could not, therefore, supply a buyer with a three-generation pedigree, nor did this disturb them at all.

Suffice it for them to know that their "Pastoure" was bred to M.'s "Patou" in the next valley or village. This simple exchange of breeding services between friends and neighbors accounts for the predominance in mountain pedigrees of Patous and Pastoures, followed by "de" (from), and then the proper name of the home territory of said animal.

At the beginning of the breed's introduction to the States, therefore, the American Kennel Club had to be liberal in lowering their standards to allow specimens to come into the country and to be shown and registered in spite of insufficient pedigrees. Otherwise there would not have been enough breeding stock made available to assure strong and wise propagation of the breed.

Peasant-owned and -reared dogs were selected for Basquaerie by M. Senac-Lagrange. He took charge of locating suitable specimens and getting them to the railroad station at Lourdes for shipment to America.

The following are important dates in the early history of the breed here:

1932: Urdos de Soum of Basquaerie carried the banner for the breed into the Miscellaneous Class at Boston's Eastern Dog Club Show on February 22.

1933: In February the Great Pyrenees obtained official recognition as a purebred breed by the American Kennel Club. On April 4 the first separate classes for Great Pyrenees were offered at the Worcester show in Massachusetts. Records were made in quick succession. Urdos de Soum became the first Great Pyrenees to place in a Working Group (at the Ladies Dog Show on June 3). Two weeks later, the first litter of Pyrenees puppies, sired by Urdos, was born to Blanchette du Givre at Basquaerie Kennels.

1934: Urdos became the first American-crowned champion at the Eastern Dog Club Show in Boston. Champion Patou of Basquaerie won

Ch. Basquaerie Gui de Noel, a son of Ch. Ibos du Val d'Aure of Basquaerie, and a sire of nine champions. 1940.

Ch. Basquaerie Bichon CD, a son of Ch. Basquaerie Gui de Noel and sire of nine champions including Ch. Basquaerie Bibelot and Ch. Cote de Neige Ariette. 1943.

Ch. Basquaerie Bibelot, a son of Ch. Basquaerie Bichon CD. Note the outstanding type. Winner of 132 Bests of Breed. Bibelot sired six champions.

a Working Group—first Great Pyrenees to achieve this honor—at the Middlesex Kennel Club in Cambridge. On June 17 Aspe du Pic du Jer became the first Great Pyrenees bitch champion, winning her title at the Ladies Dog Club show in Dedham, Massachusetts. To round out this very active year, on December 2 the Great Pyrenees Club of America was formed.

1935: This year saw the championship of the first American-bred Great Pyrenees, Basquaerie Marsous, son of Champion Patou out of Mitsou de Langladure. Basquaerie Marie Blanque, a daughter of Urdos out of Pastoure du Pic du Jer, became the first Great Pyrenees to be registered and recognized in Canada.

On September 10, the Great Pyrenees Club of America was voted a member club by the American Kennel Club. Mr. Crane became the delegate, a position which he held until 1948 when an illness forced his retirement.

In November, Great Pyrenees were shown at the Royal Winter Fair in Toronto, Canada, under National Kennel Club rules with separate classification for sexes. The breed was permanently launched in Canada.

During this year the breed was reintroduced to England by Mme. Jeanne Harper Trois-Fontaines, who secured two males and one female from the Continent, and registered her de Fontenay Kennels with the British Kennel Club.

1936: The first American-bred Great Pyrenees arrived in England to begin its six-month quarantine. And at the Golden Gate Show in San Francisco, Belle of Basquaerie, daughter of Urdos and Blanchette, became the first registered Great Pyrenees to be shown in an AKC show on the Pacific Coast.

In the summer of this year Mr. and Mrs. Crane traveled to England and the Continent, visiting Mme. Harper and meeting her foundation stock, Nethou de Langladure, Kop de Careil and Ianette de Boisy. They then went to Paris and, renting a car, drove into the château and High Pyrenees country, stopping to visit kennels and to seek out the breed in its home environment. Some of the movies taken on this trip have been reproduced for the Great Pyrenees Film Exchange and have been viewed by many in recent years.

This trip also brought to Basquaerie other imports including Maya de Langladure, Arizes and Azun de Soum, Arlette de Truchard, Khiva and Kaira du Val d'Aure, and some English Cocker Spaniels.

Over the next few years, I took further trips to the Continent: in 1937 to France, Belgium and Holland; and in 1939 to Brussels to judge the Canine Exposition Internationale of the Société Royale de Saint-Hubert. During this last visit I went to the kennels of Mme. Vandermousen in Frameries, which was near the Maginot Line. From Mme. Vandermou-

TRI-INT. & AM. CH. ESTAT d'ARGELES of BASQUAERIE

Fr. Ch. Hermes du Val D'Aure

Ch. Basquaerie Boris

Ch. Ibos du Val D'Aure of Basquaerie

Ch. Cote de Neige Niverau

Ch. Basquaerie Gui de Noel

Ch. Basquaerie Ariel C.D.

Ch. Basquaerie Houx de Noel

Ch. Basquaerie Estagel

Ch. Basquaerie Bichon C.D.

Ch. Lawrence of Combermere

Ch. Cote de Neige Symphony

Ch. Basquaerie Beau Jacques

Ch. Quibbletown Mistigris

Ch. Basquaerie Bibelot

Ch. Basquaerie Ballerina

Ch. Sunset Knoll Basquaerie Beak

Quibbletown Bouncing Bett

Ch. Loramo de La Colina

Ch. Quibbletown Gina

Ch. Basquaerie Bijou

Ch. Basquaerie Corvina

Quibbletown April Sunshine

Ch. Lorvaso de La Colina

Ch. Basquaerie Bali

Ch. Basquaerie Vicki Snow White

Ch. Quibbletown Impresario

Ch. Quibbletown Ariette

Ch. Basquaerie Bali

Ch. Quibbletown Good Time Charli

Ch. Quibbletown Carlotta

Ch. Balibasque Mister Big

Balibasque Beau of Karolaska C.D.

Ch. Quibbletown Impresario

Ch. Quibbletown Jim Dandy

Ch. Karolaska Glacier

Ch. Quibbletown Cavalier

Quibbletown Queen Bear

Ch. Balibasque Wooden Nickel

Ch. Quibbletown Billy Wink

Ch. Karolaska Glacier

Ch. Balibasque Wooden Nickel

Ch. Chip 'N Tip Quibbletown Impy

Ch. Chip 'N Tip Sonny's Reflection

The descendants of Tri-Int. & Am. Ch. Estat d'Argeles of Basquaerie, showing the influence of this dog on contemporary bloodlines in America.

1
2
3
4
5
6
7
8
9
10
11

Mary Crane with her first breeding pair, Ch. Urdos de Soum and Blanchette du Givre, pictured in Needham, Massachusetts, in 1932.

Ch. K'Eros de Guerveur of Basquaerie, the first Great Pyrenees to a win Best In Show, on September 23, 1939, at the Eastern States Exposition. Owned by Mary Crane.

E. Morgan Savage

sen I was able to purchase the bitch Koranne, a daughter of International Champion Baby du Pic du Jer. Koranne was destined to become one of Basquaerie's top brood matrons.

Mr. Crane joined me later in France and together we toured the French kennels, returning on the French liner *Normandie*. With us were six new additions to the kennel. Among these were Rhune du Pic du Jer and K'Eros de Guerveur of Basquaerie.

Perhaps no win did more to boost Great Pyrenees' popularity and prestige than that of Champion Ibos du Val d'Aure of Basquaerie. In June 1939 Ibos won the Working Group at the North Westchester Kennel Club show which was held on the Sherman R. Hoyt estate at Katonah, New York. That this was the third largest show in America of the time added much glory; it was also the show considered that year as the Specialty Show of the Great Pyrenees Club of America.

The following year, K'Eros de Guerveur gained fame for the breed by being the first Great Pyrenees to win an all-breeds Best in Show, at Hartford, Connecticut, on April 20, 1940. Continuing along the road to fame came eight other champions: Basquaerie Gui de Noel, Basquaerie Beau Estagel, Basquaerie Bichon, CD, Basquaerie Andre, La Shan Marc of Basquaerie, Basquaerie Bibelot, Sunset Knoll Basquaerie Beau and Basquaerie Bali. All not only won Working Group firsts and consistently had other placements in the Group through their careers, but most were also Best in Show winners.

While the Best of Breed winners were predominantly males, some of the great bitches over the years also deserve mention. The ones that especially come to mind are Champions Aspe du Pic du Jer, Mitsou de Langladure, Basquaerie Nana, Noella, Ballerina and Corvina; the latter two had the almost unheard-of distinction of defeating their male competitors at Club Specialty Shows!

One of the great bits of good fortune for Basquaerie and the breed in general was my meeting in Paris with Mme. la Comtesse de Sauvigny, during which I was able to persuade her to part with her European Tri-International Champion Estat d'Argeles and his brother French Champion Estagel d'Argeles, and to send both to America in the fall of 1936. Estat had been proclaimed the most perfect and beautiful Great Pyrenees in all France in 1935. So, as the exemplification of correctness of head, expression and type, we commissioned M. Fath, a sculptor designated by the French Government as an official animal judge, to do a head study, and also a full-length sculpture of him from life at his home château. One of the full-length bronzes is in the library of the American Kennel Club in New York; the other at Basquaerie. The head study is known to all members of the Great Pyrenees Club of America as that on the club pin.

M. Fath also painted for us a full copy of the famous original by Oudrey, entitled "La Chasse Aux Loupes," depicting two Great Pyrenees fighting a wolf, which at that time hung over the grand staircase in the Château de Compiegne. This now hangs at the American Kennel Club also.

However, the greatest contribution, one that will be lasting, was the ability of the two famous brothers and their cousins from de Langladure to stamp their line with the correct Great Pyrenees' type and expression. This ability has come down directly through their descendants, all Basquaerie champions: Beau Estagel, Bichon CD, Bibelot, Sunset Knoll Basquaerie Beau and Basquaerie Bali; then on to the Balibasque sires, among them Balibasque Beau of Karolaska CD, El Amor Bruno Balibasque, and their offspring. These have been and are continuing to be the top producing lines for head and expression, without which, in my opinion, one just does not have a true and beautiful Great Pyrenees.

The only other strain that I have found consistently producing the same type is the interrelated de Soum, de Langladure and du Val d'Aure family. The progenitors of these are Champions Urdos de Soum, Azun de Soum, Ibos du Val d'Aure, Gui de Noel and Basquaerie Boris. A mating of a son and daughter of Urdos de Soum was the foundation choice of Mrs. Butcher for her Cote de Neige Kennels.

Basquaerie pioneered in the field of Obedience training back in the early years of the movement in 1938. Champion Koranne of Basquaerie CD was the first Obedience degree winner; Champion Basquaerie Amie CD, CDX, the first to gain the second degree in 1941. Spurred on by the interest in obedience training stimulated by the request for "War Dogs," classes were springing up all over the East, and by 1942 Basquaerie had five Obedience title holders. They were: Champion Basquaerie Bichon CD, Basquaerie Kuri CD, Basquaerie Ariel CD and the two females already mentioned. The services rendered by the "Dogs for Defense" are noted in Chapter 8.

Basquaerie's years of glory passed into history in the late 1950s. Never was there a sadder person than I when the realization came that the kennels must be drastically reduced and practically disbanded. This was due in part to both Mr. Crane's health, which necessitated a move to Florida for half of each year, and the subsequent impossibility of finding suitable kennel management and supervision from such a distance.

However, in the dissolution of the large kennel family, representative breeding stock, male and female, of the famous and best producing lines went to Balibasque Kennels in Pennsylvania, and a few others to Soleil Kennels in Kansas. In both areas the lines carry on.

But Basquaerie has not and will not die as long as I live, for I have kept two brood matrons who carry on my favorite and best lines, as well as one youngster, Basquaerie Easter Bunny, daughter of my Champion

Basquaerie Corla's Betsy II, who hopefully will make a name for herself in the show rings of the future. My fourth bitch is Champion Karolaska Babs of Basquaerie, daughter of Karolaska's famous foundation stud, Balibasque Beau of Karolaska CD. There just is *no finis* to Basquaerie!

I am proud that through the years, Basquaerie has stood as a name of renown and honor wherever Great Pyrenees are spoken of, admired and loved. Dogs of our kennel prefix have gone, through the years, to foreign lands far and wide: England, Holland, Belgium, India, the Republic of South Africa, Brazil, Mexico and Canada.

We always attempted to do all in our power to establish and maintain the correct and true type of the Great Dogs of the Pyrenees Mountains. In the years before World War II, we bought up representatives of as many kennels and strains as possible, bringing them to Holliston, Massachusetts, in the hope of perpetuating the breed while the pressures of war threatened its very survival in its native land. We carried them safely over the war years, maintaining over one hundred individuals, breeding and showing whenever possible. We exhibited far and wide to acquaint the public with the breed's charm and beauty. We stood ready to help new breeders with advice when asked, to assist breeding programs, and gave freely of our time to further the breed's proper promotion.

Basquaerie was the fountainhead from which all the early kennels sprang: Cote de Neige, Add-En-On, La Colina, La Shan, Robwood and Combermere.

Basquaerie is proud of the successes of the breed in America and believes that a bright future lies ahead *if* breeders will put aside personal and petty jealousies and remain true to the authentic type, breeding for and rewarding in the show ring *only* those dogs and bitches which carry the correct Pyrenean type and expression. Think of the head of a Polar Bear with the ears falling down, not a Brown Bear—for you want a substantial muzzle, not a short one. And refer to your club insignia for the correct head!

I want to take this opportunity right here and now to stress that it is *not* the nature of Great Pyrenees to be overly large, tall, or in any sense "immense." This choice of a translation word to describe the breed in the original standard was ill-chosen. The breed is a large breed, true, but neither excessively tall, slab-sided, short-muzzled, droopy-jowled, too narrow or too domed in the head, nor marked with a positive stop or a round eye! They are of a large-medium size when compared with the few exceedingly tall and large breeds. So, please push far asunder any misconceptions you may now have concerning size. Let's not breed for ponies!

I bring this critique up because I have often been asked how the dogs of today compare in size with those early imports. My reply is that the average dog and bitch one sees are the same.

The initial interest in a tall Great Pyrenees came into vogue, I believe, with Champion K'Eros de Guerveur of Basquaerie, who did make a striking picture in the ring, and made himself famous by becoming the first to win Best in Show. But he was also a dog of correct Pyrenees type, not carrying the faults I mentioned above, and well deserving of his wins. However, size has become an obsession in the minds of some people ever since— but fortunately not in the minds of all! And not in the minds of those breeders whose interest centers on correctness of type and quality.

Unfortunately, all too many people are prone to speak out, giving their own ideas and appraisals to fit their own dogs. But how many who do this have really seen the dogs in their native land doing their natural chores? I say again, please don't pioneer for a new cause unless you are sure of your facts, from actual experience and not just hearsay.

Basquaerie has indeed had a long and colorful history, full of accomplishments, success and failures. We have had our share of happiness and sorrow, of good times and bad. But life, after all, means taking the bitter with the sweet. So we wish you all, newcomers to the breed and old alike, all successes in the years ahead. But *please*, one request—do not try to change the world's most beautiful and wonderful breed. The Great Pyrenees' delight and charm lie in its being what it is today. Keep it that way.

Work for the perpetuation of the *true type* of Great Pyrenees. For without those beautiful, dark expressive eyes, that elegance of head and carriage, one just does not have a real Great Pyrenees.

So, long may the breed prosper and spread. And, so too, the joy of ownership, the devotion, companionship and intelligent protection to be offered by this, the world's most beautiful dog. For to once own a Great Pyrenees is to love and want one always.

THE BASQUAERIE LEGACY LIVES ON: CH. QUIBBLETOWN T.G. OF BASQUAERIE

The passing of Mary Crane brought a very sad end to a glorious era in the history of the Great Pyrenees. However, years after her death her dogs remain an important and direct force in the breed today. In fact, her very last litter produced a dog, Ch. Quibbletown T.G. of Basquaerie, whose repercussions continue to be felt all across the country and in Canada also.

This last litter was sired by Ch. Quibbletown Billy Deaux out of Ch. Basquaerie Corla's Betsy II. Mr. and Mrs. C. Seaver Smith, Jr., of Quibbletown kennels owned the sire, and so chose the pick of the litter. They named him Quibbletown T.G. of Basquaerie.

Before T.G. was a year old, Mimi Cary, a West Coast breeder, visited Quibbletown looking for a top quality addition to her breeding program. There she saw the young T.G. and eventually convinced the Smiths to sell him to her. She took him back to Berkeley, California, and let him grow up. There he was admired and used by prominent West Coast breeders

Ch. Quibbletown TG of Basquaerie, won BOS at the National Specialty in 1980, owner-handled by Betty Wade Warmack, under French judge, Guy Mansencal. *Carl Lindemaier*

T.G. daughter, Am/Can Ch. Euskari Kaskadian Everstar, won Best of Breed at the 1980 National Specialty, owner-handled by Michael Floyd. Bred by Mimi Cary. *Carl Lindemaier*

such as JoAnn Teems (California), Dusty Hohman (California), Betty Wade Warmack (California) (to whom T.G. was later sold), Linda Weisser (Washington), Michael Floyd (Washington), Sharon Armstrong (British Columbia, Canada), and Gerald Scott (British Columbia, Canada). Through these breeders T.G. and his offspring have been an important presence at virtually every National Specialty in the United States and Canada since 1980.

1980 was the year that, for the first time, a French expert on the breed was invited to judge the National Specialty. M. Guy Mansencal, president of the R.A.C.P. (Reunion of Pyrenean Dog Fanciers, in France) and resident of the Pyrenees Mountains, had long been critical of the American Great Pyrenees he had seen in photos. In publications such as the *International Great Pyrenees Review* he had expressed the opinion that Pyrenees in the United States had lost the essential aspects of type which define the breed. He felt that the Pyrenees he had seen in photos lacked elegance in body and lacked correct expression due to heads which were too heavy, eyes which were round, not almond-shaped, loose, pendulous lips, and too much stop. After hearing this from him for several years, American breeders finally decided to throw down the gauntlet: let M. Mansencal come to the States to judge the National Specialty. To see if, after judging 150 of our dogs, he could still say there are no good Pyrenees in North America. M. Mansencal accepted the challenge with pleasure.

Breeders from all over the United States and Canada brought their dogs to participate on this historic occasion. M. Mansencal was meticulous in his examination of each specimen. His animated gestures made it clear to the audience which aspects of which dogs he liked, and, even more so, certain characteristics that he found undesirable. In the end, he pulled out five males and five females which he considered outstanding. These dogs were of several different bloodlines. However, when he made his final choices, Ch. Quibbletown T.G. of Basquaerie was chosen as the best male there. What a lovely tribute to Mrs. Crane's efforts to preserve correct type in the breed she had introduced to our shores fifty years previously.

However, M. Mansencal did not choose T.G. for Best of Breed. Rather, Best of Breed was awarded to the Winners Bitch, Ch. Euskari Kaskadian Everstar, bred by Mrs. Cary and owned by Mr. Floyd—T.G.'s daughter! What greater honor could there be than for a stud dog to be beaten by his own progeny?

In the ten years since then, T.G.'s sons and daughters and their offspring have inspired breeders all over the country. As Mrs. Weisser put it, "It's not just his own get. For many breeders, T.G. serves as a symbol of our mental image of the ideal Great Pyrenees. He was a big dog, thirty-one inches tall with a lot of body, but he was also of overwhelming beauty, his head and expression, his bearing and carriage. He made your heart stop. He had excellent topline, drive and length of stride, and a *wonderful* temperament!"

Actually bred to fewer than ten bitches, T.G. has an outstanding record of specialty-winning offspring, including the previously mentioned National Specialty winning bitch and two sons who have taken top honors at Canadian National Specialties. T.G.'s son, Am/Can Ch. Euzkotar One for the Money ("Jesse"), bred and owned by the Weissers, was Best of Breed at the Canadian National Specialty in 1982, Winners Dog at the American National Specialty in 1982, and had numerous other wins including BOB at the Northern California Specialty in 1983 and 1984. Jesse has sired many champions including Ch. Euzkotar Fancy Lovin', bred by Mrs. Weisser and co-owned by her with Carolyn Mohr (Ohio), who was RWB at the 1987 National Specialty. Jesse's grandson, Ch. Reymaree Tonto's Crackerjack, bred and owned by Jean Cave (Texas), was a multiple group placer from the classes.

Another T.G. son, Am/Can Ch. Ventisquero's Friend O' the Devil ("Taylor"), bred by Mr. Scott and co-owned by him with Mr. and Mrs. Lawrence Carr (Washington), was Best of Breed at the Canadian National Specialty in 1988 and Best Opposite Sex at the Canadian National in 1986. A Taylor son, Ch. Catalan Roman, bred by the Carrs, was Best of Breed at the Northwest Specialty in 1987. Roman's sister, Ch. Catalan Kiowa, was best puppy at the Canadian National Specialty in 1986. T.G.'s granddaughter Can Ch. Weskyuwin Hi Mountain Odyssey TT, bred and owned by Ms. Armstrong, was Best Opposite Sex at the Alberta Specialty in 1984. T.G.'s great-grandson Can Ch. Benjamin Bravo, also owned by Ms. Armstrong, was Winners Dog at the 1986 Canadian National. T.G.'s daughter Ch. Quanset D.G. of Caspyr, owned by Betty Wade Warmack, was Best Opposite Sex at the California Specialty in 1989 and Best Veteran and Award of Merit at the National Specialty in 1990.

Many of the most prominent T.G. descendants trace their pedigrees to Am/Can Ch. Euskari Kaskadian Everstar HOF ("Tubie"), M. Mansencal's choice as Best of Breed at the 1980 National. Her daughter, Am/Can Ch. Kaskadian's Image of Everstar ("Tauna"), bred and owned by Mr. Floyd, sired by Am/Can Ch. Euzkotar Hell or High Water HOF/HOF, was Best of Breed from the classes at the Canadian National Specialty under judge Alain Pecoult, Best of Breed from the classes at the British Columbia Specialty, and Best of Winners/Best Bred By Exhibitor at the American National Specialty—all in 1986!

Tubie's son Am/Can Ch. Kaskadian Skookumchuk Kid ("Chuk"), bred and owned by Mr. Floyd, is a multiple group winning dog and is siring well. Chuk's son Am/Can Ch. Kaskadian's Idyll gossip ("Jackson"), bred and owned by Mr. Floyd and Mr. Frank Ingram, was Best in Sweepstakes at the 1988 National Specialty at six months of age and Best of Winners at the Northern California Specialty in 1989. In 1990 Jackson is just starting his career as a young special, but is following in his father's footsteps. He is already a multiple Working Group winner in both the United States and Canada. Repeating the breeding of Chuk to Jackson's mother, Ch. Kas-

T.G. son, Am/Can Ch. Euz-kotar One for the Money, Best of Breed at the 1982 Canadian National Specialty, won BOB at the Southern California Specialty, breeder-owner-handled by Francesca Weisser.

T.G. son, Am/Can Ch. Ventisquero Friend O' the Devil, Best of Breed at the 1988 Canadian National Specialty , won BOS at the 1986 Canadian National Specialty under French judge, Alain Pecoult. Bred by Gerald Scott and Sandy Glas. Co-owned by Gerald Scott and Mr. and Mrs. Lawrence Carr.

Patricia Princehouse

T.G. daughter, Ch. Quanset D.G. of Caspyr, won WB and BOS at the 1989 California Specialty to finish her championship under breeder-judge, Joann Teems, owner-handled by Betty Wade Warmack.

Callea photo by *Meg*

kadian Dancin' In The Dark, produced Ch. Kaskadian Whitehope Timber, co-owned by Mr. Floyd and Mr. and Mrs. David Simon (Pennsylvania). Timber was Best of Winners at the National Capitol Area Specialty in 1989 at six months of age, finished his championship with Winners Dog, Best of Winners and Award of Merit at the 1990 National Specialty, and went Best of Breed at the 1990 Pyrenees Fanciers of New England Specialty. There are many other winners, too numerous to mention.

Thus T.G., the last of the great dogs bred by Mary Crane, is the only stud dog in recent times to sire multiple National Specialty Best of Breed winners, one American and two Canadian. It is a fitting tribute to Mrs. Crane that T.G. and his descendants have done a great part of their winning under breeder-judges. It would seem that, beyond most Great Pyrenees fanciers, owners of T.G. descendants owe Mrs. Crane a special debt of gratitude.

4

Early American Bloodlines

THE BASQUAERIE IMPORTS of Mr. and Mrs. Crane provided a firm foundation upon which to build for the future. During the growing years, a number of well-known breeders and friends of the Great Pyrenees also made important contributions to the further development of the breed in America.

COTE DE NEIGE

Among the early pioneering kennels, Marjorie Butcher's Cote de Neige stands out as a dramatic example of just what can be accomplished by a truly gifted and dedicated breeder. During a rather brief period, little more than a decade, when Cote de Neige was at its height, no kennel produced more champions, or did more to establish correct type and soundness in its bloodlines.

Marjorie Butcher was born in Canada, educated in Switzerland, received training in the opera and sang for the Washington Opera Company. A great lover of dogs from early childhood, Mrs. Butcher moved to the Berkshires and, in Pittsfield, Massachusetts, acquired her foundation female. Ch. Basquaerie Fleurette promptly whelped a litter of puppies in a coat closet—much to the surprise of all concerned. It was obvious that she had indulged in a moonlight romance with her own brother! But Mrs. Butcher said, "We had a very nice litter from her. I could see no signs of nervousness, or what you might expect from inbreeding."

The following year Fleurette was bred to Ch. Patou of Basquaerie and produced two champions, Cote de Neige Patou and Joyeuse. The bloodlines of other imports were added, the most notable being Chs. Bazen de Soum and Maya de Langladure from France, and Ch. Zayda Van Euskara from Holland.

Bazen de Soum was the dog imported by the Misses Hedge in the fall of 1930. He later distinguished himself by doing sled work for the Grenville Mission in Newfoundland. And Ch. Zayda became the first Great Pyrenees to win a Canadian Championship.

The honor role of Cote de Neige champions, well over thirty in number, included many famous winners of the day: Cote de Neige Acteur, Ariel, Ariette, Berceuse, Echo, Guerrier, Nive, Nivereau, Pastourette, Symphonie, Zephire and others. Mrs. Butcher's musical interest explains the many musical names given her dogs.

In 1944 Ch. Cote de Neige Echo became the first bitch to win the Will S. Monroe Memorial Trophy by going Best of Breed at the Great Pyrenees Club of America National Speciality. Two years later, Chs. Cote de Neige Echo and her litter sister, Ariette, won the Best Brace at Westminster. The following year Ch. Cote de Neige Symphonie became the first American-bred Great Pyrenees to win an all-breed Best in Show!

Mrs. C. Seaver Smith, a contemporary authority closely associated with Marjorie Butcher in the early fifties, recalls: "It would be difficult to find an American-bred Great Pyrenees today who does not have Cote de Neige in its background. La Shan, Esterhazy, Castellan, La Colina, Crete de Pins, Bon Chance, Robwood, Add-En-On, Be-La-Mar and Quibbletown all had, in their beginnings, at least some Cote de Neige stock.

"It would not be accurate to refer to Cote de Neige as a bloodline, as there was no true pattern of linebreeding or inbreeding. It cannot be denied, however, that through selective and perceptive breeding, Marjorie definitely established a Cote de Neige type, which we can still identify in the dogs of today. It is obvious in going over her records and photographs that the means to that end were the bitches of Cote de Neige. She seemed to have an unending supply of superb bitches and rarely was the kennel defeated in that sex."

In the forties Mrs. Butcher moved her dogs to Connecticut, where the kennel remained a small family-run operation with emphasis on quality. In the fifties she again moved to a new location elsewhere in Connecticut. Since the new property was not well suited to a large breed, Mrs. Butcher turned to her other love, the Pembroke Welsh Corgi. In a short time, Cote de Neige was to add to its fame through its top-winning Corgis.

At the GPCA Fall Specialty Dinner in 1971, Mrs. Butcher revealed some of her guiding principles:

Ch. Cote de Neige Echo, one of Marjorie Butcher's top winning bitches. Whelped in 1940. *Courtesy, Edith K. Smith*

Ch. Cote Neige Ariette I, sired by Ch. Basquaerie Bichon CD, and a litter sister to Mrs. Butcher's Best In Show winner Ch. Cote de Neige Symphonie. Whelped in 1942.
Courtesy, Edith K. Smith

Ch. Cote de Neige Ariel displays the perfection of type Marjorie Butcher sought in her bitches. Whelped 1942.
Courtesy, Edith K. Smith

I'm a strong believer that the first litter you get from a bitch is going to be your best litter. I think if you're going to plan your first breeding, you should breed the very best you want to breed.

After my first litter which was inbred brother to sister, I've never bred that close again. I have bred father to daughter, but I'd rather skip a generation.

I believe that pigmentation problems are harder to correct than lack of bone. Again, I don't think a Pyrenees is a dog that should have clumsy, overly heavy bone. I think that it should be a moderately boned dog. It should be an agile moving dog with good, sturdy bone.

We often spayed our bitches after their first litter. They're much healthier if they're spayed. We were fortunate in being able to place our bitches in homes after breeding them. They didn't have to spend the rest of their lives in the kennels. There may be exceptions to this, but this was my policy.

I think the coat of a Pyrenees should be really quite coarse hair lying absolutely flat. This coat sheds the dirt much better, and you can keep a dog with what I have called a "correct" Pyrenees coat very clean with very little effort.

I think that any little puppy that's brought into the world should have the opportunity to live. I do think that there are certain very serious faults that may warrant culling. But when you get a puppy which just hasn't quite made it, I think it's pretty sad if some good home somewhere can't be found. I think the puppy should be sold without papers along with a written agreement that it is never to be used for breeding. If you put a pet-quality puppy out and allow it to breed, then you will pull the breed quality down. A little puppy going without papers and with a signed agreement makes an awfully nice pet for someone who can't afford to pay the price for a show-quality dog.

Throughout her life Mrs. Butcher remained actively interested in the breed. Her devotion to the Great Pyrenees prompted her to serve on a committee to study the Standard of 1971. Mrs. Butcher was recognized as one of the leading authorities on Great Pyrenees up to the time of her passing in 1973.

CASTELLAN

The kennel prefix of the author, Paul Strang, came into being with the purchase of Ch. Cote de Neige Pataud from Mrs. Butcher.

While living in France in the 1930s, Mr. Strang owned a number of Great Pyrenees. These were selected from firsthand experience after visiting the shows, talking with the French breeders, and making several trips into the Pyrenees Mountains to study the dogs in their native environment.

Pataud came to Castellan Kennels in the spring of 1946, and before passing away some ten years later, this splendid dog sired innumerable litters that inherited, to a high degree, his beautiful head, keen intelligence and outgoing nature.

The goal of Castellan breeding, in the tradition of Pataud and his fine descendant, Castellan Coco, has always been to produce sound dogs of proper type and disposition, in the upper size range.

ADD-EN-ON KENNELS

The prefix of Dr. and Mrs. Carl Harris came into being in 1937 with the purchase of their foundation female, Basquaerie Hunnette, from Mrs. Crane.

Additional specimens were acquired from the Cranes and Marjorie Butcher. The first litter whelped in 1938, sired by Ch. Cote de Neige Zephire, was to establish the reputation of the kennel. Among seven puppies, six were champions by eighteen months of age, and one, Ch. Henry VIII, was a Group winner.

During the twelve years when Add-En-On was at its peak, the kennel played a major role in popularizing and promoting the breed, particularly on the East Coast, where modern pedigrees still show the Add-En-On influence. After the death of Dr. Harris in 1945, Mrs. Harris and her daughter converted their kennel into a boarding and training facility. They are the authors of the excellent *Add-En-On Kennels Course in Kennel Management.*

BATOR DE ESTERHAZY, REG.

Born in Hungary, Frank Koller's kennel name celebrates the Esterhazy nobility of his native land. During a brief period in the late forties, this suffix was used by a Giant Schnauzer breeder and during this time Mr. Koller registered his dogs under the Zold Erdo prefix. Later he reclaimed his rightful suffix and had it registered.

Frank Koller based his bloodlines on Basquaerie, La Colina and Cote de Neige. Ch. Vitz of Bator de Esterhazy and Nagy Feher of Bator de Esterhazy made an important contribution to the breed in this period. Chiogenes of Bighyo was the sire of Castellan Canichet.

Interbreeding between his foundation dogs, Frank Koller produced the sturdy, consistent Esterhazy bloodline that, with only occasional outcrosses, continues to this day.

Mr. Koller became the Great Pyrenees Club of America's representative to the American Kennel Club in 1954 and held the position until he retired from the Club in 1966. He watched the breed develop over the years, and he firmly believes that the present holds the reality of what in the past was only a wish. "Now is what we have always wanted and strived for. Now we have many Pyrenees, really good ones, and beautiful ones."

LA COLINA

Dr. and Mrs. Frederick Seward founded their La Colina Kennels at New Hampton, New York, in 1940. Ch. Lawrence of Combermere, purchased from Mr. and Mrs. George Lord's Combermere Island Kennels in Ontario, Canada, was the kennel's foundation stud dog. This was a truly beautiful dog, strong in de Soum and de Langladure bloodlines. Some fine bitches were purchased from Basquaerie and Cote de Neige.

The Sewards did not achieve instant success. Several of their younger stock were eventually shown to their championship, but on the whole Lawrence did not seem to be passing on his superlative qualities. Fanciers with less determination would have given up. Fortunately the Sewards persevered and for that we can be thankful. La Colina was, eventually, to go down in history as one of our breed's most outstanding bloodlines—and Lawrence as one of its great stud dogs.

The "open sesame" to success came when daughters of Lawrence were bred to the outcross stud dog Ch. La Shan Marc of Basquaerie. Vano de la Colina and Ch. Vistoso de la Colina were produced in this manner. Ch. Lorvaso de la Colina, a grandson of Lawrence through his sire, was to pass his fine bloodlines on to Ch. Quibbletown Impresario.

As it turned out, Lawrence of Combermere became not only a pillar of the breed, but a testimonial to the fact that good breeders, such as Dr. and Mrs. Seward, with grit and perseverance, can turn adversity into success.

LA SHAN

The La Shan Kennels of Mr. and Mrs. Bruce Layman of Waynesboro, Pennsylvania, produced a number of show winners over a period of more than a decade. Their foundation bitch, Basquaerie Anemone, was purchased from Mrs. Crane in whelp by Ch. K'Eros de Guerveur in 1943. This breeding combined the French bloodlines of de Soum, de Truchard and de Guerveur.

The mating gave birth to three champions: Ch. La Shan Marc of Basquaerie, Ch. La Shan White Belle and Ch. La Shan K'Eros de Guerveur.

La Shan White Belle became the first Great Pyrenees bitch ever to win a Working Group, scoring at the Heart of America K.C. show in 1949. Only one other bitch in the breed has ever repeated this feat.

From their de Guerveur sire the La Shan dogs inherited great size and heavy bone and also the typical de Guerveur heads. To refine the heads in their line, the Laymans purchased the stud dog Ch. Combermere Capitan from the Lords in Canada. This dog was sired by Ch. Ibos du Val d'Aure, the result of a brother to sister mating by M. and Mme. Carel in

Ch. La Shan Marc of Basquaerie, son of America's first Best In Show winner, Ch. K'Eros de Guerveur of Basquaerie. La Shan Marc was one of the breed's all-time top producers with 16 champion offspring. Owned by Homer H. Lee.

Ch. Cordelia of Koch's Knoll CD, HDF, a granddaughter of Ch. La Shan Marc of Basquaerie, sired by Milfra's El Gran Blanco Zutano. "Triksy" was the dam of six champions.
Courtesy, Dorothy Wise

Ch. Lorvaso de La Colina. A cornerstone of the Quibbletown breeding program. Sire of eleven champions. Owned by Mr. and Mrs. C. Seaver Smith, Jr.

53

France, made to capture the full effect of their parents, Ch. Estat d'Argeles and Fr. Ch. Monne de Langladure. Ch. Combermere Capitan thus brought the needed refinement to the La Shan bloodlines.

La Shan bloodlines were distributed from coast to coast: Ch. La Shan Damoiselle went to Mrs. Butcher, Ch. La Shan K'Eros de Guerveur to the Zimmermans in Minnesota, Int. Ch. La Shan Marc Aurelius to Mrs. Bethel Blendheim in Seattle, Washington, and Ch. La Shan White Belle to the Nobles in Iowa. Thus stock from La Shan, like that from La Colina, went to breeders throughout the country where they were to exert a powerful influence on behalf of the breed.

THE BREED ON THE WEST COAST

To San Francisco must go the honor of hosting the first dog show in the United States at which Pyrenean Mountain Dogs were exhibited. This event occurred in 1915 at the great exposition celebrating the opening of the Panama Canal. According to a sharp-eyed newspaperman, there were also a number of other rare breeds on display, including Basset Hounds and the Russian Aftsharkas. Of course, few if any of the breeds shown at this early gathering were pedigreed or registered with the American Kennel Club. However, it does point out the fact that San Francisco, indeed, California does have deep ties to dog shows in general, and to our breed in particular.

By the late 1940s, the breed on the West Coast was not only well underway, but was actually represented by some of the finest specimens and bloodlines in America.

Contributing greatly to the size of the California dogs was the breeding done by Mavis Miller, of **Milfra Great Pyrenees**, who imported the dog Ch. Zutano de la Colina from the Sewards in New York. Bitches at Milfra were obtained largely from two other distinguished West Coast kennels of that era, the **Val-Ken-Be** Kennels of Mr. and Mrs. R. Kenneth Evans of Portland, Oregon; and the **Be-La-Mar** Kennels of Bethel Blendheim in Seattle, Washington. As noted earlier, the Blendheims' foundation stud was Ch. La Shan Marc Aurelius.

The Val-Ken-Be breeding program contained some of the finest bloodlines of its era. Their primary stud dog, Basquaerie Dijon, made a solid contribution to West Coast Pyrenees.

The influence of his sire, Ch. La Shan Marc of Basquaerie, was even more considerable. This dog was sent to Homer Lee in northern California in 1950 by Mrs. Crane, with the hope that he would make a major contribution to California breeding. This he did, siring sixteen champions.

Among the pioneer efforts in southern California was Fran Bennet's **Pyr-Haven** Kennels. Her first brood bitch, Ch. Princess Carla, embodied

Basquaerie bloodlines. The first mating of Carla was to the famous stud dog Ch. Basquaerie Monte Cristo, owned by the King-Smiths of Los Angeles. Three champions were produced from this mating in 1953. They included Prince Albert de Mont and Carlita de Mont, both of whom became key dogs in the PyrHaven bloodlines.

Ch. Basquaerie Monte Cristo was used at stud a number of times in both southern and northern California. In northern California, his influence is to be found primarily in the offspring of a litter whelped by Ch. Cordelia of Koch's Knoll, CD ("Trisky").

Trisky was bred by Mr. and Mrs. E. A. Koch and sold to the Melvin Rhodes (**Rhopyr**). She was bred twice. The first mating, to Monte Cristo, gave birth to three champions, one of whom was Ch. Montalvo of Rhopyr. In turn, Montalvo was the sire of the breed's top producer, Ch. Rogue La Rue, about whom more will be said later. Trisky's second mating was to Ch. Basquaerie Beau Mari. This breeding also led to champions who were to leave important descendants in California, namely Ch. Odin of Rhopyr and Ch. Euskaldun Rhopyr Gracieuse.

Another Pyrenees to top the list of California producers was Hendaye Euskalrho Laustan. He, too, sired sixteen champions, and was the chief stud at **Hai-Lee**. His sire was Ch. Euskaldun Ramuntcho and his dam was Ch. Euskaldun Rhopyr Gracieuse.

Also contributing to the early bloodlines on the West Coast was the breeding of Ralph Ensign (**Ralfrans**). Ch. Quibbletown Windsor was brought to California in 1956 by the Ensigns, where he sired Ch. Count Athos of Ralfrans. This dog, in turn, sired a great many leading California show winners. The Ensigns' Jacquiline of Ralfrans was the dam of six champions, a number of them sired at the **Hai-Lee** Kennels of Mr. and Mrs. Merval Haile, by Hendaye Euskalrho Laustan. The influence of these dogs continues to be felt on the West Coast.

The combination of the bloodlines of Basquaerie, La Shan and La Colina, which was to give the West Coast a well-deserved reputation for size, was further reinforced in 1962 by the arrival of the bitch Amelia de Fontenay. Amelia was the daughter of Irving de Pontoise de Fontenay, a French dog bred by M. Delattre of **Pontoise** Kennels. Irving's sire was Ch. Drex de Pontoise, one of the truly large dogs of France.

In the late 1950s we find that three dogs of superior merit were taking the majority of the Bests of Breed at the leading California shows. Together, they embodied the best of the "old California bloodlines." They were: Ch. Odin of Rhopyr, owned by Mr. and Mrs. A. R. Hunter; Ch. Montalvo of Rhopyr, owned by Mr. and Mrs. Arthur Nevins; and Christine Palmer-Person's Ch. Euskaldun Ramuntcho, sired by Ch. Prince Albert de Mont out of Ch. Basquaerie Coquette II.

Ch. Euskaldun Ramuntcho's type was evaluated by Mrs. Crane in these words: "Never have I seen a lovelier or more typical Pyrenees head than Ramuntcho has. I would know just by looking at it that he had many crosses in his pedigree to the fine type of the famous old European Tri-International and American Champion Estat d'Argeles and his brother Estagel."

Speaking of the California dogs in general in another publication of the early sixties, Mrs. Crane wrote, "It is a real pleasure for me to write these few words about the status of Western-bred and -owned Great Pyrenees, for I have, possibly unknown to any of their owners, sung their praises very loudly ever since my last visit to the Coast in 1959. At that time, I was fortunate to have shown under me a very imposing array of these dogs and I was particularly impressed with their size and well-proportioned appearance, their excellent type and their splendid coats."

5

The Great Pyrenees Standards: Now And Then

THE OFFICIAL AMERICAN KENNEL CLUB STANDARD OF THE GREAT PYRENEES (EFFECTIVE AUGUST 1, 1990)

General Appearance

The Great Pyrenees dog conveys the distinct impression of elegance and unsurpassed beauty combined with great overall size and majesty. He has a white or principally white coat that may contain markings of badger, gray or varying shades of tan. He possesses a keen intelligence and a kindly, while regal, expression. Exhibiting a unique elegance of bearing and movement, his soundness and coordination show unmistakably the purpose for which he has been bred, the strenuous work of guarding the flocks in all kinds of weather on the steep mountain slopes of the Pyrenees.

Size, Proportion, Substance

Size: The height at the withers ranges from 27 inches to 32 inches for dogs and from 25 inches to 29 inches for bitches. A 27 inch dog weighs about

100 pounds and a 25 inch bitch weighs about 85 pounds. Weight is in proportion to the overall size and structure.

Proportion: The Great Pyrenees is a balanced dog with the height measured at the withers being somewhat less than the length of the body measured from the point of the shoulder to the rearmost projection of the upper thigh (buttocks). These proportions create a somewhat rectangular dog, slightly longer than it is tall. Front and rear angulation are balanced.

Substance: The Great Pyrenees is a dog of medium substance whose coat deceives those who do not feel the bone and muscling. Commensurate with his size and impression of elegance there is sufficient bone and muscle to provide a balance with the frame.

Faults:

> Size: Dogs and bitches under minimum size or over maximum size.
> Substance: Dogs too heavily boned or too lightly boned to be in balance with their frame.

Head

Correct head and expression are essential to the breed. The head is not heavy in proportion to the size of the dog. It is wedge-shaped with a slightly rounded crown.

Expression: The expression is elegant, intelligent and contemplative.

Eyes: Medium-sized, almond-shaped, set slightly obliquely, rich dark brown. Eyelids are close-fitting with black rims.

Ears: Small to medium in size, V-shaped with rounded tips, set on at eye level, normally carried low, flat, and close to the head. There is a characteristic meeting of the hair of the upper and lower face which forms a line from the outer corner of the eye to the base of the ear.

Skull and Muzzle: The muzzle is approximately equal in length to the back skull. The width and length of the skull are approximately equal. The muzzle blends smoothly with the skull. The cheeks are flat. There is sufficient fill under the eyes. A slight furrow exists between the eyes. There is no apparent stop. The bony eyebrow ridges are only slightly developed. Lips are tight-fitting with the upper lip just covering the lower lip. There is a strong lower jaw. The nose and lips are black.

Teeth: A scissor bite is preferred, but a level bite is acceptable. It is not unusual to see dropped (receding) lower central incisor teeth.

Faults:

Too heavy head (St. Bernard- or Newfoundland-like)
Too narrow or small skull
Foxy appearance
Presence of an apparent stop
Missing pigmentation on nose, eyerims, or lips
Eyelids round, triangular, loose or small
Overshot, undershot, wry mouth

Neck, Topline, and Body

Neck: Strongly muscled and of medium length, with minimal dewlap.

Topline: The backline is level.

Body: The chest is moderately broad. The rib cage is well sprung, oval in shape, and of sufficient depth to reach the elbows. Back and loin are broad and strongly coupled with some tuckup. The croup is gently sloping with the tail set on just below the level of the back.

Tail: The tailbones are of sufficient length to reach the hock. The tail is well plumed, carried low in repose and may be carried over the back, "making the wheel," when aroused. When present, a "shepherd's crook" at the end of the tail accentuates the plume. When gaiting, the tail may be carried either over the back or low. Both carriages are equally correct.

Fault: Barrel ribs

Forequarters

Shoulders: The shoulders are well laid back, well muscled and lie close to the body. The upper arm meets the shoulder blade at approximately a right angle. The upper arm angles backward from the point of the shoulder to the elbow and is never perpendicular to the ground. The length of the shoulder blade and the upper arm are approximately equal. The height from the ground to the elbow appears approximately equal to the height from the elbow to the withers.

Forelegs: The legs are of sufficient bone and muscle to provide a balance with the frame. The elbows are close to the body and point directly to the rear when standing and gaiting. The forelegs, when viewed from the side, are located directly under the withers and are straight and vertical to the ground. The elbows, when viewed from the front, are set in a straight line from the point of shoulder to the wrist. Front pasterns are strong and flexible. Each foreleg carries a single dewclaw.

Front feet: Rounded, close-cupped, well padded, toes well arched.

Hindquarters

The angulation of the hindquarters is similar in degree to that of the forequarters.

Thighs: Strongly muscular upper thighs extend from the pelvis at right angles. The upper thigh is the same length as the lower thigh, creating moderate stifle joint angulation when viewed in profile. The rear pastern (metatarsus) is of medium length and perpendicular to the ground as the dog stands naturally. This produces a moderate degree of angulation in the hock joint, when viewed from the side. The hindquarters from the hip to the rear pastern are straight and parallel, as viewed from the rear. The rear legs are of sufficient bone and muscle to provide a balance with the frame. Double dewclaws are located on each rear leg.

Rear feet: The rear feet have a structural tendency to toe-out slightly. This breed characteristic is not to be confused with cowhocks. The rear feet, like the fore feet, are rounded, close-cupped, well padded with toes well arched.

Fault: Absence of double dewclaws on each rear leg

Coat

The weather-resistant double coat consists of a long, flat, thick, outer coat of coarse hair, straight or slightly undulating, and lying over a dense, fine, woolly undercoat. The coat is more profuse about the neck and shoulders where it forms a ruff or mane which is more pronounced in males. Longer hair on the tail forms a plume. There is feathering along the back of the front legs and along the back of the thighs, giving a "pantaloon" effect. The hair on the face and ears is shorter and of finer texture. Correctness of coat is more important than abundance of coat.

Faults:

   Curly coat
   Stand-off coat (Samoyed type)

Color

   White or white with markings of gray, badger, reddish brown or varying shades of tan. Markings of varying size may appear on the ears, head (including a full face mask), tail and as a few body spots. The undercoat may be white or shaded. All of the above described colorings and locations are characteristic of the breed and equally correct.

Fault: Outer coat markings covering more than one third of the body

Gait

   The Great Pyrenees moves smoothly and elegantly, true and straight ahead, exhibiting both power and agility. The stride is well balanced with good reach and strong drive. The legs tend to move toward the center line as speed increases. Ease and efficiency of movement are more important than speed.

Temperament

   Character and temperament are of utmost importance. In nature, the Great Pyrenees is confident, gentle, and affectionate. While territorial and protective of his flock or family when necessary, his general demeanor is one of quiet composure, both patient and tolerant. He is strong willed, independent and somewhat reserved, yet attentive, fearless and loyal to his charges both human and animal.
   Although the Great Pyrenees may appear reserved in the show ring, any sign of excessive shyness, nervousness or aggression to humans is unacceptable and must be considered an extremely serious fault.

   An in-depth look at the Standard will be presented later in this book.

THE 1935 AMERICAN KENNEL CLUB STANDARD OF THE GREAT PYRENEES (APPROVED FEBRUARY 13, 1935)

General Appearance: A dog of immense size, great majesty, keen intelligence, and kindly expression; of unsurpassed beauty and a certain elegance, all white or principally white with markings of badger, gray or varying shades of tan. In the rolling, ambling gait it shows unmistakably the purpose for which it has been bred, the strenuous work of guarding the flocks in all kinds of weather on the steep mountain slopes of the Pyrenees. Hence soundness is of the greatest importance and absolutely necessary for the proper fulfillment of his centuries-old task.

Size: The average height at the shoulder is 27 inches to 32 inches for dogs, and 25 inches to 29 inches for bitches. The average length from shoulder blades to root of tail should be the same as the height in any given specimen. The average girth is 36 inches to 42 inches for dogs, and 32 inches to 36 inches for bitches. The weight for dogs runs 100 to 125 pounds, and 90 to 115 pounds for bitches. A dog heavily boned with close cupped feet, double dewclaws behind and single dewclaws in front.

Head: Large and wedge-shaped, measuring ten inches to eleven inches from dome to point of nose, with rounding crown, furrow only slightly developed with no apparent stop. **Cheeks:** Flat. **Ears:** V-shaped, but rounded at the tips, of medium size, set parallel with the eyes, carried low and close to the head except when raised at attention. **Eyes:** Of medium size set slightly obliquely, dark rich brown in color with close eyelids, well pigmented. **Lips:** Close-fitting, edged in black. **Dewlaps:** Developed but little. The head is in brief that of a brown bear, but with the ears falling down.

Neck: Short, stout and strongly muscular.

Body: Well-placed shoulders set obliquely, close to the body. **Back and Loin:** Well coupled, straight and broad. **Haunches:** Fairly prominent. **Rump:** Slightly sloping. **Ribs:** Flat-sided. **Chest:** Deep. **Tail:** Of sufficient length to hang below the hocks, well plumed, carried low in repose, and curled high over the back, "making the wheel" when alert.

Coat: Created to withstand severe weather, with heavy fine white undercoat and long flat thick outercoat of coarser hair, straight or slightly undulating.

Qualities: In addition to his original age-old position in the scheme of pastoral life as protector of the shepherd and his flock, the Great Pyrenees has been used for centuries as a guard and watchdog on the large estates of his native France, and for this he has proven ideal. He is as serious in play as he is in work, adapting and molding himself to the moods, desires and even the very life of his human companions, through fair weather and foul, through leisure hours and hours fraught with danger, responsibility and extreme exertion; he is the exemplification of gentleness and docility with those he knows, of faithfulness and devotion for his master even to the point of self-sacrifice; and of courage in the protection of the flock placed in his care and of the ones he loves.

Scale of Points:

(a) Head, 25 points comprised as follows:
    Shape of skull 5
    Ears   5
    Eyes   5
    Muzzle   5
    Teeth   5

(b) General Conformation, 25 points comprised as follows:
    Neck   5
    Chest   5
    Back   5
    Loins   5
    Feet   5

(c) Coat: 10 points
(d) Size and Soundness: 25 points
(e) Expression and General Appearance: 15 points
    TOTAL number of points, 100.

SOME OBSERVATIONS ON THE REVISION OF THE AKC STANDARD

With the introduction of the breed to the United States in 1933, a standard was required to register the dogs with the American Kennel Club. As a temporary measure so that the breed could be recognized and shown, Mr. and Mrs. Crane persuaded their artist friend living in Paris, Miss Clara Perry, to consult with M. Senac-Lagrange and obtain an English translation of the French Standard. The essential points were discussed, and after making minor changes Senac-Lagrange gave his approval to its final form. It was adopted by the AKC, but remained in force for only two years, after which it was replaced by the 1935 Standard.

The 1935 Standard was mainly an extension of the French view. But there are certain important differences.

The Standard contained none of the breed faults listed in the French version. The inclusion of at least some of these would have been of considerable aid to American judges and breeders unfamiliar with the finer points of the Great Pyrenees dog.

Next we come to the description of the dog's gait: "In the rolling, ambling gait it shows unmistakably the purpose for which it was bred. . . ." A further explanation of this passage appears because to many these words have implied that pacing is a common breed characteristic.

We must recall that the French version did not give a gait description. So when one was required for the AKC Standard, an attempt was made to locate an appropriate source. This led inevitably to M. Senac-Lagrange, who had firmly maintained in his notes that *at times* the Pyrenean dog adopts a gait like that described in the literature on horses (Senac was an authority on this subject also). This he described as a "broken pace," with the lateral biped beat in four-time, and not two. He was quick to point out that the same applied to the Petit Berger, a breed also given to long hours of work on the mountainside. It would seem that what Senac was describing was not the pace, with its exaggerated side-to-side rolling body motion, but a modification of it more akin to the single foot. This is undeniably a resting gait which conserves energy and momentum and can be maintained effortlessly for long periods. It must be added that Senac-Lagrange did not condone pacing in the show ring. And when a gait description did eventually appear in the French Standard, as we shall see shortly, it did not include a roll, an amble or a shuffle.

The classical working gait of the Great Pyrenees will be taken up in a later chapter.

Next, two changes were made in the dog's size and balance. The first was the lowering of the minimum height for both sexes by a half inch. The second was the specification that the shoulder height must equal body length (from withers to root of tail), thus giving a compact and well-balanced silhouette.

One significant omission is found in the head section, in which the 1935 Standard does not specify the structure or length of the muzzle. As the French state, it should be strong, of good length, slightly pointed toward the nostrils and with a *black* nose. A person reading the 1935 Standard would be perfectly free to breed a Pyrenees with a short, square muzzle (without pigment)—yet this would be completely uncomplimentary to the breed type. The 1935 Standard also does not mention that a correct Pyrenean bite is one in which the incisors meet in either a scissors or an even manner. Fortunately, the 1990 Standard does not make these omissions, and does specify the French Standard.

With these thoughts in mind, in 1938 the Great Pyrenees Club of America published a *Concise Guidebook on the Breed* which was distributed to members and judges. The Guidebook contained a list of Proposed Changes to the Standard as well as a list of *Peculiarities Characteristic of the Breed* which aided considerably in the matter of interpreting the Standard. Unfortunately, the Guidebook went out of circulation years ago. An in-depth look at the Standard will be taken up later in this book.

CURRENT STANDARD IN FRANCE
(R.A.C.P. 1970)

General Appearance: That of a dog of large size, imposing and strongly built, but not devoid of a certain elegance.

Faults: A general appearance of heaviness, without distinction, or indicating a resemblance to the Saint Bernard, Newfoundland or Leonberg. Sluggish, overweight dogs, or those having a dangerous look.

Size: Males: 70 to 80 cms (27.55 to 31.49 inches). Females: 65 to 72 cms (25.59 to 28.34 inches). A tolerance of 2 cms above these sizes is admissible for subjects of flawless type.

Head: Not too heavy in comparison to the size. The sides of the head are fairly flat; the skull is slightly rounded; the peak of the occipital bone, being visible, gives the posterior portion of the skull an ogival, vaulted form.

The breadth of the skull at its widest part is about equal to its length. There is a gentle slope to the broad muzzle which is of good length, slightly pointed at its extremity. The lips hang but little, just enough to cover the lower jaw; they are black or very strongly marked with black, as is the roof of the mouth. The nose is entirely black. The head is that of a brown bear with the ears pressed down.

Faults: Head too heavy; overenlarged skull; foreskull protuberant; a heavy or marked stop; insufficient pigment of the mucous membranes; lips sagging too much; a square head.

Disqualification: A nose other than completely black.

Teeth: A full set of healthy, white teeth is required. The incisors meet like the blades of a scissors, the uppers just overlapping the lowers without losing contact. An even bite is acceptable.

Disqualification: An undershot or overshot bite.

Eyes: The rather small eyes, of intelligent and contemplative expression, are amber brown in color. They are surrounded by tight lids, bordered in black, and placed slightly obliquely. The look is gentle and dreamy.

Faults: Round eyes, too light and prominent (staring); drooping eyelids; an evil or haggard expression; insufficient pigment around the eyes.

Disqualification: Missing pigment on the eyelids.

Ears: Placed at the height of the eyes; fairly small, triangular in form and rounded at the tips; they fall flat against the head; carried a little higher when the dog is on the watch.

Faults: Long ears, poorly formed, folded, placed too high (above eye level).

Neck: Strong, fairly short, with the dewlap little developed.
Faults: Too slender and weak, too long, too much dewlap.

Shoulders: Medium oblique. Withers broad and well muscled.

Body: The chest does not come down too far but is broad and of good length. The ribs are slightly rounded, the back is of good length, broad and straight. The rump is slightly oblique with the haunches fairly prominent. The flanks drop but little.
Faults: Sway or roached back.

Legs: The forelegs are straight, strong and well fringed. Fringes on the hindquarters are longer and thicker. The thighs are rounded but not low. The hocks are strong, clean and sharp, of medium bent. The back legs carry well-formed double dewclaws.
Faults: Straight hocks. Poor front alignment; toeing in or out.
Disqualification: Absent dewclaws; single dewclaw or poorly developed dewclaw.

Feet: Not long, compact, with slightly arched toes.
Fault: Feet too long.

Tail: Fairly long, well-plumed; carried low when not at attention, preferably with just the extremity curled; raised over the back (making the wheel according to the mountaineers) when the dog is on the watch.
Faults: A tail too bushy or badly carried; a tail too short or too long, without plumage; not making the wheel in action.

Coat: Rather thick, flat; fairly long and supple, longer on the tail and about the neck where it is sometimes slightly waved. The hair of the pants is finer and more woolly and very thick.
Faults: A short or curly coat. Lack of undercoat.

Color: White or white with spots of gray or badger color (*blaireau*), pale yellow or wolf-gray on the head, the ears and the base of the tail. The markings of the badger are esteemed the most. A few spots on the body are permitted.
Faults: Other colors than those indicated above, which denote crossbreeding.
Disqualifications: Black markings reaching to the root of the hair.

Gait: In spite of his size, the Pyrenean moves easily, without plodding or heaviness, but on the contrary with elegance; due to his angulation he moves without tiring.

Disqualifications for Males: Monorchid and cryptorchid dogs, that is to say, those having only one testicle or none at all.

Scale of Points:

Skull and muzzle (nose, lips, jaws)	....	15
Eyes	....	10
Ears	....	5
Neck, back, loin, rump	....	12
Shoulders, chest, sides, flanks	....	10
Legs and feet	....	10
Tail and carriage of tail	....	8
Coat, color, pigmentation	....	15
General appearance (expression, size, gait)	....	15
		100

SOME OBSERVATIONS ON THE REVISION OF THE FRENCH STANDARD

This standard, compiled by M. Duconte and M. Delattre, is basically an attempt to update the Senac-Lagrange standard of 1927. (See Chapter 2.) Two new sections have been added: one on dentition and correct bite; the other on gait. A few notes have been added to the Head section. Despite the changes, it is quite apparent that every effort has been made to safeguard the *true* French type. In the words of M. Duconte:

> The type, which is the result of head, coat, markings, pigmentation, expression and gait will earn 60 points out of 100. These are the principal indications of purity, and they should never be sacrificed to the anatomical points, no matter how important the latter may be. Regarding the general aspect of the Pyrenean Mountain Dog, we insist that it lack that overall heavy appearance which is common to most big dogs, such as the Saint Bernard. This is why he is qualified in the standard as being a dog with a certain elegance.

Great importance is given to the tail carriage which is regarded by the French connoisseur as a positive sign of good breeding. As soon as the dog goes on the watch, he must lift his tail quite frankly and curl it over his back in such a way that the crook at the very end reaches the back at the level of the loins. This is the *arroundera* or "making the wheel" as the mountaineers say.

The French also insist that the top of the ears be level with the eyes and lie flat against the head to give the skull its distinctive contour.

Great emphasis continues to be placed on strong pigmentation, which in France must also cover the roof of the mouth.

A scissors bite, in which the upper and lower incisors are touching, is preferred. An even bite is admissible.

There has been no loss of regard for the Pyrenean eye, which must be gentle and dreamy (the faraway look).

Regarding the gait, the remarks of M. Mansencal will suffice:

> It is while the dog is trotting that one can best judge good gait and bearing, the "arroundera," and the elegance and pride of the Pyrenean Mountain Dog. Besides the build of the Mountain Dog, which should be established by working upwards, how can a plethoric dog, which often has short legs and loose skin, be elegant?
>
> In order to have an idea of this natural elegance and pride, one needs to have seen a Mountain Dog, head held high, tail arched, trotting the Lord knows where across the grass of a Pyrenean meadow far from all human habitation.

THE BRITISH STANDARD

The first standard for the breed in Great Britain was approved by the British Kennel Club in 1936. It remained identical to the American Standard until 1955 when a policy decision by the Kennel Club (England) called for the removal of the table of points from all standards having them.

In the late sixties, British fanciers became aware that without a points designation, or a list of well-considered faults, judges were finding it difficult to decide on the relative merits of the various dogs they saw in the show ring. Under the able direction of Sqn. Ldr. Peter Gilbert (R.A.F. Retd.), who served as Secretary of the Standard Working Party and later became the Chairman of the Pyrenean Mountain Dog Club, a new standard was formulated and approved by the Kennel Club in 1972. Several important and necessary clarifications were made. A number of faults are now included, being graded in accordance with their severity.

CURRENT STANDARD FOR THE PYRENEAN MOUNTAIN DOG IN GREAT BRITAIN

Characteristics: The Pyrenean is a natural guard dog and was originally employed as a protector of the shepherd and of his flocks.

General Appearance: The Pyrenean should possess great size, substance and power, giving an impression of an immensely strong yet well-balanced dog. These qualities should be accompanied by a certain elegance resulting from a combination of the attractive coat, the correct head and a general air of quiet confidence. It is of the utmost importance that nervousness or unprovoked aggression should be heavily penalized.

Head and Skull: It is very important that the head should give an impression of strength with no sign of coarseness; it should not be too heavy in proportion to the size of the dog. The top of the skull, as viewed from front and side, should show a definite curve so as to give a somewhat domed effect and the breadth of the skull at its widest point should be about equal to the length from occiput to stop. The sides of the head should be nearly flat and of a good depth. There should be no obvious stop and only a slight furrow so that the skull and muzzle are joined by a gentle slope. The muzzle should be strong, of medium length and with slight taper near its tip. The nose should be absolutely black. When viewed from above, the head should have the general form of a blunt "V" well filled in below the eyes.

Eyes: The eyes should be almond-shaped and of a dark amber-brown color. The close-fitting eyelids should be set somewhat obliquely and should be bordered with black. Drooping lower eyelids should be penalized. The expression should be intelligent and contemplative.

Ears: The ears should be fairly small and triangular with rounded tips, the root of the ear being on a level with the eyes. Normally the ears lie flat against the head, but may be slightly raised when the dog is alert.

Mouth: There should be a complete set of healthy even teeth, the incisors meeting in either a scissor or a pincer bite. The two central lower incisors may be set a little deeper than the others but this should not be regarded as a serious fault.

The lips should be close fitting, the upper ones extending downwards just sufficiently to cover the lower. They should be black or heavily marked with black in common with the roof of the mouth.

Neck: The neck should be fairly short, thick and muscular. Some dewlap is permitted.

Forequarters: The shoulders should be powerful and lie close to the body. There should be medium angulation between the shoulder blade and the upper arm. The forelegs should be straight, heavily boned and well muscled. The elbows should not be too close to the chest nor should they stand off too far from it, so that a good width of stance and a free striding movement are obtained. Pasterns should show flexibility, but no weakness.

Body: The chest should be broad and of sufficient depth to reach just below the elbows. The sides should be slightly rounded and the rib cage should extend well to the rear.

The back should be of a good length, broad, muscular, straight and level. Dogs usually have a more pronounced waist than bitches, giving a greater curve to the lower body line.

Hindquarters: The loins should be broad and muscular with fairly prominent haunches, the rump should be slightly sloping and the tail should be set on so that the topline curves smoothly into it. Male animals should have two apparently normal testicles fully descended into the scrotum.

The thighs should have great strength and be heavily muscled, tapering gradually down to strong hocks. The stifle and hock joints should both have medium angulation as seen from the side.

The hind legs should each carry strongly made double dewclaws and lack of this identifying characteristic is a very serious fault.

The hind feet may turn out slightly, but the legs themselves when viewed from behind should be straight. Pronounced cowhocks should be heavily penalized.

Feet: The feet should be short and compact, the toes being slightly arched and equipped with strong nails.

Gait: It is very important that the gait should be unhurried, and one should gain the impression of a large dog propelled by powerful hindquarters moving steadily and smoothly well within its capacity, yet able to produce bursts of speed. At slow speeds the Pyrenean tends to pace.

Tail: The tail should be thick at the root and should taper gradually toward the tip, which, for preference, should have a slight curl. It should be of sufficient length to reach below the hocks and the thick coating of fairly long hair should form an attractive plume. In repose, the tail should be carried low with the tip turned slightly to one side, but as the dog becomes interested the tail rises and when he is fully alert it should be curled high above the back in a circle.

Coat: The undercoat should be profuse and composed of very fine hairs whilst the longer outercoat should be of coarser texture, thick and straight or slightly wavy but never curly or fuzzy. The coat should be longer around the neck and shoulders, where it forms a mane, and toward the tail. The forelegs should be fringed. The hair on the rear of the thighs should be long, very dense and more woolly in texture, giving a "pantaloon" effect. Bitches tend to be smoother-coated than dogs and usually have a less developed mane.

Color: (a) Mainly white with patches of badger, wolf-grey or pale yellow, and (b) white: (a) and (b) are of equal merit and judges should show no preference for either. Areas of black hair, where the black goes right down to the roots, are a serious fault.

The colored markings can be on the head, the ears and at the base of the tail, but a few patches on the body are permitted.

The nose and eyerims should be black. The presence of liver pigmentation or pink is a serious fault.

Weight and Size: The shoulder height of a bitch should be at least 26 in. (66 cm) and of a dog 28 in. (71 cm). Most specimens will exceed these heights by several inches and great size should be regarded as absolutely essential, provided that correct type and character are retained. The weight of a bitch should be at least 90 lb. (40 kg) and of a dog 110 lb. (50 kg). (These weights apply only to specimens of minimum height and taller ones should weigh considerably more.) Weight should always be in proportion to height, giving a powerful dog of great strength. Excess weight due to fat should be penalized.

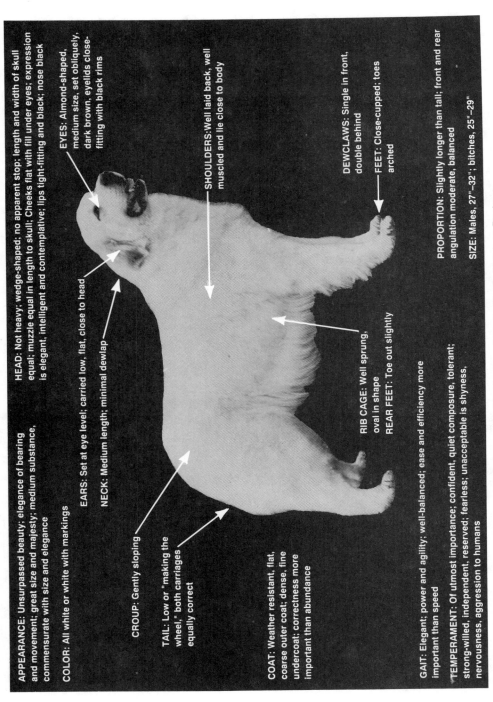

APPEARANCE: Unsurpassed beauty; elegance of bearing and movement; great size and majesty; medium substance, commensurate with size and elegance

COLOR: All white or white with markings

HEAD: Not heavy; wedge-shaped; no apparent stop: length and width of skull equal; muzzle equal in length to skull; Cheeks flat with fill under eyes; expression is elegant, intelligent and contemplative; lips tight-fitting and black; nose black

EYES: Almond-shaped, medium size, set obliquely, dark brown, eyelids close-fitting with black rims

EARS: Set at eye level; carried low, flat, close to head

NECK: Medium length; minimal dewlap

SHOULDERS: Well laid back, well muscled and lie close to body

CROUP: Gently sloping

TAIL: Low or "making the wheel," both carriages equally correct

DEWCLAWS: Single in front, double behind

FEET: Close-cupped: toes arched

RIB CAGE: Well sprung, oval in shape

REAR FEET: Toe out slightly

PROPORTION: Slightly longer than tall; front and rear angulation moderate, balanced

SIZE: Males, 27"–32"; bitches, 25"–29"

COAT: Weather resistant, flat, coarse outer coat; dense, fine undercoat; correctness more important than abundance

GAIT: Elegant; power and agility; well-balanced; ease and efficiency more important than speed

TEMPERAMENT: Of utmost importance; confident; quiet composure, tolerant; strong-willed, independent, reserved; fearless; unacceptable is shyness, nervousness, aggression to humans

Visualization of the Standard, modeled by Ch. Quibbletown Duchess.

6

An In-Depth Look at the Standard

No PYRENEES has yet been bred who can fulfill all the ideals of our breed Standard. No dog is perfect. Yet some are better in type than others. In the Standard, we find both an incentive to correct breeding and a measure by which success in the show ring can be acknowledged.

The character of the Great Pyrenees will be discussed in Chapter 7. As a trusted guardian and a worker of single-minded purpose, no other breed is its rival. However, this discussion will not deal primarily with the character of the dog, except that where character is a quality of the part we are discussing, it is reason enough to insist upon the perfection of that part.

GENERAL APPEARANCE AND SIZE, PROPORTION AND SUBSTANCE

The Great Pyrenees, like other breeds, has its own unique composition. This is what sets it apart from other breeds. The Standard describes our breed as a dog of elegance and unsurpassed beauty combined with great size and majesty. We should note that this is all part of the dog's immediate appeal and, indeed, it is inseparable from its composition. Good composition adds not only to the aesthetic appeal of the dog, but also allows the dog to carry on with its appointed tasks under circumstances in

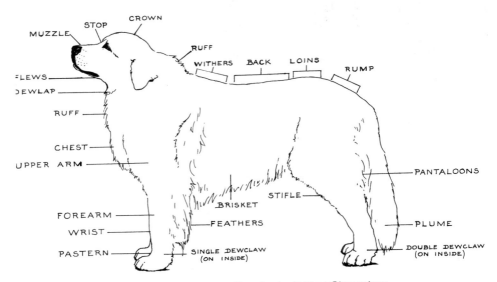

Topographical Anatomy. Drawing by *Bridget Olerenshaw*

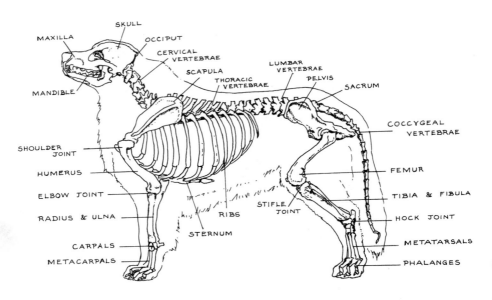

Skeletal Anatomy. Drawing by *Bridget Olerenshaw*

Ch. Cote de Neige Symphonie, Winner of over one hundred Bests of Breed, and the first American-bred Great Pyrenees to win a Best In Show. Owned by Marjorie Butcher.

Ch. Cote de Neige Pastourette, a nearly perfect bitch. Note the head and expression and overall elegance. Owned by Mr. and Mrs. C. Seaver Smith, Jr.

which the poorly constructed one falters or breaks down. Hence, as the Standard says, "his soundness and coordination show unmistakably the purpose for which he has been bred, the strenuous work of guarding the flocks in all kinds of weather on the steep mountain slopes of the Pyrenees."

A Great Pyrenees of proper proportions will tell us at a glance that he can guard a flock, pull a cart, climb a mountain, pack a load or attack a predator—all with equal ease and determination. Its conformation must be judged by the principle that it is, above all, a powerful and well-coordinated working dog.

The Standard gives the shoulder height of males at 27 to 32 inches, and females at 25 to 29 inches. We would suppose that in any breed such as ours in which the height of the specimen is not defined within a narrow range, a difference of opinion will always exist within the fancy as to what constitutes the ideal height. This has always been the case, not only in today's fancy but in bygone years. A glance at the old breed descriptions will show that height ranges have not always been in agreement. In his 1927 treatise, M. Senac-Lagrange explains that the Standard's height limit was fixed at 32 inches because, although one heard of specimens reaching as much as 36 inches in the 1800s, no dog of his day had been known to measure over 32 inches.

Whatever height the dog attains, it can be only part of the complex of qualities which confer to the Great Pyrenees an imposing appearance. A tall, lightly boned dog will not give the appearance of great overall size and majesty, while a short, cobby dog will never appear elegant. We need to consider height, weight, substance, muscular development, angulation, coat, head and expression, temperament, balance, bearing and movement, for all of these are part of the dog's grandeur, charm, appeal in the show ring and success in the field.

The Standard gives the minimum weights for specimens of minimum height, 100 pounds for a male of 27 inches and 85 pounds for a 25-inch bitch. Larger dogs will often weigh much more, even as much as 150 pounds for a 32-inch male. Each dog has its own ideal weight which contributes to its overall balance. Balance in overall construction and movement is more important than single factors such as height, weight or bone.

The Standard says there should be sufficient bone and muscle to provide a balance with the frame. This contributes to the breed's unique combination of power and elegance. A Pyrenees with bone like a Newfoundland must be considered very faulty, as must one with the bone of a Borzoi.

The Great Pyrenees is longer than tall and, thus, should never appear short backed like a Boxer. Yet the breed is not low-slung and should stand over a good deal of ground. The height from the ground to the elbow is about equal to the distance from the elbow to the withers.

HEAD AND EXPRESSION

More than any other aspect, the beautiful head and expression defines a dog as a Great Pyrenees. It allows one to be absolutely certain that this is not just any big, white livestock guardian dog, but the magnificent white-furred lord of the Pyrenees. From time immemorial the shepherds of the Pyrenees Mountains have insisted on the wedge-shaped head with good fill under the eyes and no apparent stop, and the almost mystical "Pyrenean Expression." To achieve correct expression, everything must be perfect—skull shape, muzzle, mouth, pigmentation, ear set, eye shape and color, even the neck and its carriage of the head.

The head is not massive. It should never appear too large in proportion to the body. It must be carried regally on a good length of neck. A lovely ruff provides the ideal setting for the perfect head. The cranium is approximately as broad as it is long, and the muzzle is about equal in length to the back skull. The head is built all in one piece. The sides of the skull blend into the flat cheeks which provide good fill under the eyes. The muzzle is of good length, tapers from the cheeks and is gently blunted at the tip. From the pitch-black nose the topline of the muzzle rises almost imperceptibly to the eyes. There follows a gentle, gradual slope up to the top of the skull. There a slight sagittal crest can be followed to a palpable occipital. The occipital protuberance and slight nuchal cresting provides attachment for powerful neck muscles. The skull does not, therefore, fall away abruptly at the back.

Eyes must be almond-shaped. Round eyes completely destroy expression. The iris is a deep, rich brown. The color should, however, never appear dull. This gives insight into the French Standard's description of the eyes as "ambered" brown, not to indicate a yellow eye, but rather, to indicate a certain brightness. The eyes are set obliquely, the outside corners rise slightly. Some breeders describe this aspect as "Chinese" or "Asiatic." The almond shape and oblique set bring the eyes alive. Full black eyerims contribute greatly to expression.

Ears are small to medium in size, an overly large ear detracts, as does a rose ear. It is very important that the ears be set and carried properly. One cannot judge expression in a dog whose ears are raised at attention. Only when they are lowered to the level of the outside corner of the eye does the correct head achieve that soft, contemplative expression characteristic of the breed. They should also be placed toward the rear of the skull, where they are carried low and close to the skull, often half hidden in the ruff. Very subtle changes in the position of the ears can tell us volumes about the dog's mood. A Pyrenees should never have to raise its ears in the show ring to show that it is attentive.

Lips must be tight, very close-fitting. The upper lips should fall only enough to cover the lower lip—never below. Loose, sagging lips are very faulty.

A lovely head and expression on this male—Ch. Basquaerie Nuvalari of Pondtail, bred by Carolyn and Bruce Hardy.

A slightly rounded crown as seen from the front, that would be acceptable to most breeders. Notice the position of the ears — set at a level with the eyes and carried low and close to the head.

Peter Bickle

Teeth are strong and regular, the canines being especially well developed. Scissors bite is preferred. An even bite is acceptable. Undershot, overshot, wry or any other malocclusion is seriously faulty. However, dropped lower middle incisors are common and are perfectly acceptable to most breeders.

Pigmentation is of great importance. Eyerims, nose and lips must be black. All the better if the palate, pads and nails are also black. Some breeders and judges will excuse a "snow nose." However, as the dog in the show ring must be judged as it appears on the day of the show, any color other than absolute pitch-black must be considered faulty. There are dogs whose noses remain pitch-black all year round. Thus breeders would do well to avoid snow noses as a sign of pigment breakdown.

NECK, TOPLINE AND BODY

The ideal topline is straight and level. It should never drop away like that of a German Shepherd. The back and loin are well-coupled, straight and broad. The chest should reach about to the elbow and extend well to the rear. In many cases where the chest does not reach to the elbow, it is not the chest but the lack of shoulder angulation which is to blame. There is a slight but noticeable tuck-up. The croup is sloping, never flat. The tail is set on low following the slope of the croup. The bony part of the tail is of sufficient length to reach or hang below the hocks. The bones at the tip of the tail frequently form a U or kink called a shepherd's crook, which is highly esteemed by many breeders. Any exaggeration of the crook, such as a spiral, is undesirable and often accompanies poor tail carriage. In routine situations, the tail is usually carried low. However, when excited, the Pyrenees carries its tail in a full circle over its back with the tip just touching either side of the loin. This is called the *arroundera,* or "making the wheel." A tightly curled tail like the Samoyed's is incorrect. Although some other livestock guardian breeds have similar carriages, this tail carriage is unique to the Great Pyrenees among AKC breeds.

FOREQUARTERS

The Standard calls for well-laidback, well-muscled shoulders. A sound front assembly is a must. An essential feature of the well-constructed front is a strong pastern with enough bend, or slope, to take the weight off the column of bones at the moment of impact, thereby transmitting the shock via tendons and ligaments (which absorb shock) rather than via cartilage and bone (which do not). The extremely steep, or straight, pastern may cause knuckling over at the wrist joint. On the other hand, a weak pastern slopes too much, thereby stretching the ligaments and breaking down the

Two early Cote de Neige Pyrenees—at home in the mountains.

Press Pictures

Ch. Pyr Pastures Ivy Du Bousquet on top of Mt. Mansfield. Owners, Arlene and Philip Oraby.

Arlene Oraby

foot. The front legs carry single dewclaws. The close-cupped feet are thickly padded with well-arched toes. A working Pyrenees with a long, thinly padded or splayed foot is "off on the wrong foot" as far as structure is concerned. The toes are webbed.

HINDQUARTERS

The Standard calls for moderate angulation in balance with that of the forequarters. The upper and lower thighs should be well muscled and of the same length, "rounded but not low," as the French say. This leads to moderate angulation at the hock joint. There is medium length from hock to foot. Thus, well let down, short hocks are very undesirable.

The rear feet of the Great Pyrenees have been subject to great misunderstanding by judges. When standing or moving, the feet toe-out slightly. This is a breed characteristic. It must not be confused with cow-hocks. The hocks move parallel to one another with no bobbing or wavering. It is believed that the slight toeing out provides the Pyrenees with greater traction and balance going up steep slopes. Double dewclaws must be present. They are found just above and usually webbed onto the rear feet.

COAT

The correct Pyrenees coat is both functional and attractive. Preference must always be given to correctness of coat rather than mere abundance. The outer coat must be quite coarse and flat-lying in order to shed rain and keep the undercoat and skin dry and warm, and so as not to mat or pick up debris. The outer coat is thick and is especially long on the tail, the backs of the thighs and elbows, and over the rump. The outer coat can be straight or wavy but should never be curly or cottony. Highly undesirable is the stand-off coat as seen in the Samoyed, Pomeranian and Chow. The undercoat is dense, fine and woolly. It is shed for the summer and returns for the winter. The correct coat requires very little care. A ruff is usually present, often more pronounced in males. This gives protection to the vulnerable throat area. It also contributes to the beauty of the dog. As the head is not massive, an especially well-developed ruff often leads to the remark "Oh, he looks just like a lion about the head."

COLOR

The Great Pyrenees may be all-white or white with markings. Both are equally desirable. The markings may cover up to one third the dog's

Diagonal pairs of legs moving in unison, propelled by strong hindquarters.

J. Clawson

Correct movement, smooth and efficient, showing good, balanced reach and drive without exaggeration.

J. Clawson

body but not more. Markings are usually gray or badger (a mixture of gray and tan hairs). However, other acceptable colors are frequently seen such as tan. Tan may range from beige to champagne to sandy tan to even a quite reddish color known as arrouye, sometimes called redheads. Gray can range from nearly black to very soft pearl gray. Markings can appear on the ears, head, side, and along the midline from shoulders to root of tail. All the above colorings and locations are very characteristic of the breed and are equally correct and desirable. The shepherds in the Pyrenees often preferred a dog with a full mask and a spot at the base of the tail. They referred to this as "*U ca pla p'apat.*" Symmetry is not required, although a half mask often does detract from expression. Ticking is not desirable but is not a serious fault. Puppies are frequently born with masks and body spots which fade out during the first year leaving traces in the undercoat of the adult dog.

GAIT

In bearing and carriage, the Great Pyrenees exhibits supreme elegance, power and agility. In gait we should expect to see the pride and majesty of a Pyrenean Mountain Dog at age-old duties of surveying and defending the flock; as the Standard says, showing "unmistakably the purpose for which he had been bred."

When going away, the rear feet might appear too close together due to the double dewclaws, but the hocks should tell a different tale. In a restricted show ring, space must be made to exhibit the attributes of the dogs as they are gaited individually. The length of stride of a good-sized, correctly moving Pyrenees swallows up the average show ring in a few steps. Pyrenean movement is efficient, ground-covering and tireless. It is neither exaggerated nor ponderous; nor does it pace. The stride should never appear awkward, stilted or restricted. Correct Pyrenees side gait is a joy to behold. It has an ethereal, uplifting quality all its own. The dog becomes a celebration of elegance, power and authority.

TEMPERAMENT

The Great Pyrenees should present a picture of quiet, confident self-possession. As a livestock guardian rather than a herding dog, it should evidence no desire whatsoever to chase or nip. It is quickly bored with mundane situations such as dog shows. It is affectionate with its family, but may appear reserved with strangers, depending on how much socialization it has had. However, any sign of fear, shyness, nervous agitation or aggression to humans would be an extremely serious fault, and such a dog must not be used for breeding.

Ch. Maranatha Pyragon Apollo CDX enjoys a dip in the pool.

Rhonda Dalton

7

The Character of
the Great Pyrenees

"**I** SAW MY FIRST *animated snowdrift* some ten years ago," wrote Mr. Strang in 1935, "stretched in front of a busy Paris cafe, taking up considerably more than his share of the sidewalk. He struck me then as the most beautiful dog I had ever seen and a more intimate association with the Great Pyrenees has since convinced me that his character is on a par with his looks."

The Pyrenean character, to which Mr. Strang refers, has been clearly set forth in the breed Standard. Let us consider these two passages:

First, "He possesses a keen intelligence and a kindly, while regal, expression."

And second, "Character and temperament are of utmost importance. In nature the Great Pyrenees is confident, gentle and affectionate. While territorial and protective of his flock or family when necessary, his general demeanor is one of quiet composure, both patient and tolerant. He is strong-willed, independent and somewhat reserved, yet attentive, fearless and loyal to his charges, both human and animal."

In *The New Complete Shetland Sheepdog* Maxwell Riddle, respected American judge and author, wrote the following on Sheltie character. It applies to all breeds:

Is a dog loyal who follows the children to school? Is it one which shadows its master? Will it attack the charging bull which threatens its owner? If the owner engages in a fight with another, will the dog attack the owner's opponent? Will the loyal dog rush into the street and drag a child out of the path of a car?

Dogs do these things. But they rarely have the chance to prove themselves. The dog which shadows its master may do so out of innate fear of being alone, rather than out of loyalty. Similarly, the dog which barks when strangers approach may be doing so out of fear, and may feel no sense of loyalty.

Similarly, it is the rare dog in any breed which does not show affection for its master and family. This is a quality of being a dog. So, as in the case of loyalty, this tells us nothing about the breed's character.

So, in attempting to describe the qualities that set the Great Pyrenees apart from other breeds, we must take into account three special qualities which are either stated or implied by the breed description. They are:

- He is a working dog bred for a specific purpose.
- He is a natural guardian. This aptitude has been refined through genetic selection.
- His keen intelligence is reflected in his innate ability to discriminate between friend and enemy—in a word, dependability.

While no one can deny that the Pyrenean's benevolent expression and a certain bearlike lovability are part of his charm, to the peasant and shepherd who developed the breed as we know it today, a working dog needed something more than charm. Let us consider the historical background of our present-day Pyrenees. What are the attributes of character we expect to find in today's dog? This account, written by Robert Leighton in *The New Book of the Dog* (1911), will serve as an example:

> In the beginning of the summer the Pyrenean shepherds moved their flocks from the lowland pastures to the mountains, where they remained for a period of four to five months, often at an altitude of five thousand feet about the sea level. The dogs accompanied them, and in a country infested with bears and wolves there could be no better or more faithful and courageous guardians. Gifted with an exceedingly keen sense of hearing and an excellent nose, the Pyrenean Dog was accustomed to mount sentry at night over the sleeping flocks; and if a marauding Bruin should approach, or a stealthy pack of wolves draw nigh, he knew it from afar, and was ever alert to warn his master, or himself hasten to the attack, and the wolf or bear who should face him would have to deal with an exceedingly formidable foe, whose quickness of decision and adroitness in combat might be compared with the trained skill of the fighting dog of the arena.
>
> So trusting was this canine guardian of the fold, that the shepherd could with confidence leave him at intervals of two or three days at a time, knowing that during his absence the dog would tend the sheep unaided, never deserting his post of duty.

For yet another description of Pyrenean character, we turn to the description given by the Argeles-Gazost Standard of 1907:

A family group living on a sheep ranch in Virginia. *Linda Walraven*

Possessing a courage against all odds, combined with immense strength and the power of his jaws, nothing stops him or makes him retreat. At night he continues to bark to show he is on guard. He does not sleep for a moment. He inspects the surrounding neighborhood without wandering too far, unless he finds the trail of a dangerous animal, and only returns when he knows the danger to the flock is over. The true Pyrenean never sleeps at night, but rests and sleeps during the day in case his vigilance fails (during the night). He distinguishes himself from other large breeds by his devotion to everything he is expected to guard, principally children.

To quote M. J. Dhers, a French connoisseur of the late twenties and thirties, "The characteristics of this true type are their utter fearlessness, a total lack of nervousness, and an apparent desire to mind their own business and have strangers do likewise."

From these accounts it is not hard to picture the character of the dog. First, it put duty above all else. It worked in extremes of weather, in gales of rain or snow—often alone. Isolated on the mountain slopes with just its sheep to protect, it was expected to show reserve toward strangers. Under the right circumstances, it must be suspicious, even hostile. A stranger could be a thief. And a shepherd would never consider leaving his flock, if he were not sure it was well protected by his Pyrenean guards.

In turn, each dog would need to recognize its master and his helpers and submit to their orders.

A Pyrenean would have to act with boldness and determination when the wind brought the scent of an enemy. A shy or nervous animal would lack the self-confidence to react appropriately to a plausible threat. An overly dependent dog who shadowed its master could never be relied upon to take over in the absence of its owner. The shepherds expected these things from their dogs, and bred them for it.

A dog that attacked or bit without provocation would have been a menace to everyone including the villagers. Lady Morris once remarked after a visit to the mountains, "I never met a mean dog," and certainly a shy or untrustworthy Pyrenees would not have been tolerated in the restricted economy of the herdsmen.

So we find that a Pyrenees of correct character is steadfast, responsive and self-sufficient. It has inherited, to an uncanny degree, an understanding of man's ways. Lithe and quick of action, it is capable of enduring hardship, exposure, and any degree of activity. It is undisputably one of the most intelligent dogs in the world and certainly one of the most picturesque and beautiful. It exemplifies, as no other breed can, the attributes one looks for in a devoted companion and worker.

More than just a guardian of the flock, the Great Pyrenees is a superb watchdog. From the chronicles of the early life and adventures of the Pyrenees dogs on the royal estates of France, three, narrated by M. Duconte, a French authority and breed historian, show how the Pyrenean performed this time-honored service. The first is the story of the Château de Foix:

This castle was built on steep rock, difficult of access. Its prison cells and secret dungeons were continuously occupied by brigands and highwaymen who tried to hold up and rob travelers passing through this area to Spain. Thieves also attacked mountain flocks which were insufficiently guarded. So many were these brigands that there was scarcely room for them in the prison nor sufficient men to guard them. So a certain number of Pyrenean Mountain Dogs were brought in, their keen sense of smell and nocturnal vigilance making them proof against any surprise. The Pyrenean shepherds had, in fact, for a long time beforehand, trained their dogs to chase thieves as well as wild animals. And so Foix acquired its guard of Pyrenean dogs; and from then on it was well guarded.

The second account is based on a document in the National Library of France, telling that in 1407 the Château de Lourdes had both a square and a round tower, both of which were surrounded by a high wall. Between the wall and the towers was an open passage, round which Pyrenean dogs patrolled on watch to give the alarm:

The dogs seemed endowed with intelligence enough to recognize suspicious behavior of criminals and yet never to attack any honest man. These qualities were particularly precious at a time when a cowl literally made the friar. But there was one occasion when it didn't work as planned! One of the officers of the castle, wishing to put the guard dogs to test, disguised himself in the garb of a wandering friar and then made his nightly rounds. He was set upon by the angry dogs in the twinkling of an eye, and was in grave danger when luckily the clever beasts recognized him and so he was spared.

Still another ancient document, found in the archives at Fuxéennes, related that in 1391, following a treaty of succession to Gaston Phoebus, Comte de Foix, King Charles VI decided to go pay a visit to his cousin who was waiting for him in his castle at Mazeres:

Before getting to Mazeres the King rode through a region stocked with huge white cattle wearing silver bells about their necks. Knights disguised as shepherds were running in all directions trying to get the herd out of the way. Enormous mountain dogs with thick long coats were engaged in helping them. Suddenly a bull charged the King! One of the shepherds attempted to catch it by the horns and pull it to the ground, whilst the dogs, hanging onto its ears, dragged it back to the herd and so saved the King!

Thus we can vouch that our Pyrenean has always been considered an ideal watchdog, even from the earliest times. Only a person who knows dogs very well would dare to advance upon a Great Pyrenees on guard. The sound of a warning growl, not to mention the explosive bark which follows, would cause any trespasser to keep a respectful distance.

A Pyrenees is adept at cannily blocking the approach of a suspicious intruder. The bushy mane rises in anger and lips are raised to expose a fang. Skillful at cornering and holding until help arrives, keen intelligence and powers of discrimination allow the breed to distinguish the suspicious intruder from the friend who belongs.

A charming account of Pyrenean character is found in *The Power of the Dog* (Maude Earl), a piece written by A. Croxton-Smith as a tribute to his beloved Pandora:

As the heavy train steamed into Willesden, sounds of barking directed me to the compartment in which the pup was traveling. When the hamper was opened the most delightful little Teddy Bear imaginable bounded out and proceeded to introduce herself. A mass of white fluffy down, with here and there a splash of lemon, eloquent dark eyes, and plump as the proverbial partridge. That was Pandora as we first knew her. Time only served to strengthen and crystallize the early impressions. With manners as charming and irreproachable as her looks, before many days had passed she had won all hearts, becoming an important member of the household. That wise head of hers held brains which led her instinctively to adapt herself to her surroundings, and fall in with the habits and wishes of the human gods who formed her little world. Visitors, though tolerated as necessary evils, were regarded with signal disapproval, heavy bark and bared teeth warning that no evil intent must be harbored towards the inmates of the home.

As Pandora grew older the downy coat was shed, profuse long hair taking its place in gradual transition, and she became more and more intelligent, until we agreed that we had never, among our host of canine friends, met one so sensible. None, too, could be more expressive. When on mischief bent she displayed it with a roguishness of demeanor that earned absolution for the misdeed almost before it was perpetrated.

Greatly did she delight in a game of "catch as catch can" on the lawn with the children. Entering into the spirit of fun she would romp around in endless gyrations, busy tail extended to the full a few inches from hands ready to grasp, but she could calculate to a fraction, twisting and dodging with the art of a football player, until pity impelled her to pretend she could go on no longer.

One could fill a book relating Pandora's escapades, but further recital might weary. Let mention of her adventure with the garden hose suffice as an example of the rest. The curious serpentine length stretching out on the lawn interested her vastly, and when she heard the sizzling noise made by the air escaping from the nozzle as the water came on, down went her nose to investigate. A sudden jet full in the face caused a precipitate retreat, and now as the hose appears there is much commotion at a diplomatic distance.

Certainly no other breed is more ideally suited for the role of child's companion and protector than is the Great Pyrenees. Perhaps in the joy and carefree abandon of a child, a Pyrenees sees a kindred spirit. In the company of children it seems sublimely happy whether enjoying a romp, a tussle, a game of tag, pulling some kind of conveyance or merely doing

Kimberly Mardi Gras and friend. Owned by Brenda Judson, Carabrae Kennels, England.

nothing but listening to their chatter. Ever conscious of its own strength, it seems more gentle than the smallest lap dog, yet, should danger appear in the form of a molesting stranger, thief or trespasser, its deep warning bark is usually enough to handle the situation. If not, its size, strength and fury most certainly will.

When a Pyrenees wants attention it has a way of slapping you with its paw. It always sleeps with its back against a door which opens inward, so as not to be taken by surprise, a fact which caused the shepherds to refer to their Patous as "mat dogs."

The breed gets along well with other dogs and household pets. A Pyrenees would much prefer to ignore the harassment of a smaller dog and will usually fight only as a last resort. However, two mature Pyrenees of the same sex often do not get along well together as house pets. This is particularly true of males.

When a Pyrenees turns its attention to the affairs of its family, its powers of deduction are uncanny. Let something out of the ordinary happen, such as packing a suitcase, and a Pyr becomes all eyes and ears. An alert family will go to almost any length to conceal their plans from their household Pyr—but it always finds them out! Even the accidental jingle of a choke collar brings any Pyrenees, napping in a remote corner, straight to the door, insisting upon a walk. A Pyrenees reads your dress and mannerisms as you read the evening paper—and for much the same reason: to find out what's going to happen next. The difference is, the Pyrenees is usually right, and you aren't.

There is no doubt that the Great Pyrenees is a highly intelligent animal. It always knows what's expected of it and its ability to understand the subtle nuances of its master's voice and expression are second to none. Add to this a desire to do everything required to win its handler's praise, and you have a dog that is easy to train for obedience work.

To train a Pyrenees, one should approach the task in a leisurely fashion and keep the exercises, at first, reasonably brief and varied. As with any intelligent species, perfunctory and repetitious exercises are apt to bore.

A part of the breed's innate intelligence is an almost uncanny prescience, an ability to know or sense danger well in advance, and to take action to safeguard, as illustrated in this anecdote: One evening in the late 1930s Mrs. Carl Harris, of Add-En-On Kennels, was traveling with her husband and their dogs in Mississippi when they decided to stop for the night, by the side of the road, to camp. She then set out to take her favorite dog, Henry VIII, for his nightly walk, and had gone only a short distance when suddenly Henry sat back and refused to go any farther—indicating his desire that they return at once to the camper. Mrs. Harris became quite exasperated and tried to coax him to continue, but the wise dog steadfastly refused and they eventually returned to the trailer. The following morning

Henry again went for a walk with his mistress and in due course they returned to the same spot as the night before. There, before the pair, was an abandoned cistern! Had Henry not sensed the danger the night before, the two would have continued on (according to Mrs. Harris) and plunged to their deaths.

Perhaps the character of the breed is best exemplified by the intelligent and kindly expression to be found in the eye of the well-bred dog. A look which has been classified as faraway, contemplative, perhaps a little melancholy, yet possessing, too, a serenity acquired through association with the high, wind-swept mountain slopes and distant vistas that make up the magnificent grandeur of the Pyrenees Mountains.

The vocabulary of the Great Pyrenees is a subject which has interested fanciers for many years. With a little experience one can learn not only which dog is barking, but can tell, within limits, just what it is talking about. The joyous bark of greeting is different from the short, excited yapping of the same dog chasing a rabbit. The plaintive whine of an uneasy dog in trouble is quite different from the wheedling whine of a dog overjoyed by attention.

The range of different barks is certainly extensive. The dog is hungry or has overturned its water bucket and is thirsty. Another animal is running loose; there is a snake in its pen; it smells fire; it has caught its feet in the fence; it is answering the call of another dog in the distance on a moonlit night; each emotion is qualified by a particular bark. And besides barking, whining and howling, our dogs growl; there are different growls for different occasions. Greeting, with suspicion, another dog; protective growling in defense of its property, master, food pan or bone; the low grumbling, deep-in-the-throat growl when angered and about to attack.

But of all the different vocalizations of which our dogs are capable there is one that stands out above all others. This is the voice of authority that, in the night, calmed restless sheep in the fold, assured the shepherd of the area's security and told potential troublemakers that the camp was well guarded.

Writers, from the earliest days of our breed's history have spoken, in passing, of this distinctive Pyrenean bark. This remote ancestral trait is certainly a vital characteristic of our breed.

Calm, low-registered, powerful but muted, this is the voice of the Great Pyrenees at its age-old post, telling us all is well.

Leading the flock to summer pasturage.   *Mary Crane*

VilleVieux pups with sheep.

8

The Great Pyrenees: A Worker for All Reasons

LIVESTOCK GUARDIAN

First and foremost the Great Pyrenees is and has always been a guardian of livestock, particularly sheep, but also goats, cattle, llamas and other exotics. Great Pyrenees were first brought over by Lafayette as a gift to George Washington. They were intended to help prevent losses to predators. However, use of the dogs did not become widespread. It wasn't until recent years that the Great Pyr was able to prove its mettle in its ancestral role.

During the late 1960s ranchers started looking for an environmentally sound alternative to the poisons they were using to protect their flocks from predators. The results were overwhelming. The dogs saved the ranchers thousands of dollars. In many cases an entire lambing season would go by without a single loss. In 1969 the U.S. Sheep Experimental Station in Dubois, Idaho, launched a program to study the effectiveness of European livestock guardian dogs. The project is still in progress under the capable direction of Dr. Jeff Green.

The Pyr bonds with the flock and protects them instinctively. Thus no real training is needed, although ranchers must learn proper management techniques for optimal success. There are three important characteristics of a good livestock guardian. First and most important, it must not show aggression or even playfully chase the livestock. Second, it must stay with the stock. Third, it must protect them from predators. This can range from a warning bark to an all-out fight to the death.

There are many, many success stories. The following two will serve to illustrate the Pyr's value as a livestock guardian. The first comes from Missouri's *Marshfield News*.

The predators referred to in Missouri as "wolves" are actually both coyotes and coy-dogs, the latter being hybrid crosses with feral dogs, often attaining greater size than their wild canine cousins. Some time ago, a pack of these animals fell upon T. H. Macdonnell's sundry stock dogs, killing one and mangling several others. The dogs lost all spirit for fighting and, at the howl of the pack, would always turn tail and flee to the security of the house or barn. Macdonnell is a serious rancher and raises a fine strain of Herefords. At calving time, predator losses were seriously undermining his breeding program. After trying several different breeds and finding none suited to the work of protecting his calves, Macdonnell acquired a Pyrenees named Polly. She proved her worth, at least as far as Mrs. Macdonnell was concerned, by showing the cattle that the family garden was not the proper place to take their evening snack!

Polly needed no special instructions to size up the situation as far as the wolves were concerned. One late afternoon when icy sleet was falling, a wild pack was heard in the lower pasture. Polly and a stock dog sped down to the quarter-mile fence, but the Collie, smelling the wolves and recalling his recent encounter, turned and ran back to crouch, trembling between the rancher's legs. The Pyrenees continued on to the half-mile gate and turned into the woods. As Macdonnell arrived he saw a large silver animal (at first he thought it was his Pyrenees) lunge from behind a bush and grab his bitch by the throat, throwing her to the ground. But she tore free and the two animals met head to head, rearing high and snarling in the heat of combat. The outcome was obvious—the pack leader was no match for the Pyrenees, and turning tail he fled with Polly in close pursuit. The leaves were scraped bare where the animals fought. As the rancher went on he eventually came upon three newborn calves with Polly standing guard, open-mouthed, smiling, and breathing heavily. There wasn't a mark on her!

Unfortunately, this was not to be the case after the next encounter. The coyotes, having superior numbers, fought as a pack. Some of them worked behind her and tore at her tail and hindquarters. As she crawled back to the ranch, her tail was dangling from a four-inch stub. After two operations and an inevitable tail amputation, Polly returned to her family with a sorely wounded dignity. For weeks she hid herself under the bushes so nobody could make fun of her sorry appearance.

Interestingly, the loss of her tail never affected her balance or agility. One might forgive a dog for losing its spirit after such an experience, but in Polly's case such sympathy would have been wasted. Rather than diminishing her courage it made her only the more determined to hold her supremacy in her own territory. The cattleman quickly availed himself of the chance to acquire a companion for her—this time a mature male. Today, no four-footed interloper sets foot on this cattle ranch!

The second account appeared in the *GPCA Bulletin* in 1972, and starred Suki and Yukon, a bitch and a dog belonging to Jack and Carolyn Nix of rural New Mexico.

One summer afternoon the barking of Suki was heard from the ranch and peering through binoculars it was apparent that she was being attacked by a pack of coyotes. As Jack searched for his rifle, Yukon sped to the rescue. Hackles up in rage, he joined his mate and scattered the coyotes, who beat a hasty retreat. As Jack arrived, the reason for the fracas became apparent. There before them was the carcass of a calf, its throat a gaping hole. Both dogs immediately lay down beside the calf, and although implored repeatedly to return to the ranch, they simply would not budge until collars and leashes were sent for.

Thus the Great Pyrenees—guard and fighting dog extraordinaire when the need arises—retains an ancient heritage.

SLED WORK

Although the original work of the Great Pyrenees was to protect livestock, the breed is highly adaptable and can be used for nearly anything.

A Great Pyrenees named Bazen de Soum lived in North Newfoundland in the 1930s. He loved to do sled work. Here is his story in "his own" words:

One winter day my mistress, Anna Kivimaki and I decided to show the Newfoundlanders that a sled pulled by a Great Pyrenees and two huskies could make the difficult trip from St. Anthony to Canada Bay, a distance of eighty miles, and return. Of course, in those days dog sleds were the chief form of transportation. And if you had business in Canada Bay, you really didn't have much choice.

The morning broke bright and clear, but the going was sort of rough for us at the start because the two huskies were young and inexperienced. As a matter of course, the heaviest dog is usually hitched to the shortest trace as his weight is more effective well to the rear. But when our team finally hit its stride, I was in the lead, the other two milling around on equal length traces behind.

Weather changes with lightning rapidity in northern Newfoundland. On the second day out the temperature dropped and the snow began to fall in a thick blanket. Visibility was down to fifty yards. It was time to think

Bazen de Soum in Massachusetts, just prior to his departure for Labrador in 1932.

Three Alaskan pioneers hauling the family's fuel. On the far side is Balibasque Beau of Karolaska CD, HOF; on the near side is Quibbletown Queeka Bear HOF. In front, pictured at six months of age is their daughter, Ch. Karolaska Polar Bonni Bear, who became the top winning bitch in America.

about shelter. The Green Wood *tilt* (log cabin) was five miles away but in the wrong direction.

However, there was an island called Hare Island in the arm of the coastal bay. My mistress had heard that men went there in the seal season to hunt and live in a little shack on the island.

Although she had not actually seen the shack, she decided that this was to be our destination. The sun the day before had broken up the ice, so there was water between the shore and the arm. We crawled along the winding trail among the scrub trees for an exhausting mile before we could finally get out onto the ice.

At this point, my two helpers attempted a mild revolt. Driven back by the blizzard, the huskies tried to get at the seal meat which was tied on top of the komatik in a burlap sack. However, I would allow no such insubordination. With bared fangs I warned the huskies in no uncertain terms that the meat was forbidden! One crack of my mistress' whip settled the matter. Two huskies thought better of their rascally attempt to sneak the food.

We were all nearly exhausted when we sighted the island. After a bit of searching, we found a very small log cabin complete with a rusty stove for warmth. We knew if the huskies were allowed loose they would hightail it back to civilization. So after we were all fed, I crowded the two huskies under a bunk and stretched out in front. When one stirred the least bit, I growled a warning.

That night we were joined by a party of six men who had come to hunt seals. The blizzard continued for three days, during which time my mistress and the hunters swapped yarns and played a card game called Auction. This was particularly hard on her knuckles, which rapped the table every time she put down the card that took the trick.

As the third morning dawned clear and cold, I led the team off to a fine start. At one point while crossing the ice a gleam of water suddenly appeared. But by cutting quickly to shore the danger was averted. The next day we were again in good form and my mistress rode part of the way on the sled. And on the third day the wind died and we arrived in Canada Bay well before nightfall.

After a four-day rest, during which my mistress looked into the affairs of the Mission sawmill, we prepared for the return journey. On the first day it rained and so we were all exhausted by the time we got to the first *tilt*. The next day was bitter cold. But by now we were in top form. Toward evening we sighted Hare Island. Our friends, the sealers, had seen us coming and had begun to heat tea on the roaring stove.

The next day was ideal. The sun was bright; the snow was hard, and we fairly flew as our mistress shouted the magic words: "Home, home, home!"

My mistress told me we held a record for being the smallest team to make this journey. I was very proud because she said to everyone, "The success was all due to Bazen, our leader, and a real companion on any trip."

PACK DOG

The demand for the Great Pyrenees as a working dog, and a pack dog in particular, is increasing. Here is Rod Perry's account of backpacking with a Pyrenees, written in 1970 and published in the *Pyr-Alaskan:*

My brother, Al, and I are photographers and we own a Great Pyrenees who not only works almost daily, but is a veritable necessity to the continuation of our professional activities. A company that we formed is involved in the production of nature, adventure and travel motion pictures. Our packs containing food and gear for extended bush forays were back-breaking enough before we cast our hats into the cinematography business. But the addition of fifty odd pounds of camera equipment and film soon led to the realization that we had to find a gimmick.

We began to consider all possibilities in the realm of mountain transportation—from mechanical conveyances to mules, llamas to yaks. One idea after another was discarded. Reasons for this ranged from mechanical breakdown to difficulty in providing feed. Many of the wilderness routes we take will stop a goat and bog a snipe. Nothing we could think of could follow us over these courses.

Then we considered dogs. Perhaps our answer lay somewhere within the canine fraternity. But they'd have to meet several requirements. They must be able to haul sizeable payloads for long distances over difficult terrain. Prerequisites for this would be great size, strength, endurance and willingness to work. Obviously, we could not tolerate a dog that tended to give chase or bark at the sight of game. Thus, an animal of calm disposition and trainability was needed. Could any dog measure up? We investigated the various breeds to see if any fitted our needs. We finally purchased a year-old Pyrenees bitch named "Sugar" from Ted Rumsey of Eagle River.

After a period during which Sugar received strict Obedience training from Al, we decided it was time for her to make her first trip into the mountains. Al strapped a pack to her back and they were off on a forty mile jaunt. Many dogs, new to the game, take time to adjust to the weight and swing of the load. Sugar just fell into the job as if she'd done it all her life. No hesitation, not even as much as a wondering glance at the strange encumbrance on her back. Al had placed it there and to her that was reason enough to pack it.

At first the load collided with a log here or a rock there and caught on a protruding branch. But she has since learned just how far the bags protrude and now seldom experiences any difficulty. She discovered that if she jumped over a downed log she would high center on the pack bottoms. Now she jumps on top of the log with all four feet before she continues over. She sizes up other difficult situations at a glance and has become very adept at picking her own way around places that would hang her up.

By late Fall she had packed about 500 miles. Not many Pyr owners have the opportunity to see what really hard work will do for their dogs' muscle tone. To witness her corded muscles methodically sauntering over the mountain under more than half her weight in moose meat makes one shake his head in disbelief. But when a grueling day is done and her pack is finally removed, to watch her romp and beg for a game of tag is worthy of a Charlie Chaplin double take!

While on one filming jaunt, Al and Sugar located a mineral lick that attracted about a hundred white Dall Sheep. While filming them Al frequently left Sugar for long periods on "Stay" as he searched for interesting camera angles. Not once did she show any inclination to rush the animals. Perhaps their similarity to domestic sheep awakened age-old instincts.

As Al and Sugar left the mountain near dusk one day, they jumped a black bear at fifteen yards. Sugar growled a warning and showed some willingness to mix it with the bruin. A sharp command from Al kept her at heel.

We feel that Sugar would tackle a bear if one of us were charged while filming. It is hoped that we never require these services of her. I'm sure that with its lightning quickness and great strength, an average-sized black bear would be a match for more than one Pyrenees in a fight to the death. A lone dog burdened with a heavy pack would give a bear little trouble but the distraction might just give us time to make a getaway.

Most breeds constitute a health hazard in Bear Country. Bowser as readily chases the bruin as he would the neighbor's cat. The big difference in comparing bear and cat chases is that when the very irate she grizzly is pounding after Bowser, he runs to you for protection! A downright unsanitary situation.

However, the Great Pyrenees is usually content to mind his own business. If trouble comes his way, he is not one to back down; but he doesn't go out and look it up. So Sugar is a real advantage in Bear Country.

Sugar adapts well to new and unusual situations. The first time we introduced her to a canoe she came aboard as if she were an old voyager. She has since canoed over 200 miles and has never given us any trouble. One time after we upset the canoe in the rapids, she even brought Al's down jacket ashore.

The Great Pyrenees has other advantages that make the breed an asset to an operation like ours. Low metabolism is one. Even carrying up to a two-week supply of dry dog food, Sugar still packs a good share of our camping equipment. Another advantage is the beautifully photogenic quality of these animals.

Lately, Al has been preparing Sugar for the Anchorage Fur Rendezvous weight-pulling contest. She has taken to the sled work readily. After only ten days of pulling in our firewood, she is breaking loose and pulling over four times her weight.

Incidentally, Sugar did indeed enter the weight-pulling contest and finished second among twenty-three entries, pulling the fantastic weight of 1,325 pounds! Most of her competition came from the Saint Bernards, weighing 150 to 200 pounds. The winner was a part Pyr and part Husky who pulled 1,375 pounds. From the reports we received, it appears that most of the weight was pulled by the Pyr part.

For the lover of winter sports, the Great Pyrenees has other unique and interesting uses. A French breeder tells of his experience in crossing the Alps on skis from Nice to Lake Leman with eight Pyrenees. Some of these were dog porters and others served as guides, forging ahead but stopping with infallible instinct at dangerous snow, thereby finding the safe paths. When the slopes become too gradual for downhill skiing, the dogs served as horses, pulling their master through the glistening powder at nothing less than a gallop. His dogs were also used for life-saving work. They were trained to bring back a piece of clothing from the lost traveler and then lead the rescue party back to the scene.

A delightful story of the intelligence of a Great Pyrenees comes from Mary Crane:

> Frenchmen of all walks of life seem to be in complete agreement on the fact that the Pyrenees is the most intelligent dog in the world. As an illustration let me cite a tale that may be hard for most of you to believe. Some years ago a personal friend of mine, living in southern France, told of an instance that she herself witnessed. It is, therefore, told with the utmost sincerity. One of the dogs was trained to fetch water from the village square. He would carry a bucket in his mouth, go to the trough, turn on the spigot, fill the pail, turn off the spigot, and carry the brimming pail home.
>
> When I told this to my veterinarian he laughed and said, "That's all right, but you better leave out the part about turning off the spigot." And the rest of you may feel the same.

DRAFT DOG

You may wonder if today's Great Pyrenees are the workers they used to be in days gone by. Actually, today's Pyrenees are often given the chance to prove they have the capabilities they once had in the past.

A Pyrenees has done guard duty in the 4-H Dairy Barn at the Sonoma County Fair in California for the past several years. During the day he wanders about the barn, sleeping atop the tack box or happily playing with the children who come by. There is a sign fixed to a stall with the words "Guard Dog On Duty—Keep Away!" Adults read and believe. Small children ignore the sign and stop to pet the fluffy dog and are greeted with a wet tongue instead of bared teeth.

Nighttime is a different story, though. Here Barbo has the run of the barn and challenges every visitor with a fierce bark. He admits only those who belong. Despite security problems and thefts from other barns, the dairy barn has never been molested.

Barbo is an example of the working Pyrenees at the Poste de Pompier Ranch of Kitty and Norm Carpedus. Kitty and Norm believe that the way to bring out the best in a Pyrenees is to give the chance to work at traditional European tasks, guarding livestock and pulling carts. And they have proven it, not only with their own dogs, but with many from unhappy homes who are given to them as a last resort.

Ch. Cavalier Michel — a modern undercover agent. What precious contraband do you carry? Breeder-owner Charles McConnell.

The entertainment between games at Dodger Stadium. Allan and Randy Baab with four of their Companion Dogs.

Thousands of visitors to the Renaissance Pleasure Faire in Northern California, Mrs. Carpedus tells us, enjoy the sight of Pyrenees pulling children in colorful carts. Few realize that these are not "Sunday cart-pulling Pyrs," but dogs who make their living at this, or similar work, the year around.

One of these dogs, named Snow, is used regularly around his owner's ranch as a draft animal. One wet winter a number of small trees had floated down the creek during a flood and lodged against the fence. To make the field usable, the trees had to be removed, but the ground was too wet for a tractor. With a heavy chain attached to his work harness, Snow half-floated, half-pulled the trees and branches from the field, then snaked them up a small hill and along a gravel road for a total of more than 300 yards.

On his fifth trip out of the field, his sixteen-year-old owner looked up to see an SPCA truck on the road. The Humane Officer watched as Snow approached off lead, tail wagging, doing what he loved best. The officer grinned and shook his head. "I got a call that a dog was being abused. If you see one, let me know." Turning to leave he remarked, "Now that's what I'd call a *real* working dog!"

GUARD DOG

The amazing intelligence of the Pyrenees dogs, as well as their capacity to act with prudent foresight, is shown by two incidents narrated by Dr. Edmond S. Bordeaux (*Messengers from Ancient Civilizations*). Both are delightful examples of the traits we look for in our present-day Pyreneans:

My summers of childhood were spent on my family's estate in Dordogne, France. And inextricably linked with my memories of the hundreds of acres of giant walnut trees, apple orchards, the centuries-old stone buildings, and the stern matriarchal figure of my grandmother were the magnificent Pyrenean Mountain Dogs which guarded our estate.

All of the dogs were of breathtaking beauty and immense size—their snow-white coats covering lean muscles, toned to perfection by their daily romps with the small shepherd boys. These boisterous games of wrestling, hide and seek and tag were welcome diversions from their daily schedule of hard work. For these dogs were, first and foremost, guardians of the highest caliber, using their amazing intelligence in feats of strategy that would shame a general.

One example I will always remember was the "incident of the apple thieves," an event which made a peculiar impression on my young mind. Toward the end of every summer, our hundreds of huge apple trees were loaded down with dark red, juicy beauties waiting to be harvested and sent to market, all protected from greedy view by a high stone wall which surrounded the entire estate. But the determination of small boys is a powerful thing, and on this day, two clever little entrepreneurs had spirited away from their father's tool shed a stepladder, letting their common sense be overruled by the thought of how sweet that first bite of stolen apple would taste. They found a likely spot and hoisted one side of the stepladder over the wall. Then they climbed up merrily, all prepared to come down the other side. However, their well-laid plans did not materialize! The boys did not know that the five Pyreneans had heard them long before they had the ladder in place. But, intelligent strategists that they were, they did nothing—only came to a spot near the plotted crime and waited and watched, silent and unmoving. One of them stationed himself near one of the many dog-size openings that were to be found all along the perimeter of the stone wall, clever little doors which allowed a dog to get out, but which could not be reentered. And the moment that both little criminals were on top of the wall, ACTION! One dog rushed through the wall opening and got to the ladder in time to prevent either of them escaping as they had come, three dogs stayed at their post to prevent the culprits from descending into the orchard, and the fifth dog ran for the gardener. Such teamwork!

The end was woefully predictable. The good gardener arrived, removed the stepladder and thanked the boys for bringing him such a fine one which he could certainly use. He also told them that to steal from one's neighbors is a very bad thing, and if they had come to the front gate and asked, he would have given them each a bag of apples. Then he went outside, let the Pyreneans back in through the gate, and left the boys to jump off the wall, go home without a stepladder, and meditate on the sorrows of a life of crime.

Another example of the amazing intelligence and teamwork shown by the Pyreneans concerned again a small boy—this time, the son of a houseguest who wandered where he was warned not to go. The forbidden spot was a large cistern full of water, just a small swimming pool to an adult, but dangerous for a small child who did not know how to swim. But hanging over the cistern was a very large pear tree, and at this time of year its branches were heavy with juicy golden pears, made all the more tempting by their forbidden location. The worst happened: The little boy reached for a pear and fell into the water, but luckily his howls were heard by the five Pyreneans before he had a chance to take a breath and howl again. When the dogs reached the cistern, one jumped in immediately and grabbed the child's jacket in his teeth, holding the screaming boy afloat. The others stayed where they were and waited until the dog in the water had dragged his protesting charge to the side. Then all four, scrambling and pushing, managed to pull the child out of the cistern and on to the ground (fortunately, the water level was high). The boy's clothes were in shreds after this overenthusiastic rescue, but he was safe and whole—though it was a long time before he went pear hunting again!

THE GREAT PYRENEES AS A SOLDIER

The association of our Great Pyrenees with the Armed Forces is another subject which bears mentioning. As a War Dog his practical value has always been somewhat restricted because of his coat color. At night, or against a green background, he stands out as an easy target for enemy fire.

But in an arctic or alpine campaign he is the ideal dog for pack work or messenger service. Here his white coat blends with the snow and ice. It also provides protection against the sleet, snow, and the extremes of cold. No other breed can lay claim to so many advantages to an army operating in the Nordic climes.

Luz and Pastoure of the de Loubonnieres Kennels both saw action with the Alpine Chasseurs in the Italian Campaign in the Second World War. Both were wounded in action and lost their lives. They were buried on the scene of battle, high in the Alps, and will long be remembered for the gallant service which they gave to their native France.

In 1942 ten Great Pyrenees were shipped from Framingham, Massachusetts, to Front Royal in Virginia to begin training for the Arctic Campaign. A second and larger contingent was dispensed to Camp Rimini in Montana where they were later joined by the first. The dogs were trained to work in rotation, three dogs assigned to one man. They were taught to carry forty-pound packs of ammunition, machine guns weighing up to sixty pounds, and lastly, to pull a toboggan laden with Red Cross supplies. On the success of the program, the Defense Department reported, "Of all breeds tried out for pack work, the Great Pyrenees are proving themselves most satisfactory."

Although the progress of the war led to the cancellation of the proposed Arctic Campaign, several dogs were dispatched to active duty in Greenland and Newfoundland. Returning servicemen brought reports of their success. But by August 1943 the last had been returned to his owner.

Ch. Basquaerie Brinker was one of those that had been away for about a year. His dewclaws had been removed "to prevent their catching and tearing in deep snow," according to the Army report! He received both an honorable discharge, as well as a Certificate of Honor "in recognition of his loyal service to our nation during this great War."

Reports of the use of Pyrenees as War Dogs antedate the above. The French Army before the turn of the century was said to favor a cross with a Pyrenean dog for ammunition portage "on account of his strength which enables him to carry as many as five hundred cartridges." And there are documented reports of Pyreneans serving as First Aid Dogs in World War I.

WORKING THE SHADY SIDE OF THE ROAD

There is also another Pyrenean tradition which has, understandably, been given little public exposure. It, too, deserves a place in a chapter on the Working Pyrenees. What follows comes from the pen of Paul Strang:

On the afternoon of the 26th of May, 1775, Louis Mandrin, the king of smugglers, was led to a scaffold erected in the front of the cathedral in the public square in Valence, France. Five thousand people jammed the area and crowded the surrounding rooftops. After a short speech, in which he warned the school children that crime does not pay, Mandrin was brutally executed.

Mandrin's "crime does not pay" speech proved prophetic. He had been captured, illegally, by a commando-type French raiding party over the border in Savoy, which was then under the jurisdiction of Sardinia. Charles-Emmanual III, King of Sardinia, protested vehemently against the action and withdrew his ambassador to France. Louis XV, in turn, dispatched his most prestigious diplomat, the Count de Noailles, to smooth over the affair. Hostilities were averted but, in France, the public outcry refused to die down. Books and pamphlets rolled from the presses. Epic and heroic songs glorifying Mandrin became the rage. Thousands of portraits and engravings of the popular hero were sold.

Of particular interest is the fact the Mandrin legend mentions his huge and faithful companion, supposedly a mountain dog, purchased in Nice in 1748. And from some of the illustrations I have seen, it is apparent to me that this dog was a Great Pyrenees. We shall probably never know positively but in any case the association would be symbolic in the extreme for, from the earliest records of our breed we know him, not only as a protector of the flock, but as a smuggler's companion and helper.

Of all the animals that have been used to carry contraband goods, the dog is, of course, the most intelligent. Robert Leighton wrote in 1911:

Travelers on the Continent may often notice the dogs kept at the various *octroi* cabins on the frontiers. They are used to assist in the detection and pursuit of smugglers, at which work they are remarkably clever; but there is even a more active and cunning class of dog employed by the contrabandists themselves who train them to evade the vigilant *dounier* and his canine assistants, and to carry consignments of illicit goods across the frontiers at night and in stormy weather, the loads of silk, lace, tobacco, spirits, or other taxable commodities being packed in small compass about their bodies and covered with a false coat. The method of training these smuggling dogs is that of implanting in their minds a rooted fear of all men in uniform, and they are taught to make their journey by unfrequented paths; consequently they steer clear of the uniformed guards at the frontier stations, and make their way to their destination by secret routes which are frequently changed.

An intelligent Obedience class in New Mexico. From left to right: Ch. Andre El Encantado de La Luz CDX, owned by Nancy Wood; Cynthis Lyon, owned by Richard Davison; Diane's Frosty Bear, owned by Diane Thomas; Skeel's Juliet of Corrales, owned by Doris Thomas; Valle del Oso Yeti, owned by Carla Greth; Dar-Jan's Bright Angel, owned by Doris Thomas; Ha-Bou-Scha, owned by Bob Jones. The *Long Sit* and *Long Down*.

The police dogs are seldom a match for these cunning four-footed contrabandists.

The situation in the Pyrenees is, in several respects, unique. In the east, toward the Mediterranean, live the Catalans, speaking an ancient Roman tongue not easily understood by outsiders. And in the west are the Basques, who also have their own language. Quasi-control of the mountain passes between France and Spain has rested, for centuries, in the hands of these two population groups who are a closed society. Smuggling, for many, simply became a way of life. Imagine the difficulties of a detective sent from either Paris or Madrid in trying to obtain any information whatsoever in the mountains. One spoken word and he is immediately recognized as a potential danger!

Certainly any farmhouse, on either side of the border, had a perfectly legitimate reason for owning a big, strong Patou. He was there to "guard the sheep." The fact that he might be perfectly suited for a quick jaunt, over the border, in the dead of night, with a twenty-pound illicit pack on his back was incidental.

Actually, while the gradual disappearance of bears and wolves is usually given as the reason why our breed became scarce in his homeland there is another, and quite distressing reason, I have been told. This is the fact that trigger-happy border guards destroyed so many of the dogs in the early years of this century.

Most of the people I questioned on the use of Pyrs in the border traffic on my recent trip to the Pyrenees took great pains to assure me, "Yes, but that's all in the past." Planes, cars, boats and bribed officials have made smuggling a big business so there really was no place, in this day and age, for anything as unsophisticated as a dog.

Perhaps so. I must have been dreaming that morning, when, standing on the little balcony of my hotel room at dawn, in the tiny mountain village, I thought I heard a guarded whistle. And thought I saw something that looked like a Pyr carrying saddlebags disappear with his master behind quickly closed doors.

THE GREAT PYRENEES IN OBEDIENCE

As an intelligent and easygoing animal, the Great Pyrenees does not lend itself to precise, repetitive obedience performances. However, with enough motivation, perseverance and teamwork, top scores and titles are possible.

Ch. Koranne of Basquaerie CD pioneered the field of obedience, earning her CD in 1938. In 1942 Basquaerie Amie CDX was the first to earn an advanced title. In the years since, many stalwarts achieved success in the obedience ring. Interest in obedience began to expand in the late sixties. There are now over 300 Pyrs that have earned a CD, and some

Ch. Koranne of Basquaerie CD. The first
Obedience titleholder in America, 1938.

Percy Jones

Am/Can Ch. Can OTCH Peerage Wolftrap Kid Jubilee AM/CAN/UD AM TD HOF and her
daughter, Ch. Wolftrap's Spotnick in Orbit CDX. Both owned and trained by Nancy
Woodward.

Peerage Wolftrap Kid Coulomb UD, clearing the *Bar Jump* in the Utility class. Owned and trained by Nancy Woodward.

Ch. Maranatha Pyragon Apollo CDX performing the *Retrieve Over the High Jump*. Bred by the Coombs, owned by Rhonda and Joe Dalton.

Joe Dalton

fifty have entered the GPCA's Obedience Hall of Fame with CDXs. Their accolades are well deserved!

Only a handful of Pyrs have gone on to complete tracking and utility titles. The most famous of these is undoubtedly Nancy Woodward's Jubilee. Her full title is: Am/Can Ch. Can OTCH Peerage Wolftrap Kid Jubilee Am/Can UD, Am TD HOF. She is the only American-bred Pyr ever to become an Obedience Trial Champion (OTCH) and is the most titled Pyr in America.

For information on obedience training, consult *How to Raise a Puppy You Can Live With,* by Neil and Rutherford (Alpine), and *Mother Knows Best: The Natural Way to Train Your Dog,* by Carol Benjamin (Howell Book House). The current AKC Official Rules for Obedience Trials are available free from AKC, 51 Madison Ave., New York, NY 10010. Most areas have puppy socialization classes where you can start your puppy off on the right foot beginning at eight weeks.

THERAPY DOGS

Increasing numbers of Great Pyrenees and their owners are becoming active in therapy dog work, or "pet-oriented therapy" as it is sometimes called. The dogs and their owners visit senior citizen centers, hospitals, schools for handicapped children and many other places where people do not normally have access to pets.

The results can be dramatic. In one instance, an occupational therapist in Michigan, Brigitte Doxtator, took her Pyr, Badine de la Brise ("Nikki"), to a nursing home in downtown Detroit. The residents were thrilled to meet Nikki, and in spite of her size, there was not enough of her to go around. However, there was an elderly lady in a wheelchair who did not participate. Nikki kept trying to go to her but the other residents told Brigitte not to bother, that the woman had not spoken a word or shown any interest in anything for over five years. Finally, Nikki succeeded in approaching the lady and gently nuzzled her hand. Ever so slowly, the woman turned and looked at her, then stroked her head. "I know you," she said with vocal cords weak from years of disuse. "I used to know you." And she sighed, and hugged Nikki and wept silently into her ruff.

Therapy work is a wonderful way of serving the community. It doesn't seem like work at all. It is more like visiting friends. The dogs love it, and it is good public relations for the breed and for dogs in general. Pets and show dogs alike can participate. All it takes is a good stable temperament and a little basic obedience.

Becoming involved is usually easy. The largest organization is Therapy Dogs International (TDI), to whom goes the credit for promoting therapy work all over the country. Many kennel clubs and other dog groups have programs also. Texas has a state-wide therapy program called Paws

Rivergrove's Virginia Bluebell brings a little joy into the life of an elderly gentleman. Owner Susan Tucker

Happy faces all around as Lysette de la Brise visits the senior citizens' center. Breeder-owner Patricia Princehouse. *Patricia Princehouse*

Across Texas. Director, Virginia Hyatt is especially impressed with the work Ch. Reymaree Mr. Bojangles TT ("Bono"), owned by Jean Cave, has done with handicapped children and the elderly. "I don't care what the Standard says, Pyrs were bred to do," she insists. "These dogs were born to do therapy work!"

On a visit to a hospital for crippled children, a four-year-old girl in braces and crutches wanted desperately to walk Bono. She took the lead, looked him in the eye (they were about the same height) and wrestled her way across the room with Bono walking patiently beside her, empathizing with her determination, encouraging her with gentle nudges. The nurses explained that this little girl had long ago given up and refused even trying to walk. When she kissed Bono good-bye, she promised him, "I'll practice walking every day."

Dogs, patients and owners agree, it is a wonderful way to spend an afternoon! Susan Tucker in Virginia has been involved in therapy work since 1982 with her dogs, Ch. Tip 'n Chip Beaucoup de Joie CD TDI and Rivergroves Virginia Bluebell. She enthuses: "The wonderful response from the residents and the anticipation as they wait to see 'their dog' has proved the value of this program so many times. . . . What boundless pleasure our dogs give!"

And the Pyr shall lie down with the lamb! Pup and lamb on Huny Mountain farm.

Fay Knox

114

9

The Modern Great Pyrenees in America

<hr>

WITH THE DISAPPEARANCE of Cote de Neige, La Colina and some of the other early kennels from the show scene in the late forties, the banner of the breed passed into the hands of a new generation. The breed is now well represented from coast to coast.

Foremost among the show and breeding kennels in America in the past four decades is **Quibbletown,** founded by C. Seaver and Edith Smith of Taunton, Massachusetts.

Quibbletown came to the forefront in the very early 1950s. During the next forty years their bloodlines have continued to maintain a prominent position in show rings and breeding programs from coast to coast. Quibbletown has now finished in excess of 160 champions carrying the kennel prefix.

Edith Smith acquired her first Great Pyrenees nearly fifty years ago while still an undergraduate at Radcliffe. Cote de Neige Guerrier was a familiar figure on the college campus and at the Fogg Museum at Harvard. As an art major, Edith Smith spent many hours in the museum. Guerrier shared her dormitory room.

Two years later when she married, the Smiths decided to show their dog, and Guerrier became their first champion. Between 1951 and 1955, the Smiths began their kennel by acquiring all the best stock owned by Marjorie Butcher.

Ch. Quibbletown Carlotta HOF won BOB under Judge Wm. L. Kendrick on the way to a Group placement at the 1964 Camden County Kennel Club Show, just three weeks before she whelped. She was a very influential producer. *Shafer*

Ch. Quibbletown Billy Wink was a Group and Specialty winner in the late '60s. Bred, owned and handled by Mr. and Mrs. Smith, Billy Wink is shown here scoring a win under the late, great Alva Rosenberg. *Roberts*

Ch. Soleil Serein Ami HOF won the Working Group under Judge Maxwell Riddle at the Mid-Del Tinker Kennel Club Show. Bred, owned and handled by Jack Magoffin. *Petrulis*

Mrs. C. Seaver Smith with her first puppy, Ch. Cote de Neige Guerrier.

Early Quibbletown champions benched at Westminster. Pictured left to right are Parfait and Mistigris. Ch. Quibbletown Mistigris went BOB at Westminster in '54, '56 and '57. Bred and owned by Mr. and Mrs. C. Seaver Smith, Jr.   *Stephanie Rancou*

"The kennel got its name," Mrs. Smith told us, "while we were living at New Market, New Jersey. There was a market in the town which explained that, in colonial days, it had been called 'Quibbletown,' since the farmers would bring their produce to the square and then quibble over the prices."

Two of the early standouts at Quibbletown were Ch. Cote de Neige Actrice and her daughter Ch. Cote de Neige Ariette II. They were direct descendants of Ch. Cote de Neige Ariette, a litter sister to Ch. Cote de Neige Symphonie, America's first homebred Best in Show winner. Mrs. Smith recalled: "Our early breeding efforts were plagued with problems which don't exist today. Vaccines were less than reliable, and more than one promising puppy was lost to disease. In 1951 hepatitis struck many American kennels, and Quibbletown came close to being wiped out. Those dogs who survived had hard-pad and lived thereafter with damaged feet. The battle against parasites was difficult and discouraging without the aid of today's more sophisticated drugs. We relied heavily on 'Early Bird Puppy Wormer.' While sulfa drugs were available, as well as the early antibiotics, their side effects were damaging in many cases. When we watch our veterinarians in surgery today, with complex anesthesia procedures and total life-support systems available, we remember the days when few veterinarians owned an x-ray machine and surgery meant an ether cone."

In the fifties and early sixties Ch. Quibbletown Easter Token and Ch. Quibbletown Bon Chance, campaigned by the Linewebers, swept the National Specialties with seven combined wins. Ch. Quibbletown Mistigris achieved 105 bests of breed and 37 Group placements.

One of the most successful Quibbletown show winners of this period, and a dog whose production was to be of great significance to the breed in the years to follow, was Ch. Quibbletown Impresario HOF. Impy holds the record at Quibbletown with eighteen champion offspring, many of which have been outstanding winners and producers in their own rights.

While Impy was making his mark in the East, in the Midwest Ch. Quibbletown Chanson de Geste became the first Quibbletown BIS winner.

Ch. Quibbletown Jim Dandy HOF/HOF began his show career by winning the National Specialty from the classes at fifteen months of age. Mrs. Smith reminisced about Dandy, who left a legacy of ten Quibbletown champions. "This beloved dog was our friend, companion, house dog and resident character of twelve years and is still sorely missed by his family."

Ch. Quibbletown Billy Wink, a multiple Group winner, was campaigned in the middle sixties. In the late sixties and early seventies, Ch. Quibbletown Falstaff, owned by Frances Glover, was a multiple Group winner and won the National Specialty twice.

In the seventies and early eighties, two dogs followed Ch. Quibbletown Impresario HOF/HOF as the predominant sires in the ongoing linebreeding program. They were Ch. Quibbletown Billy Deaux HOF and Ch.

Quibbletown Step Aside. Their impact on the breeding program is being passed on to this day. Step Aside was part of a brace, together with his litter sister, that won five Best Braces in Show and an additional two Working Group Braces. Step Aside's son Ch. Quibbletown Justin Time is now making his mark as a sire and is acquitting himself well in the show ring with limited showing. One of Quibbletown's greatest bitches was Ch. Quibbletown Dutchess, Best Opposite Sex at the National Specialty in 1961 and dam of Ch. Quibbletown Beaucoup II and Ch. Quibbletown Chanson de Geste—both of which were Group winners before the age of two. Ch. Quibbletown Carlotta HOF whelped nine champions. Several famous winners and producers from the Impy-Carlotta breeding made a profound impact on the breed in North America. Special mention must also be made of Quibbletown Queeka Bear HOF, the foundation bitch for the Kentopps' **Karolaska** Kennel. Queeka was the dam of two Best in Show winners and several Group winners in the early seventies.

In 1971, for the second time in the history of Quibbletown, the Smiths campaigned a dog that did not bear their kennel name: Ch. Karolaska Glacier HOF. The first dog so campaigned was Ch. Lorvaso de La Colina HOF in the fifties. Glacier came to live with the Smiths in 1971. He shattered all marks with an awesome ten Bests in Show, fifty-six Group Firsts, sixty-one other Group placements, two National Specialty Bests of Breed and two Regional Specialty wins to become the top winner in the history of the breed. Glacier's phenomenal career was tragically terminated at its height by his untimely death from bone cancer.

Quibbletown's record at National Specialties from 1953 to 1973 began with Ch. Quibbletown Easter Token (three), and continued with Ch. Quibbletown Small Fry (two), Ch. Quibbletown Meringue (one), Ch. Quibbletown Bon Chance (four), Ch. Quibbletown Beau Olard (one), Ch. Quibbletown Jim Dandy HOF (two), Ch. Quibbletown Falstaff HOF (two) and Ch. Karolaska Glacier HOF (two) for a total of seventeen nationals in twenty years.

Mrs. Smith explained the reasons behind Quibbletown's success:

Quibbletown is a true bloodline, not merely a kennel prefix. Because we stood almost alone in the early years here in the East, we developed and maintained perhaps a larger colony than we would have liked. We determined to be totally self-sufficient, to linebreed—with extensive culling—in an effort to produce litters even in size, type and soundness. Via our Cote de Neige stock we had the type we wanted, since those early dogs were almost all close to the lovely Estat d'Argeles of Basquaerie.

In the late 1950s we added our one outcross dog, Ch. Lorvaso de La Colina, who corrected any deficiency we felt we might lack in soundness. Laurie finished his championship in 1958, at the age of nine years, and also won the Working Group. This dog produced hindquarters, balance and good feet with remarkable consistency. Once Laurie had been incorporated into

Ch. Karolaska Puffin,
HOF. Owned by Elli
Pasicznyk of Maleens.

Ch. Skeel's Bonnie won a Group Third
under judge Arthur Zane, at Lewiston,
ID; owners Evelyn Stuart and Carrie
Stuart Parks. *Roberts*

Ch. Barqueill Status Quo HOF, bred
and owned by Frankie Glover, won a
Group Second under judge Mary Crane.
Klein

our breeding program, we felt we were on the right track. Laurie was the sire of eleven Quibbletown champions, including Impresario.

Our hope has always been that, within our linebred colony, we can afford the luxury of purely visual breeding, and that any dog and bitch may be mated without danger of a genetic disaster. Though we do not offer stud service, we have always welcomed Quibbletown-bred bitches who are brought back to be bred and thus continue a linebreeding pattern.

We are pleased that our stock has been wholly or in part the foundation of many of today's most respected kennel names.

These names include: **Tip 'n Chip** (Illinois), **Cavalier** (Washington), **Barqueill** (Delaware), **Karolaska** (Washington), **Elysee** (Colorado), **VilleVieux** (Illinois), **Limberlost** in Ontario, Canada, and many others.

During the eighties, Mr. and Mrs. Smith devoted an increased amount of time to dog show judging. In 1986, finding it nearly impossible to hire competent kennel help in Taunton, they had all of the Quibbletown breeding and show stock transferred to the care of Patricia Milliman just outside Geneva, New York, where the bloodlines continue in a carefully monitored linebreeding program. Following Mrs. Smith's untimely death early in 1989, all of the dogs were transferred to a co-ownership consisting of Patricia Milliman and C. Seaver Smith. A respected all-breed judge and thus frequently on the road, Mr. Smith feels completely confident leaving the dogs in Ms. Milliman's hands: "Pat's care and dedication to our lovely breed cannot be extolled too highly!" Thus the story of Quibbletown now spans six decades with many more years of breeding and showing yet to come.

While Quibbletown was getting underway on the East Coast in the fifties, another kennel, 1,800 miles to the west, began a modest breeding program which was to grow in prominence over the next twenty years, culminating in a major contribution to the show scene in the early seventies.

This was **Soleil**, owned by Mr. and Mrs. Jack Magoffin of Sterling, Kansas. Jack and Dorothy became actively interested in showing and breeding in the late forties. Their first Pyrenees, Sunshine O'Cobermere, left a permanent legacy in her name Soleil, the French equivalent for Sunshine—which became the kennel prefix.

The next Pyrenees to arrive at Soleil was Ch. Basquaerie Marechal, purchased from Mrs. Crane after he finished at the National Specialty in 1947 under judge Mme. Harper Trois-Fontaines. The vibrations of Marechal were felt in the Midwest in the late forties, where he was campaigned successfully to a number of Working Group placements.

Next came Lady Jeanne, Sunshine's puppy who finished in 1949, then Basquaerie Jacqueline, daughter of the multiple BIS winning Ch. Basquaerie Beau Estagel, who was writing the record book in the East.

In the late fifties, the Magoffins began to campaign their dogs in a manner which won fame and admiration for the breed. Ch. Pondtail Ra-

Ch. Tip 'N Chip Sonny's Image HOF. A ranking producer with sixteen Champion get, he was owned and handled by Judith Cooper. *Booth*

Ch. Trottenfox I'm A Tuff Tip 'N Chip made history by becoming the first Great Pyrenees to win a Working Group from the Puppy class. Owned by Judith Cooper and Nan Hall Hamilton. *Schley*

Can/ Am Ch. Ventisquero Samson The Great, Winners Dog at the California Specialty in 1976, under Eng. judge Peter Gilbert. Owned and handled by Henry Hanemaayer.

phael of Basquaerie and Ch. Pondtail Tattoo of Basquaerie arrived in 1958. Both were English imports.

Ch. Soleil Baron HOF, a Raphael son, achieved multiple Group placements and in 1965 was named the breed's first top producing sire.

The acquisition of Ch. Rogue la Rue HOF, bred by Mr. and Mrs. Floyd Bolden of southern California, was to be a major factor at Soleil. In Rogue's background were some of the best of the early Basquaerie bloodlines in California.

By 1975 Rogue was the top producing sire in the history of the breed with twenty-seven champions.

Rogue's son Ch. Soleil Serein Ami HOF opened doors for the breed in the Midwest. He was the breed's top winner in 1967 and had a lifetime record of twenty-nine Group placements.

The most widely known of the Rogue sons is Ch. Soleil Pierre de Blu Crest HOF ("Pierre"). Pierre was campaigned by Vic and Sue Capone of Poco Pyrs Kennels in the early seventies. In 1970 Pierre broke the five-year hiatus during which no Pyr had won Best in Show. Four more Bests in Show followed and a total of eighty-seven Group placements, three National Specialty wins, a Regional Specialty win and innumerable Bests of Breed. One of Pierre's most poignant wins was at the 1974 National Specialty in Rock Creek, Maryland, under English judge Mrs. Joan Passini-Birkett. At ten years of age, Pierre came out of retirement to win first the veterans' class and then the Breed. He was known as the "Pyrenean Pathfinder," paving the way for contemporary Pyrenees in the Working Group and Best in Show rings. Pierre sired thirteen champions.

Additional Soleil champions to distinguish themselves in the Working Group are: Ch. Basquaerie's Clown by Golly, Ch. Soleil Rayon, Ch. Soleil King's Image, Ch. Soleil Gai Lance, and Ch. Cobberidge Adam HOF.

Soleil stock has been widely dispersed and has served, at least in part, as the foundation for a number of fine contemporary kennels including **Skeel** (Idaho), **Marwell** (Alaska), **Cobberidge** (Wisconsin), **Chantilli** (Washington), **Snowmass** (California), and **Ventisquero** in British Columbia, Canada.

In the words of Dorothy Magoffin, "The tall, fragrant cedars that are on the north side of Soleil have become the final resting place for those wonderful, affectionate friends who, like troopers, went many miles with us. In thirty-one years the names are many and I wouldn't say that one was greater than another, for each had the qualities that set them apart, to us and to the breed."

The Great Pyrenees fancy sustained a major loss with the passing of this great and generous lady on May 17, 1974. The Soleil line continues in a reduced capacity under the direction of Jack Magoffin and his niece Kim Clark.

The **Tip 'n Chip** kennel of Mrs. Roy Peavey and her daughter Judith Bankus-Cooper has earned a reputation for breeding and showing a distinguished line of Great Pyrenees winners. Over one hundred champions bear the Tip 'n Chip prefix, including numerous Group, BIS and National Specialty winners.

This kennel came into being in 1948 with the acquisition of its foundation bitch, Basquaerie Dawn, bred by Mary Crane. Two more females that were to play an important role in the Tip 'n Chip bloodlines were Basquaerie New Dawn and Soleil Ting Tang Paddy Wack.

In the late 1950s the kennel came to the attention of the fancy with the breeding of Ting Tang Paddy Wack to Ch. Soleil Rayon. A trio of top-winning Pyrenees were produced: Ch. Tip 'n Chip's Gentille Amie, Tip 'n Chip's Massif Mont-Blanc and Ch. Tip 'n Chip's Mountvalea. The first and third were shown as a brace; a fourth pup from this breeding won both his championship and a CD Obedience title.

The next important influence on the kennel strain came in 1963 when a litter out of Gentille Amie was sired by Ch. Basquaerie Bali HOF. This produced four champions, including Tip 'n Chip's Luchon, who won Best of Breed at the National Specialty in 1967 under judge Mary Crane.

In 1966 Ch. Tip 'n Chip's Mountvalea was bred to the BIS winner Ch. Quibbletown Chanson de Geste to produce Ch. Tip 'n Chip's Mont-Chanson ("Sonny"). The kennel then added Ch. Tip 'n Chip's Quibbletown Impy HOF ("Q.T."), a daughter of the well-known Impresario-Carlotta breeding, that was BOS at the 1967 National Specialty. These dogs served as the foundation for the contemporary Tip 'n Chip winners and producers.

Judith Cooper writes: "Sonny left a definite impression on the breed in his short life. He died at twenty months of age after siring only three litters. Among these, one truly outstanding litter whelped by Q.T. was born on March 18, 1968. Sonny was a top producing sire in 1969, with a total of eight champions, two of whom were Group winners."

The Sonny-Q.T. litter mentioned above included six puppies that were raised by a foster mother, a Collie, because of milk toxicity. They were: Ch. Tip 'n Chip Sonny's Image HOF, Ch. Tip 'n Chip Sonny's Reflection HOF/HOF, Ch. Tip 'n Chip Sonny's Pride and Joy, Ch. Tip 'n Chip Sonamara Chanson, Ch. Tip 'n Chip Sonny's Angelique and Tip 'n Chip Sonny's Impression CD. Q.T. was top producing dam in 1969 and was also the dam of Ch. Tip 'n Chip Sonny's Quaes-Tor HOF, a multiple Group winner.

Ch. Tip 'n Chip Sonny's Reflection HOF/HOF finished his championship and went on to a Group 4 from the puppy class. He won the Midwest specialties back to back in 1970 and 1971. He won a total of 112 BOB's, and 35 Group placements including six Group Firsts. He was top producing sire in 1973 and sired over a dozen champions including 1975's Top Winner, Ch. Pyrstrom's Ringmaster HOF and several specialty winners including Ch. Tip 'n Chip's Sonny's L'Air HOF/HOF.

Ch. Basquaerie Bali HOF was Winners Dog at the 1958 National Specialty and the foundation sire at Carolyn and Bruce Hardy's Balibasque Kennel.

Ch. Starlaxy Barycentre (left) shown taking BOS in Futurity to his sister, Ch. Starlaxy Bellatrix under judge Mary Crane at the Futurity of the 1981 National Specialty. Presented by breeder-owners Bob and Judy Brown.

Ch. Tip 'n Chip's Sonny's Image HOF sired over sixteen champions including several specialty winners. A Reflection son, Ch. Tip 'n Chip Sonny's Sundance Kid HOF, was BOW at the National Specialty in 1973 and BOB at the Colorado Specialty in 1976 under judge Paul Strang. In 1975 he was the year's Top Producer with seven champions. Five of these were out of Ch. Tip 'n Chip's Roxanne HOF, one of the kennel's top producers, including Am/Can Ch. Tip 'n Chip Sonny's Side Up HOF/HOF, a multiple BIS winner and National Specialty winner who was number one Pyr and number ten Working dog in 1979.

Nan Hall Hamilton of **Trottenfox** Kennels has worked very closely with Mrs. Cooper and produced a number of top winners including Ch. Trottenfox I'm a Tuff Tip 'n Chip, who was the first puppy in the history of the breed to win a Group First from the Puppy Class. Tuffy's daughter, Ch. Trottenfox Sheza Tuff Tip 'n Chip HOF, took BOS at the National Specialty in 1986 and is the breed's all-time top producing bitch with twenty-five champion produce. Sheza's son, Am/Can Ch. Tip 'n Chip's Pride d'Argeles HOF was a multiple BIS winner.

In the eighties, Tip 'n Chip has continued its winning ways with many impressive showings at National Specialties. At the 1982 National Specialty, Ch. Tip 'n Chip Ice Capades won the Puppy Sweepstakes, and then went on to win BOB over numerous adult specials. Ch. Tip 'n Chip's High Interest was BOS at the 1985 and 1986 National Specialties. In 1988 Ch. Tip 'n Chip's Beau Brummel was BOW at the National Specialty. Ch. Tip 'n Chip's Star Trottenfox came out of the Veterans class to win BOS at the National Specialty in 1989.

An entire book could be written about the winnings of Ch. Rivergroves Run For The Roses HOF/HOF ("TR"), a dog with a largely Tip 'n Chip pedigree, co-owned by Mrs. Cooper and breeder Jean Boyd. In the late eighties, TR smashed all records with a stunning forty-eight Bests in Show. Shown by Jean's husband Wayne Boyd, TR trekked thousands of miles and beat over 50,000 other top show dogs before retiring in 1990. In 1989 TR added a National Specialty BOB win under judge Paul Strang to his voluminous list of wins. TR's influence as a sire will undoubtedly be felt for years to come as he is already a Hall of Fame producer with Specialty, Group and BIS winning get.

Tip 'n Chip has provided foundation stock for other kennels, including **Trottenfox** (Illinois), **Rivergrove** (Maryland), **Starlaxy** (Wisconsin), **Summerhill**, and many others. Judith Cooper says: "Our family is continuing into its third generation with Pyrenees; my two daughters, Marcy and Laurie, have started to take an active interest in grooming and showing." Thus it is clear that the Tip 'n Chip bloodlines are in safe hands for many years to come.

Balibasque Kennels in Pennsylvania began in 1960 when Carolyn and Bruce Hardy bought their first Great Pyrenees, Ch. Dji of Bator de Esterhazy ("Melody"), from Frank Koller. Next came the lovely Ch. Basquaerie Clown's Folly. With the acquisition of Ch. Basquaerie Bali HOF and other fine Great Pyrenees from Mrs. Crane's breeding stock, the idea of establishing a kennel took root. Bali had started his career with winners dog at the National Specialty in 1958 and was already a multiple Group placer when he came to the Hardys. Mary Crane had written describing Bali's pedigree as follows: "This is the very finest of Basquaerie pedigrees— containing all our most famous names and bloodlines." To Bruce and Carolyn Hardy, it made sense to continue these bloodlines and the tradition which had produced them. They named their kennel to include that beautiful Bali, combined with Basque, and thus Balibasque was born.

During the sixties when the Basquaerie kennel was reduced, breeding stock representative of the most famous and best producing lines came to Balibasque. These included Ch. Basquaerie Jolly Clown, Ch. Basquaerie Tyna, Ch. Basquaerie Winter's Fog, Ch. Basquaerie Laika and Ch. Basquaerie Vicki's Snow White ("Vicki").

Vicki's story is unique. She originally went to Florida with the Cranes. However, as the hazards of heartworm were not well known in the early sixties, Vicki became a victim. Back to Boston she came with a clump of worms obstructing the flow of blood through her heart. She entered the Massachusetts General Hospital as a patient and underwent surgery to remove the mass. Mrs. Crane was warned, "Another bout of heartworm will do her in!" The Cranes could not take her back to Florida, so Carolyn Hardy took her and showed her to her championship. The highlight of Vicki's career provided her mistress with one of the greatest thrills of her life. The gal who had survived open heart surgery was named WB at the Great Pyrenees Club of America National Specialty in 1969.

Breeding at Balibasque has always centered principally on the bloodlines of Basquaerie. Mrs. Hardy writes: "There is one important physical characteristic of the Great Pyrenees that so impressed us that we decided to concentrate our efforts to retain it true to the standard. That's the physical appearance of the head. The Pyr head is likened to that of the brown bear but with the ears falling down. The pigmentation must be excellent. In our opinion, this is what identifies the Great Pyrenees and keeps him from being just another big, long-haired dog. Bali had one of the most beautiful heads we have ever seen. He always seemed to hand the same excellent type down to his offspring. And to Jolly Clown goes credit for producing puppies with beautiful black pigmentation. To start with such excellent stock was sheer luck, but it has taken planning to continue these qualities."

Bali was bred to Ruth Eveland's foundation bitch, Ch. Blancura of Bator de Esterhazy. This mating provided a useful outcross to the Basquaerie line. This resulted in the male puppy that was to become Ch. Balibasque Mister Big. A mating between Bali and Clown's Folly produced Ch. Basquaerie Nuvalari of Pondtail, who was exported to Mrs. Passini-

Ch. Basquaerie Vicki's Snow White, Winners Bitch at the National Specialty in 1970, handled by her owner, Carolyn Hardy. *Evelyn Shafer*

Balibasque Beau of Karolaska CD— Sire of two Best In Show Great Pyrenees and a Group Winning bitch. Bred by Carolyn and Bruce Hardy and owned by Karolaska Kennels.

Ch. Balibasque Sugar Bear Brie won BOB at the 1990 Pennsylvania Specialty under Judge Carolyn Hardy. Owned by Dave, Maureen and Dillon Simon. *Kernan*

Birkett of Pondtail kennel in England. Nuvalari added much to the breeding picture in Great Britain. Among other accomplishments, Nuvalari was grandsire to Champion Bergerie Knur, Supreme Best in Show at Crufts in 1970.

A great-grandson of Ch. Bali, Am/Can Ch. Balibasque Roland, sired South Africa's Ch. Balibasque Teddy Bear du Chateau, who helped establish the breed in that country through the efforts of Josef and Inge Briechle.

Over the years, Balibasque has continued to carry on the Basquaerie bloodlines. Bruce's death in 1984 saddened the entire Pyrenees community. However, Carolyn continues to operate Balibasque true to their original goal of producing Great Pyrenees of correct type and soundness. Keeping an eye on the bloodlines in the breeding programs of other, younger kennels, she continues to pull back into her present breeding program those old Basquaerie lines.

Current Balibasque pedigrees frequently show the old Basquaerie Great Pyrenees in the fourth or fifth generation. For example, Am/Can Ch. Kaskadian Joy of Balibasque has Ch. Basquaerie Corla's Betsy II, bred by Balibasque, as her great-granddam. Her great-grandsire is Ch. Balibasque Wooden Nickel. Ch. Basquaerie Jolly Clown is Joy's great-great-grandsire. Jolly Clown is in the fourth generation of Am/Can Ch. Balibasque Pumpkin Pie and her brother Ch. Balibasque Top of the Line, and in the fifth generation of Am/Can Ch. BelleAmi Jolly of Balibasque and the young male Balibasque Top Secret.

Mrs. Hardy has not been an AKC judge for several years but remains very active as a breeder and exhibitor. She sees a bright future for Balibasque. In her words: "With my nephew, Robert Manning, and Nicole Craig as partners to carry on the Balibasque tradition, the future is looking good. Breeding to standard to produce correct type with soundness of body and temperament is the basis of that tradition. As a companion/guardian dog, trustworthy and dependable temperament is essential in any continuous breeding program. To keep that beautiful head with no apparent stop, that excellent, black pigmentation, that pretty expression associated with correct type, and that elegant, effortless movement associated with the soundness of a working dog are lifetime goals."

Over the years, Balibasque has provided foundation stock for many breeding programs including **Karolaska** (Washington), **Starlaxy** (Wisconsin), and **Galesway** (New Jersey).

The key to the success of the **Karolaska** Kennel of Carol and Richard Kentopp is to be found in the fortuitous blending of the bloodlines of Quibbletown and Balibasque. While luck certainly played a part in the beginning, only the Kentopps' care and dedication to their line have resulted in the consistent winning of Karolaska dogs in the past two decades.

Rick and Carol Kentopp moved from North Carolina to Alaska in

1967 to homestead a wild tract on the side of a mountain overlooking the harbor at Anchorage. With them came their foundation pair, Balibasque Beau of Karolaska CD HOF ("Chief") and Quibbletown Queeka Bear HOF. During the first winter, while the Kentopps lived in a rough cabin, the dogs were required to haul tanks of propane gas up the mountainside. The original homesite was soon replaced with a modern home and up-to-date kennel, but the dogs were still expected to pull their share of the load when the need arose.

The first Karolaska litter was born the following summer. The first puppy born was to become a champion and BIS winner. This was Ch. Karolaska Polar Nero HOF, owned by Dr. and Mrs. James Giffin of **Elysee** Kennel (Colorado). The next litter, a repeat breeding, produced Ch. Karolaska Glacier HOF, owned by Mr. and Mrs. C. Seaver Smith, Jr., that became the top-winning Great Pyrenees in America in the early seventies, winning the National Specialty in 1972 and a total of ten Bests in Show. The Kentopps kept a sister, Ch. Karolaska Polar Bonni Bear, who became the top-winning bitch in the country. A Working Group winner, Bonni's career was highlighted by BOS at the National Specialty, and a Regional Specialty win.

On the passing of Bonni in 1975, Carol Kentopp wrote, "She was our beloved house girl. We have a great affection for all our dogs, but there is always that special one, and that was Bonni."

In 1970 the Kentopps acquired Ch. Quibbletown Sock It To 'Em HOF from the Smiths. Bred to the offspring of the original pair, "Clyde" made an important contribution to the development of the Karolaska bloodline, and sired some dozen champions. Clyde bred to Queeka produced Ch. Karolaska Kuskokwim Kid HOF, one of Karolaska's most influential sires. Virtually all contemporary Karolaska Pyrs trace back to Clyde, Chief and Queeka.

Another Balibasque dog was added in the mid-seventies. This was Ch. El Amor Bruno Balibasque HOF, a Ch. Balibasque Wooden Nickel son. Bruno produced pups with lovely heads, among them Ch. Karolaska Misty Lady, who was BOB at the National Specialty in 1978, breaking a hiatus of over twenty-five years during which a bitch had not won top honors at a GPCA National. Another Bruno daughter, Ch. Karolaska Puffin HOF, is the only Great Pyrenees bitch in the history of the breed in America to win BIS at an all-breed show. Puffin had earlier distinguished herself, first by winning BOS from the puppy class at the California Regional in 1976, then by going WB, BOW and BOS at the National Specialty that same year.

Karolaska dominated the Great Pyrenees show scene all over the country in the seventies and eighties. They have produced over 160 champions, including six National Specialty BOB winners, nine BIS winners, twenty Group First winners, a total of thirty-three Working Group Placers and countless winners at Regional Specialties.

Ch. Karolaska Bolshoi Baranova HOF was BOB at the National Specialty in 1975 and went on to be a BIS winner. His brother, Ch. Boris Goudonov Baranova, bred and owned by Dr. and Mrs. Arthur Shaible of **Baranova** (Alaska), finished at the National under Mrs. Crane in 1976. Ch. Karolaska Captivator HOF/HOF, owned by Mr. and Mrs. Joseph Gentzel of **Aneto** (Georgia), was a BIS winner and took the Eastern Regional Specialty from the classes in 1976. Yet another BIS winner is Ch. Karolaska Juan Carlo d'Arctic HOF, co-owned by the Kentopps and Mrs. Joan Pearson of **Pyrson** Kennel (Texas). Mrs. Pearson based her foundation on Karolaska, and owned Ch. Karolaska Kivalina II HOF/HOF, mother of Ch. Pyrson K'laska of Summerhill HOF/HOF, top producing sire in the history of the breed.

Ch. Sunshine of Karolaska HOF/HOF, owned by Anne and Alan Rappaport of **VilleVieux** Kennel (Illinois), won the National Specialty in 1982 and was a multiple BIS winner and sire and grandsire of multiple BIS winners. Ch. Karolaska Bristol Bay HOF/HOF was BOB at the National Specialty in 1985 and was a multiple BIS winner and top winning Pyr in 1985. 1986 saw Brenda Jackson's (**Breglenn** Kennel, Michigan) Ch. Karolaska Kaballero Kid HOF/HOF ("Sam"), a Group winner, go BOB at the National Specialty under judge Carolyn Hardy. Both Bristol and Sam were later exported to Mr. and Mrs. Mochizuki in Japan to help improve the breed in that country. Bristol's mother, Ch. Karolaska Honey's Abby HOF and Ch. Karolaska Nero's Clover HOF are among the breed's three all-time top producing bitches. In addition to those mentioned above, countless breeding programs are based on the Karolaska bloodline, including **Avancer** (Wisconsin), **Pyr Haven** (Wisconsin), **Montalvo** (Oregon) and **Shadowrun** (California).

In 1971 in the seemingly unlikely location of a historic landmark district of downtown Chicago, VilleVieux Great Pyrenees was established by Anne and Alan Rappaport and their twelve-year-old daughter, Tracey. In the years since, VilleVieux has accounted for more than seventy champions, the kennel's most notable achievement being three successive generations of Specialty winning and all-breed BIS winning dogs.

The Rappaports acquired their first Great Pyrenees to guard hearth and home from urban predators, a task the grandson of BIS, BIS Ch. Soleil Pierre de Blu Crest HOF/HOF, Montagnard de VilleVieux, performed well. In 1978 VilleVieux relocated in suburban Barrington, but several litters were whelped and champions finished while in Chicago.

Ch. Starlaxy Anson de VilleVieux was VilleVieux's first champion from its first litter. Mrs. Rappaport handled Anson to Best of Breed at the Centennial Westminster show, having transported him to New York City on a chartered bus along with twenty-eight other people and seventeen dogs of various breeds.

Reading, observation and long conversations with Mary Crane of

Ch. Sunshine of Karolaska HOF/HOF won a BIS at the Corn Belt Kennel Club, May 28, 1984. Handled by his owner, Anne Rappaport.

Basquaerie and Edith Smith of Quibbletown eventually led to the direction Ville Vieux is now pursuing. Mrs. Rappaport writes: "We feel ourselves fortunate to have known Mary and Edith, both very capable women, and to have been able to avail ourselves of their knowledge and experience. Mrs. Crane repeatedly stressed the importance of type, type and type. Mrs. Smith put together the genetic foundation enabling breeders to produce a sound breed type for generations to come. Time, financial and physical restraints combine to make breeding extremely difficult for present-day breeders, in addition to not having a Mrs. Crane nor a Mrs. Smith available as a resource."

As a result of their exposure to Ch. Karolaska Polar Nero HOF, and his brother, Ch. Karolaska Glacier HOF, the Rappaports concentrated their efforts on a tightly disciplined linebreeding program which has resulted in a distinct type. The kennel's first BIS winner was Ch. Sunshine of Karolaska HOF/HOF ("Lucky"), sired by a brother of Nero and Glacier. Lucky was an excellent producer. His son, Ch. Ville Vieux Yankee Sunshine HOF, also a multiple BIS winner, in turn sired Ch. Ville Vieux Le Roi HOF, the kennel's current multiple BIS winner. Bred to Lucky daughters, Le Roi has produced Ch. Ville Vieux Daphne, the 1990 Westminster BOB winner, and a multiple Group winning son, Ch. Carillon Gallavant.

Ville Vieux is the foundation upon which several kennels have begun building, including **Carillon** of Mr. and Mrs. Blacklidge, **Chanterelle** of Mr. and Mrs. Beck, **Her-Gor** of Renate Craig, **Barranca**, which is the kennel name being used by Ron and Delores Neal in respect for their very good friend, the late Lillian Williamson, a well-known Old California breeder, and **Baleklif** of Bob and Louise Edwards. Anne Rappaport concludes: "Each generation of Pyrs is but a link in the chain. Our hope is that the breed is no worse off for our interference than when we began; perhaps somewhat better."

Jean Groves Boyd of **Rivergrove** Kennel in Maryland became interested in the breed in 1967. While living in Michigan, she acquired Me Llamo Tonya de Montbleu HOF and successfully showed her to a CDX obedience title in straight shows with scores in the 1900s and a High in Trial. In 1970 she added Am/Can Ch. Poco Pyrs King Crusher HOF/HOF, a son of Ch. Soleil Pierre de Blu Crest HOF/HOF. Crusher became a multiple BIS and Specialty winner. Then came Ch. Tip 'n Chip Sonny's L'Air HOF/HOF, who proved herself a formidable competitor with multiple BOBs at Regionals and BOS at the 1979 National Specialty. This Group winning bitch is the top winning Great Pyrenees bitch of all time with over fifty BOBs and nine Group placements. L'Air is the only bitch in the GPCA Show Dog Hall of Fame. Bred to Crusher, L'Air produced many Rivergrove winners. In the late seventies, Jean married Wayne Boyd and moved to Maryland.

Rivergrove continued its winning ways into the eighties. Ch. Rivergrove's J. A. Wonderwoman went BOS at the National Specialty in 1984. At eighteen months, Crusher-L'Air son, Ch. Rivergrove's Crusher's Rerun HOF ("Blackeye"), became the youngest Pyr ever to win a BIS. He went on to be a multiple BIS winner before two years of age. Blackeye had a brilliant future ahead of him. However, tragedy struck Rivergrove's when the young star was killed in a freak accident. Luckily, Blackeye had sired two litters and Mrs. Boyd was able to salvage his line.

In the early eighties Mrs. Boyd bred two of her bitches, Blackeye daughters, Ch. Rivergrove's Rerun's Remaid HOF, and Ch. Rivergrove's Crusher's J. P. HOF to Jan Brown's Ch. Pyrson K'laska of Summerhill HOF/HOF ("Macho"). The resulting pups made quite a showing at the National Specialty in 1985. One of the most striking was the young bitch, Ch. Rivergrove's Goes To Hollywood, who went BOS in Futurity, Best Bred By Exhibitor and RWB.

This was, however, a mere foreshadowing of what was to come. One of the Macho-Remaid pups, Ch. Rivergrove's Run For The Roses HOF/HOF ("TR"), had finished his championship in 1984 at one year of age. In 1986 he won a total of fifty-two Group placements and topped it off with a BIS. In 1987 he won an astonishing ninety-four more Group placements and seven more Bests in Show. Judy Cooper then became a co-owner. TR really came into his own in 1988 with thirty BIS and seventy Group Firsts, and was the number two dog all breeds. In 1988 he was the first Pyr to receive the Quaker Oats Award, given to the dog winning the most Group Firsts. In 1989 he added a National Specialty win under judge Paul Strang to his list of feats, as well as another ten BIS. TR retired in 1990 with 10 Specialty wins, 48 Bests in Show, 162 Group Firsts, 372 Group placements and 483 Bests of Breed, having beaten over 50,000 dogs. He won the Kal Kan Pedigree Award for the most BOBs in 1987, 1988 and 1989. He was the number two producing sire in 1988 with six champions. He is the top winning Great Pyrenees of all time, the top winning Working dog of all time, and is among the Top Ten Dogs All Breeds of all time. He is by far the most winning Great Pyrenees the world has ever seen.

Many other Rivergrove's Pyrs have distinguished themselves in the BIS and Group rings. Additional BIS winners include: TR son, Ch. Rivergrove's Excuse My Dust HOF, which entered the GPCA Hall of Fame in only one week of showing; Am/Can Ch. Rivergrove's If Looks Could Kill, the top winning Pyr of all time in Canada with over thirty Canadian BIS, and top winning dog breeds in 1990; Am/Jap Ch. Rivergrove's The Black Is Back with multiple BIS in Japan; Ch. Riverain Pepa-Mint Pance HOF. Ch. Rivergrove's Levi Genes HOF/HOF is the youngest Pyr ever to finish a championship, aged six months, eleven days, and the youngest ever to win a Group, aged ten months. He is a multiple Group and Specialty winner and was the breed's Top Sire in 1988, and in 1989 tied for that honor with his brother, Ch. Rivergrove's For Your Eyes Only HOF, also a Group placer. Ch. Rivergrove's Here Is The Black HOF, co-owned by

Best In Show winner, Ch. Rivergrove's Crusher's Re-Run HOF, breeder-owner, Jean Boyd.

Cott/Francis

Ch. Rivergrove's Re-Run's Remaid HOF with great granddaughter. Remaid received a Silver Certificate for her record of champion production. Bred by the Perrys; owned by Jean Boyd.

Lucy Zorr

Elli Pasicznyk of **Maleens** (California), is a multiple Group and Specialty winning dog, as is Ch. Rivergrove's Romance The Stone HOF, who was top producing sire in 1987. TR's sister, Ch. Rivergrove's Winterwood Isis, a Group winning bitch owned by Jan Brown of **Winterwood** (Colorado), was top winning bitch in 1987 and 1988. Ch. Rivergrove's Re-Run Rides Again is a multiple Group winner. Ch. Rivergrove's Designer Genes HOF, a Specialty winner, was the Breed's Top Producing Bitch in 1987 and 1988, and tied for the Number One Producing Dam in the Working Group in 1988. TR's sister, Ch. Rivergrove's Billy Jean HOF, tied with Remaid for top producing bitch in 1989. L'Air, Remaid and Designer are all Silver Certificate Producers.

Many breeders have chosen a Rivergrove foundation for their breeding programs. In addition to those mentioned above, the **Pyrless** Kennel of Drs. Robert and Valerie Seeley (New Jersey) has finished seven champions of Rivergrove and Tip 'n Chip background. Susan Tucker of **Thorn Hill** (Virginia), Donna Osborn of **Truly** (Maryland) and Donna Coffman (Maryland) have all finished numerous champions and are working closely with Jean Boyd.

Maranatha was founded by Nancy and Whitney Coombs in New Jersey in 1972 and was relocated to a 185-acre farm just south of Gettysburg, Pennsylvania, in 1986. It is a medium-sized kennel with about twenty dogs ranging in age from puppies to senior citizens. Maranatha shows and breeds on a controlled basis: one or two carefully genotypically planned high quality litters per year. The linebreeding program was begun under the encouragement and teachings of Edith and Seaver Smith. Early on, the Coombs were also influenced by guidance from Frankie Glover and Mary Crane. Maranatha's foundation dogs came from Quibbletown and Karolaska. This combination produced the 1988 GPCA National Specialty BOB winner, Ch. Maranatha Space Commander. In recent years, the breeding program has been successfully expanded to include the strengths of the Starlaxy bloodline. Mr. Coombs has served several terms as president of the Great Pyrenees Club of America.

Kaskadian Kennel had its beginning when Michael Floyd lived in southern California. He acquired his first Pyr, Jason de Costa Lota, from the Baabs, and successfully showed him to American and Canadian Championships and American and Canadian Companion Dog Obedience titles. With a move to Washington state in 1973, Mike gained the support and enthusiasm of his parents and expanded the breeding program. Mrs. Floyd was known for spinning Pyr hair, which was available in abundance. Mike's Am/Can Ch. Pyr Haven High Drift HOF ("Jim"), bred by Fran Bennet of the original Pyr Haven Kennels in California, was very prominent on the show scene in the late seventies. Mr. Floyd handled him to many Group placements and multiple American and Canadian Bests in Show. Jim was the first Pyr to win a BIS on the contiguous West Coast. He was of "Old California" breeding and through that went back rather quickly to Basquaerie.

Following Jim's retirement, Mike was quickly back in the spotlight. This time it was with Am/Can Ch. Euskari Kaskadian Everstar ("Tubie") who went BOB at the National Specialty in 1980. Tubie's daughter, Am/Can Ch. Kaskadian's Image of Everstar ("Tauna"), started her career by going Best in Sweeps at the Northwest Regional. In 1986 she was Best Bred By Exhibitor, WB and BOW at the National Specialty under judge Carolyn Hardy. At the Canadian National Specialty that same year, Tauna was WB, BOW, and BOB from the Bred By Exhibitor Class. She did the same thing at the BC Regional and finished her Canadian championship with five-point majors.

A Tubie son, Am/Can Ch. Kaskadian Skookumchuk Kid is a multiple Working Group winner. Chuk's son, Am/Can Ch. Kaskadian Idyll Gossip ("Jackson") started his career with Best in Sweeps and BOS in Futurity at the 1988 National Specialty and won WD and BOW at the Northwest Regional. He has just started his career as a special and already has numerous Group Firsts at large shows in both the United States and Canada. Jackson's brother from a repeat breeding, Ch. Kaskadian Whitehope Timber, co-owned with Dave and Maureen Simon of **Whitehope** (Pennsylvania), started his show career with BOW from the 6–9 Puppy Class at the National Capitol Area Regional Specialty, and finished his championship by going WD, BOW and Award of Merit at the National Specialty in 1990, finishing with three five-point majors. Timber then went on to win BOB at the 1990 PFNE Regional.

Other Kaskadian Group placers include Ch. Kaskadian Euzkotar Bandit and Am/Can Ch. Kaskadian Summertime Blues. At the 1982 National Specialty, littermates Ch. Kaskadian All That Jazz and Ch. Kaskadian Kit of Marcris were Best in Futurity and BOS in Futurity. Numerous other Kaskadian Pyrs have won at Specialties. Mr. Floyd has recently joined forces with Mr. Frank Ingram. Many breeders across the country have used Kaskadian dogs as foundation stock or outcrosses.

Breeding at Kaskadian has centered on preserving correct expression and movement. Mr. Floyd says: "I like pretty dogs. I want a soft expression and a beautiful eye. For me, head and expression are the most important thing, to achieve those beautiful dark, almond-shaped eyes that just draw you right in. Soundness is, of course, very important, but type *must* come first. Similarly, temperament is of the highest importance and must never be sacrificed. Size is difficult. I like tall Pyrs and I am not happy that I have given up some size in order to get the type and movement I want. But, again, type must come first."

Another important kennel in the Pacific Northwest is **Euzkotar**. Mr. and Mrs. Lawrence Weisser got their start in Pyrs in 1965 in California

Ch. Maranatha Space Commander won BOB at the 1987 National Specialty under judge Seaver Smith. Bred, owned and handled by Nancy Coombs. *Ashbey*

Ch. Kaskadian's Image of Everstar, a multiple Specialty Winning Bitch bred and owned by Michael Floyd, won Best In Sweeps at the Northwest Regional Specialty under breeder-judge Joann Teems.

Carl Lindemaier

and later moved to Washington. Their daughter, Francesca, grew up with Pyrs and was very active in Junior Showmanship, winning Best Junior Handler at Westminster in 1980. The key to the Weissers' success lies in their continued linebreeding of Old California bloodlines with occasional outcrosses. Their foundation bitches were Ch. Pyr Oaks Lady Eva and Vascones Agerketa Euzkotar. These bitches were a blend of Quibbletown and Rhopyr, heavily bred on Basquaerie.

In 1971 they acquired Ch. Karolaska Kaskabar Euzkotar, first-born son and first champion out of Ch. Karolaska Polar Bonni Bear. He was bred to both bitches.

In the mid-seventies, the search for a dog of type, elegance and campatible pedigree was fulfilled by breeding to Ch. Quibbletown T.G. of Basquaerie. Daughters of the original bitches bred to T.G. produced National Specialty BOB Am/Can Ch. Euskari Kaskadian Everstar and Canadian National Specialty BOB Am/Can Ch. Euzkotar One For The Money ("Jesse"). Jesse was also WD, BOW at the 1982 National and BOB at Regionals.

Other outcrosses were made to Ch. El Amor Bruno Balibasque and to the exceptional French import bitch, Nemausa du Font Buis de La Chenaie, both of which are grandparents to Ch. Euzkotar Dire Straits, that went BOB at the 1990 National Specialty. The breeding to Bruno produced five champions including the Group winning dual Hall of Fame dog Am/Can Ch. Euzkotar Hell Or High Water HOF/HOF.

The primary aim of the breeding program is to produce a line of elegant, typey dogs that maintain dual-purpose potential. From every litter, some dogs are placed in show homes and some as livestock guardians. All of the many champions, including those who have been honored at National and Regional Specialties and in the Group ring, have brothers and sisters on farms and ranches. The current senior stud dog, Ch. Euzkotar Ibn Ibn Koshare HOF, has sired numerous champions, is sire and grandsire of multiple Working Group and Specialty winners, and is known as a producer of excellent working livestock guardian dogs throughout the western United States.

Mrs. Weisser writes: "We are dedicated to dual-purpose dogs of type, elegance, balance, soundness and good health. As the kennel enters its third decade, devotion to the *complete* Great Pyrenees, free of exaggeration, successful in the show ring, the living room and on the range, continues unabated."

Euzkotar Pyrs have been incorporated into breeding programs throughout the United States, including **Kaskadian** (Washington), **Reymaree** (Texas), **Pompier** (California), **Mistry** (California), **Whitehope** (Pennsylvania), **Pyrcrest** (Ohio), **La Brise** (Ohio), **Weskyuwin** (British Columbia) and **Ventisquero** (British Columbia) among many others.

The **Skeel** Kennel of Evelyn and Ned Stuart has been actively engaged in breeding and showing Great Pyrenees since 1960. Located in the heart of the Bitterroot Mountains in northern Idaho, the dogs soon became an important part of life on the ranch. The Stuarts' first breeding pair was Ch. Soleil Teddy of Skeel and Ch. Soleil Diana of Skeel. They were soon followed by Ch. Soleil Cozann HOF who was in whelp to Ch. Rogue La Rue. From this combination came several distinguished offspring for both kennels: Ch. Soleil Serein Ami HOF, Ch. Skeel's Bonnie, Ch. Woodruff of Skeel and Can Ch. Skeel's Honeybee. Cozann is a Hall of Fame producer with seven champions.

Two other important additions to the Skeel bloodline were Ch. Soleil Winni Too of Skeel and Ch. Soleil Ami Sustenter HOF. Winni was a Rogue daughter out of Ch. Soleil Coquette and a litter sister to Ch. Soleil Pierre de Blu Crest HOF/HOF. Ami was a Rogue son out of Ch. Soleil Milou. Several of the above have placed in the Working Group.

Ned and Evelyn's daughter, Carrie Stuart Parks, grew up with Pyrs and is very active in the Pyrenees world. Among other activities, she chairs the GPCA Service Dog Committee. Carrie is an artist and her Pyrenees watercolors are much sought after.

Skeel Pyrs have made important contributions to several other bloodlines, including **Snowmass** (California), **Cobberidge** (Wisconsin), **Ventisquero** (British Columbia) and **Marwell** (Alaska).

In Delaware, the **Barqueill** Kennel of Frances Glover and Ed Cloud got its start in the mid-sixties. Barqueill's foundation trio were Ch. Quibbletown Terrible Tyrant, Ch. Quibbletown Patrician and Ch. Quibbletown Wishful Thought. Through the years, Ms. Glover and Mr. Cloud have emphasized the maintenance of type and soundness through a careful line-breeding program.

One of the early stars at Barqueill was Ch. Quibbletown Falstaff HOF, top winner in 1969, and two-time National Specialty winner. When Falstaff won the National in 1971, English judge F. S. Prince remarked, "He epitomized for me the ideal of the breed Standard." Am/Can Ch. Barqueill Avant Garde HOF, a multiple Group winner, won the Canadian National Specialty in 1975, and a BIS in Canada in 1976.

In recent years Barqueill has produced many Specialty, BIS and Group dogs. A few of the most notable are Am/Can Ch. Barqueill Pyr Of The Realm HOF, who took the Midwest Specialty from the Veteran Class, Can/Am Ch. Barqueill Devastator HOF, and Am/Can Ch. Barqueill No Saint HOF.

Starlaxy is the prefix of Dr. and Mrs. Robert Brown of Jackson, Wisconsin. The Browns became interested in Great Pyrenees in 1966. Their foundation bitch, Balibasque Touche, was bred to Ch. Tip 'n Chip's Mont-Chanson. This gave them Ch. Galaxy's Bellatrix. She, in turn, was bred to Ch. Tip 'n Chip's Sonny's Reflection HOF/HOF. This produced Ch. Starlaxy Ursa Minor who was WB at the National Specialty in 1973. Several other Starlaxy dogs have done well at Specialties, including Ch. Starlaxy Sunmont Cassandra, who was WB at the 1982 National, and Ch. Starlaxy Regulus, who went WD from the Puppy class at the 1986 National. Ch. Starlaxy Bellatrix and her brother Ch. Starlaxy Barycentre took Best in Futurity and BOS at the first GPCA national Specialty Futurity under judge Mary Crane. Ch. Starlaxy Benjamin Indus HOF was a multiple Group winner. Additional Hall of Fame dogs include Ch. Starlaxy Gauguin Pyrfection HOF, Ch. Starlaxy Christmas Jupiter HOF and Ch. Starlaxy Halley's Comet HOF.

The Browns have worked tirelessly on behalf of the breed. Dr. Brown has been the AKC delegate for the Great Pyrenees Club of America for many years, and is an AKC judge of Great Pyrenees and several other breeds. Mrs. Brown served ten long years as GPCA secretary before retiring in 1990. She has been the driving force behind the GPCA titleholders books for many years and continues in that position.

Dr. Dusty Hohman and JoAnn Teems of **Snowmass** have combined their talents to produce numerous champions in California. They started with a foundation of Soleil and Marwell and co-owned, with Mrs. Betty Wade Warmack, Ch. Cobberidge Adam HOF, a top producer. In the seventies they outcrossed to some of the best Starlaxy dogs. They campaigned Ch. Starlaxy Benjamin Indus HOF to many wins in the Working Group. Ch. Quibbletown T.G. of Basquaerie was also very important. In the eighties another outcross dog, Ch. Tip 'n Chip Hawleys Magnum, was added to the kennel. Mrs. Teems moved to Washington state in 1990 where she is continuing the Snowmass breeding program. She is an AKC judge and secretary of the Great Pyrenees Club of America.

The **Caspyr** Kennel, in Fair Oaks, California, of Betty Wade Warmack and her husband, Larry, has been active in the breed since 1970. Betty's dog, Ch. Quibbletown T.G. of Basquaerie, out of Mary Crane's last litter, has had a profound influence on the breed in the West. T.G.'s daughter, Am/Can Ch. Euskari Kaskadian Everstar, was BOB at the 1980 National Specialty, where T.G. went BOW and BOS. Central to the current breeding program at Caspyr is the multiple Specialty winning T.G. daughter, Ch. Quanset D.G. of Caspyr.

The **Pyr Haven** Kennel of May Lu Vandenavond in Wisconsin became active in Pyrs in the mid-seventies. The foundation bitch, Ch. Karolaska Angel of Pyr Haven HOF, produced fifteen champion offspring. Angel's daughter, Ch. Trottenfox Sheza Tuff Tip 'n Chip HOF, is the top producing bitch of all time with twenty-five champions. Many Pyr Haven dogs have done extremely well at Specialties and in the Group and BIS ring. Ch. Pyr

Haven Shawnee White Eagle is a Group winning bitch. Ch. Pyr Haven Tonto Indian Summer HOF, the kennel's current BIS winner, is proving himself a valuable sire.

The first breeding pair was brought to Alaska in the early sixties by Charles Bergland of **Wolfsong**. These were: Tip 'n Chip Aubisque (a sister to Luchon) and Tip 'n Chip Matanuska (brother to Mont-Chanson).

Ruth Marcy of **Marwell** finished two of these, Ch. Wolfsong Skookum Jim, a Group placer, and Ch. Wolfsong Tanana Girl. Mrs. Marcy later outcrossed to Skeel. Daughters Renee and Rhonda were very active in Junior Handling. In the Breed ring Renee showed her Ch. Pyrolyn's Clever Boy V. Marwell HOF to BIS and Group wins.

Elysee is the prefix of Dr. and Mrs. James Giffin in Colorado. They purchased their first Pyr, Soleil Coquette de Neige from Jack and Dorothy Magoffin in 1969. Shortly thereafter they obtained their foundation stud, Ch. Quibbletown Oliver Twist, from the Smiths. These two produced several champions including Ch. Elysee Racquette Ruff. In 1972 they added Ch. Karolaska Polar Nero HOF, who went on to become a multiple BIS winner. Jim writes, "This splendid dog embodies the best qualities to be found in our breed and is responsible, in part, for the keen interest in the Great Pyrenees which motivates this author."

Galesway Kennel of Gale Armstrong in New Jersey came into being in the early seventies. Mrs. Armstrong has linebred Balibasque to consistently finish champions year after year. Her emphasis is on correct type and movement. Many of her champions have been used as models in commercial advertising for large firms.

Joseph and Mary Ann Gentzel of **Aneto** in Georgia got their start in Pyrs in the early seventies. Early on they met with success with their BIS winner Ch. Karolaska Captivator HOF/HOF. Since then they have bred numerous Group placers primarily from Karolaska and Quibbletown bloodlines. The Gentzels also own Pyrenean Shepherds.

Jack and Charlotte Perry of **Pyreau** have been involved in Pyrs since the late sixties. They have been a great asset to the GPCA as well as the NCAGPC. The Perrys bred the mother of the Top Winning Pyrenees of all time, Ch. Rivergroves Run For The Roses HOF/HOF.

Grand Prix of Jo Anne Bergen in Virginia bases its breeding program on Karolaska bloodlines. Mrs. Bergen has finished several champions. In the early eighties, Mrs. Bergen published *Pyrenees World*, an international magazine in the tradition of the *International Great Pyrenees Review*, both of which united Pyr fanciers from around the world.

142

Prominent on the show scene in Colorado is **Pyr Peak** Kennel of Mr. and Mrs. William Burstow. The Burstows began in the late seventies. Their foundation stud, Ch. Kobil's Louis Pastoure, won BOB at the 1984 National Specialty, was a Group placer, and won Best Veteran Dog at the 1988 and 1990 National Specialties. Louie's daughters, Ch. Pyr Peak D.D.'s Hell On Wheels and Ch. Pyr Peak Misty Morning, made quite a showing at the National Specialty in 1984 where their dad was BOB. Misty Morning was BOS in Sweeps, while Hell On Wheels was BOB in Futurity and went on to win WB and BOW at seven months of age. Louie's son, Ch. Pyr Peak Bob Barker Tip 'n Chip, is a multiple Group winner and placer. Breeding at Pyr Peak centers on correct type in head and body conformation, and excellent movement.

Forrest and Marilyn Droster of Wisconsin became involved with Great Pyrenees in the sixties. Their **Whispering Pines** Kennel was founded on Soleil lines, and outcrosses have been made to Starlaxy, and also to a French male, Pollux du Pic de Montaigne, whom they imported and co-owned with John Cobb of **Cobberidge**. One of their most famous champions is Ch. Whispering Pines Licharre, a Group placing dog. Licharre's brother from a repeat breeding, Am/Eng Ch. Whispering Pines Andre, was exported to Maggie Ashby of **Valcarlos** in England and is the only Pyr to win championships in both the United States and England. There he was stud dog of the year three years in a row, and produced English and Scandinavian champions, plus several additional CC winners. Both the Drosters and the Cobbs were very active in Pyrs in the seventies but have now reduced their involvement.

In Ohio, **La Brise** is the affix of Mr. and Mrs. Joseph Princehouse, their daughter, Patricia, and son, Steven, in Colorado. Their involvement in Pyrs began in the early seventies when eight-year-old Patricia announced that she wanted a dog as big as a horse. They started with a foundation of Soleil and Balibasque. The children's involvement in 4-H sheep projects resulted in a small flock of thirty head of Suffolk, which allowed the Pyrs to prove they could still fulfill the task for which they were originally bred.

A high school summer abroad program took Patricia to France for two months in 1979. Arriving just in time for the Paris championship show, she immediately fell for the lovely expressions and effortless side gaits of the French Pyrs. She joined the Great Pyrenees Club of France (R.A.C.P.) and returned to the States with Patoune du Grand Baou, daughter of the famous Int/Fr/Lux/Bel Ch. Jason du Grand Baou. A succession of some ten French imports followed including Ch. Samy du Domaine de Nardesca, who finished his American championship at the age of ten months, and Can Ch. Uxem du Grand Baou (co-owned with Gerald Scott, British Columbia), who sired the 1986 Canadian National Specialty Winners Dog,

Ch. Kobils Louis Pastoure won Best of Breed at National Specialty. Owned by
Wm. and Brenda Burstow. *Callea*

Ch. Whispering Pines Licharre won BOB at the PFNE Regional Specialty
in 1984 under judge Joan Passini-Birkett from England. Owned by Marilyn
Thell. Bred by Mr. and Mrs. Forrest Droster. *Ashbey*

Can Ch. Benjamin Bravo, owned by Sharon Armstrong (British Columbia).

Patricia has made five extended trips to France. In 1983 she took Clowne de La Brise to France and took RWB at the French Specialty in Lacommande in the High Pyrenees. Clowne obligingly came into heat while in France and was bred to a French champion. 1983 also saw the purchase of the Princehouses' first Pyrenean Shepherd, Ch. Urrugne de l'Estaube ("Blythe"), which went on to win the National Specialty twice in a row. Patricia has served four terms as president of the Pyrenean Shepherd Club of America.

Breeding at La Brise aims for four things: excellent temperament, correct head and expression, large size and correct conformation and movement. Patricia writes: "We breed for type. Correct type encompasses all aspects of the dog, including temperament and working ability. An extremely typey dog is *necessarily* sound. A sound dog is not necessarily typey."

Ms. Princehouse is an honorary lifetime member of the Great Pyrenees Club of France (R.A.C.P.). She often acts as a liaison between the R.A.C.P. and the Great Pyrenees Clubs of America and Canada, promoting exchanges of judges and translating information.

In 1969 John and Mary Milliken of Colorado were introduced to Great Pyrenees. They were smitten by the size and lovely personalities of the dogs. In the mid-seventies, they purchased two bitches from Soleil and had one bred to Ch. Cobberidge Adam HOF. From this litter they obtained the foundation stock for their own kennel, **Ripples**. Through their breeding program they tried to maintain the same qualities that originally attracted them to the breed.

John passed away in 1981, and Mary carried on, forming an alliance with Penny Numbers of **Pendouglas** in Canada. Their co-bred dogs carry the **Rip'n'Pen** prefix. In 1984 the Great Pyrenees Club of Canada awarded Mrs. Milliken the O'Dell-Easson Sportsmanship award. Thus far she is the sole recipient of this award.

Ripples has owned or bred Great Pyrenees carrying over thirty titles. These include American and Canadian championships as well as Obedience titles. Besides showing, Mary's Pyrs are also reliable livestock guardian dogs and, mainly, lovable family guardians. Ripples' motto is: "Great Size—Great Love."

Jerry and Carolyn Ferguson of **Dastekde** have been active in the breed in Colorado since the early seventies. Their Ch. Karolaska Joli Bon Copain was a multiple Group placer.

Also in Colorado is Jan Brown's **Winterwood** Kennel. Winterwood has successfully combined Tip 'n Chip and Karolaska to produce over thirty-five champions, Specialty winners, and Group winners and placers. Jan's Ch. Pyrson K'laska of Summerhill HOF/HOF is the Top Producing

Great Pyrenees of all time. Her Ch. Rivergrove's Winterwood Isis is a multiple Group winner and was top winning bitch in 1987 and 1988.

In Maine the breed is well represented by the **Pyrfection** kennel of Janet Jo Roberts. Starting with a foundation of Dar-Jan, Ms. Roberts added a Starlaxy outcross in the mid-seventies. Notable Pyrfection Pyrs included Ch. Starlaxy Gauguin Pyrfection HOF, who was very competitive in the Group ring, Ch. Pyrfection Henri Matisse HOF and Ch. Pyrfection Chance A Bear HOF.

Tom and Sue Perkins of **Nor'Easter** moved to Maine in the late eighties, taking their Maranatha foundation stock with them. There they brought in the Euzkotar bloodline and have finished several champions.

Texas boasts many winners. In San Antonio, **Summerhill** Kennel of Gary and Lynne Gomm has finished over thirty champions and has had several winners in the Groups. The line is based primarily on Tip 'n Chip with outcrosses to Karolaska. The Gomms' foundation bitch, Ch. Tip 'n Chip Cactus Flower HOF, is a Hall of Fame producer. Perhaps the most famous dog carrying the Summerhill name is Ch. Pyrson K'laska of Summerhill HOF/HOF ("Macho"), owned by Jan Brown. Macho is far and away the breed's top producer of champions. A Macho daughter, Ch. Summerhill Flora of Huny Mountain HOF, was a multiple Group placer and was the Top Winning Great Pyr bitch in 1983. She was very important in the breeding program in the eighties, and she is deeply missed by her family. Ch. Summerhill Winterwood McP is a Group First winner and multiple Group placer. Other multiple Group placers and Hall of Fame Pyrs include Ch. Summerhill Gandalf The White, Ch. Summerhill's Rainflower HOF and Ch. Winterwood Summerhill Baron. The Gomms also own a Pyrenean Shepherd.

In the Dallas area, Jeri Ondrusek of **Jerico** has been active for many years. She has utilized Karolaska bloodlines, and imported Ch. Gagnous D'Auverniac ("Hobo"), of French and Limberlost breeding from Canada, that has produced well for her. She also owned the BIS winner Ch. Chilkoot's Sno-ball of Maleen HOF.

Reymaree was started in 1980 by Jean and Doyle Cave, and has finished a dozen champions. The emphasis of the breeding program has been sound, typey dogs in the upper size range. The search for just the right outcross led to the National Specialty in 1982. There the decision was made to incorporate Sunmont and Euzkotar lines into the breeding program. In the mid-eighties Am/Can Ch. Euzkotar Hell Or Highwater HOF/HOF ("Tonto") was acquired on co-ownership. Before his tragic death at age eight, he amassed an impressive array of Group wins. Tonto was bred to Ch. Sunmont Pride and Joy to produce Ch. Reymaree Tonto's Crackerjack ("Dude"), which had several Group placements from the classes, and Ch. Reymaree's Queen Of Hearts, Best Bred By Exhibitor at the 1989 National Specialty. Jean has continued the breeding program with crosses to Kaskadian dogs. Doyle and Jean have owned Pyrenean Shepherds since 1987. Jean is currently the secretary of the Pyrenean Shepherd Club of America.

In Michigan there has been sustained interest in the Great Pyrenees. Mr. and Mrs. Gerald Goulet's **Pine Pointe** Kennel was founded on Rivergroves and Tip 'n Chip, and has finished many champions. The Goulets also own a Pyrenean Shepherd.

Dr. Gail Knapp and Lynn Thigpen of **Galen** Pyrs have finished several champions from Karolaska bloodlines. Also Karolaska-based is **Jenstin** of Mr. and Mrs. Steve Decker. Ch. Jenstin Noah's Inspiration was BOB at the 1987 Detroit Regional Specialty and again at the 1990 Milwaukee Regional.

Brenda Jackson's **Breglenn** Kennel has had a great deal of success. Her Ch. Karolaska Kaballero Kid, co-owned with Mike Patrick (Ohio), was BOB at the 1986 National Specialty. Ch. Breglenn's Innui of Pyramount was WB at the 1985 National. Mrs. Jackson has recently relocated to Ohio.

Sue Ansel established her **Wyndsong** Great Pyrenees in 1977 with the purchase of Ch. Starlaxy Ambling Abbey. Her male, Ch. Starlaxy Wyndsong Waterloo, was WD at the 1983 National Specialty. Her twelve years' experience as a veterinary assistant aided her tremendously in her efforts to operate a limited breeding program of high quality. Am/Can Ch. Wyndsong Wildwood was BOB at the Detroit Regionals in 1985 and 1989. "Woody" was BOB and BOS at the Ohio Regionals in 1985 and 1986. His littermate, Ch. Wyndsong Polka Dot, has won multiple BOS at the Detroit and Ohio Regional Specialties. Her son Ch. Wyndsong Whitney was Best in Futurity at the 1987 National Specialty.

Patricia Alteri of **Es-Pyr-It** obtained her foundation sire from Audrey Handwerk of **Handwerk** Kennel, which was very active in the late sixties and seventies in Michigan. Pat's Ch. Esprit Blanc won the Canadian National Specialty in 1972 and several Group placements in the States. Her Specialty winning Ch. Sundown of Saskatu was important to the breeding program over the years. Her newest stud dog is Ch. Persephone's Stepping Stone, bred by Mr. and Mrs. Jerry Davito of **Persephone** in Illinois.

Mr. and Mrs. Paul Turner of **Wildwood** have been involved in the breed since 1965. Perhaps the most famous dog of their breeding is Ch. Tip 'n Chip Sonny's L'Air HOF/HOF, the top winning bitch of all time, owned by Jean Boyd.

Steve and Mary Berman on **Snowbear** have long been actively involved in the breed. Steve has twice served as editor of the GPCA Bulletin

Ch. Snowbear's Glamour Girl owned by Steve and Mary Berman.

Ch. Pyr Oaks Lady Eva, Linda Weisser's foundation bitch at Euzkotar.

and has an outstanding collection of books on Pyrs and dogs in general. The Bermans have finished many champions, most recently the lovely Ch. Snowbear All American Girl, who was WB at the Detroit Specialty.

Gary and Lana Schwictenberg of **Avancer** in Wisconsin finished numerous champions in the seventies and eighties. Their Ch. Karolaska Misty Lady was BOB at the 1978 National Specialty. Misty's daughter Ch. Avancer Amorous Annie was BOS at the 1983 National.

Dan Russler of **Glynn Farm** in Wisconsin became a Great Pyrenees fancier while still in high school, but waited until after medical school and marriage to JoAnn Neuman to become actively involved in the breed. Their foundation stock came from the Starlaxy bloodline. Dan and JoAnn continue to be fascinated by the big dogs' interaction with and protection of sheep, and maintain a flock of Targhees. Dan is chairman of the GPCA's Livestock Guardian Dog Committee. Their dogs have also proved themselves in the show ring. Their Ch. Glynn Farm's Rock of Cashel was Best in Futurity at the 1983 National Specialty and has since been used by numerous other breeders as an outcross for their lines, as has Ch. Glynn Farm's Shepherd's Song.

BelleAmi in Missouri got its start in 1980 when Steve Williamson received Neigerie Fozwell T Bear as a wedding gift from his bride, Sally. They quickly fell in love with the breed and added Ch. Balibasque Belle, the inspiration for their kennel name. Since then they have owned or bred twelve champions including the multiple Group placer Ch. BelleAmi's Razzle Dazzle, Ch. BelleAmi's Serendipity and the well-known Ch. BelleAmi Jolly of Balibasque, owned by Carolyn Hardy. Ch. BelleAmi's Wild about Harry was WD/BOW at the 1990 Milwaukee Regional Specialty.

Mr. and Mrs. George (Skip) Mohr IV own **Pyrcrest** Great Pyrenees in Ohio and bred their first litter in 1977. Their first champion, Ch. White Oaks Cacherro Manso CD, was High in Trial at the 1983 National Specialty. In the mid-eighties Skip and Carolyn outcrossed to Euzkotar bloodlines, bringing in Ch. Euzkotar Pyrcrest Aerosmith, brother to the 1990 National Specialty winner. Ch. Pompier Euzkotar Fancy Lovin' was RWB at the National Specialty in 1989. Fancy's son, Pyrcrest Fancy Free Theory, was Best in Sweeps at the 1989 Ohio Regional.

Also in Ohio are **Almac** of Kathleen McCue and **Marais** of Barb Berkesch. Kathleen and her sister, Carolyn, got their start in 1972 in California, and named their kennel after their parents, Alma and Mac. Kathleen moved Almac to Ohio in the early eighties. Kathleen showed her foundation bitch, Ch. Maleen's Rociente ("Rikki"), to BOB at the California Specialty in 1979 and 1980. Rikki's daughter, Ch. Almac Mountain Mist CD HOF, was the top producing bitch in 1983 and 1984. Misty's daughter, Ch. Almac Winterwood Serendipity, was WB, BOW at the 1989 National Specialty. Almac Carbon Copy of Macho was WD at the 1984 National. Almac Pyrs have taken Best or BOS in Futurity at the Nationals in 1986, 1987 and 1988, and in Sweeps in 1986 and 1989. In addition to over thirty championships, Almac Pyrs have finished seven CD and one CDX Obedience titles. Ch. Winterwood Almac Dante CD was High in Trial at the National in 1989 and Highest Scoring Pyr in 1989. Ms. McCue says, "My goal is to produce good temperaments first in sound, healthy dogs which exemplify correct type."

Barb Berkesch of **Marais** started with the Group placing Ch. Rivergroves Richelieu. At the 1989 National Specialty, her Ch. Almac Serendipity was WB, BOW and Sara's son, Ch. Almac Obvious Choice, co-owned with Cheryl Angelone, was Best in Sweeps and WD from the Puppy class.

Mr. and Mrs. Ted Jarvis of **Jarde** began with a foundation of Basquaerie. Ch. Basquaerie Hamilcar of Jarde and Ch. Basquaerie Dido of Jarde both won at specialties in the late seventies. Outcrosses have been made to Starlaxy and to Tip 'n Chip.

Neigerie of Michael Patrick has had much success at specialties and in the Group ring. Mike's foundation bitch, Ch. Karolaska Aleutia Neigerie HOF, was a multiple specialty winner. Ch. Neigerie Native Dancer and Ch. Neigerie Solicitor have been valuable producers both for Neigerie and in the breeding programs of other breeders.

California boasts many breeders. **Shadowrun** of Dorothy Sisco got its start in the eighties with a foundation of Karolaska. Ch. Shadowrun Chance HOF was BOB at the 1988 National Specialty and is a BIS and Group winner. His brother, Am/Can Ch. Shadowrun Sundance, co-owned with Marie Klimek, is a Group winner in Canada. Their sisters, Ch. Shadowrun Chardonnay and Ch. Shadowrun Serena, were BOS at the 1988 and 1989 Southern California Specialties. Shadowrun Brut Montpierre HOF, co-owned with Mr. and Mrs. Lawrence Peel, is a BIS and Specialty winner. Ch. Shadowrun Moonringer, co-owned with Maxine Martin, was BOB at the 1989 California Specialty.

Mr. and Mrs. James Lasley got their start in Pyrs in 1977. Their foundation bitch was Ch. Almac Lasleys' Mystery, of Maleen and Karolaska breeding. Bred back to her grandfather, Ch. Basquay's Teddy Bear HOF, Misty produced Ch. Gabriel's Mystery Star and Mex Ch. Mistry's Audrey Rose. Star and Rose were mascots for the San Diego Special Olympics for many years.

An outcross was made to Ch. Euzkotar Natani. This produced Ch. Mistry's Lancelot, valued for his size, type and soundness. Three litters were bred from Lance and Rose with excellent results. A daughter, Ch. Mistry's Toasted Almond has produced several promising youngsters, including Mistry's Brandy Alexander, which took First in the Open Class at the 1990 National at nineteen months of age. Further Pyrs of Euzkotar Breeding have been added, notably Ch. Euzkotar Sunmont Mistry and Ch. Denali of Crane Creek. To further enhance type and size, a French import bitch, Tigresse du Domaine de Nardesca, was leased from the Princehouses in 1987 and bred to Ch. Euzkotar Kaskadian Andante, owned by Mike and Cindy Thrall.

Mr. and Mrs. Roger Tuepker of **Bousy Rouge** have finished several champions, primarily from Tip 'n Chip lines. The Tuepkers are the proud owners of Ch. Bousy Rouge Bentley, Ch. Tip 'n Chip Fascination, Ch. Wyndsong Whitney, Best in Futurity at the 1987 National, Ch. Wyndsong Wally Bee and Ch. Tip 'n Chip Cat Ballou.

De Fer Kennel got its start in 1964 when Mr. and Mrs. Charles Doran acquired their first pair. Their first litter produced six champions. They were active throughout the sixties and seventies, finishing titles in both conformation and obedience. Their breeding program was based on Quibbletown and Old California bloodlines. Mrs. Doran continued the De Fer line, while Mr. Doran, in 1982, began **C and D** Kennels. Mr. Doran has been showing actively ever since, and has completed twenty-nine titles, breed and obedience, since 1982. Several of their dogs are Group placers. Mr. Doran is an AKC judge of the Working Group.

Maleens of Elli Pasicznyk has been active since the seventies. Ms. Pasicznyk's foundation was Old California bloodlines. She co-owned Ch. Basquay's Teddy Bear HOF, a Specialty winner bred by June Palmer of **Basquay** in Utah. A Teddy daughter, Ch. Maleens Rociente, was BOB at the California Specialty. Karolaska blood was then added to produce a number of top competitors. Maleens Ms. Cream Puff Nikki HOF is the dam of two BIS winners. Ch. Maleens Kismet was BOS at the 1984 National Specialty. Elli's Ch. Rivergroves Here Is The Black HOF is a Group winner.

Allan and Anita Baab's **Costa Lota** Kennel was very active in both breed and obedience in the 1960s and 1970s. They gave several other breeders their starts in Pyrenees.

Catherine De La Cruz of **Poste de Pompier** has been involved in breed, obedience, livestock guardians and rescue work since she began in the breed in 1968. She has finished numerous champions and Obedience title holders. Numerous Pompier dogs have done well at Specialties.

A word must be said about Californian Rhett Feng, an ardent fancier of the breed who died prematurely in 1989. Mr. Feng was a true student of the breed. His search to understand correct type in the Great Pyrenees led him to Europe where his excellent photographic skills preserved what he found there for others to see. He imported several Pyrs from France and Belgium, primarily of Comte de Foix breeding. For several years he published the *Great Pyrenees Import Directory* in an attempt to unite and educate enthusiasts in the United States and Canada. Mr. Feng had many friends in Europe and North America. He left his papers and photographs to the Southern California Club. They will be an invaluable resource in years to come, and a fitting legacy to a man who truly loved the Great Pyrenees.

Cavalier of Mr. and Mrs. Charles McConnell began in Pyrs in the mid-1960s. Their foundation stud, Ch. Quibbletown Cavalier HOF/HOF, was a top show dog in his day with 139 BOB, 19 Group placements including several Firsts, and a BIS which was won at ten years of age! He was top producer in 1971, 1972 and 1974. Other Cavalier dogs have also had success in the Groups and at Specialties.

There is great interest in the breed in the Pacific Northwest. Larry and Nancy Carr of **Catalan** have been active since the early seventies. They have used primarily Euzkotar and Esterhazy lines, and have recently imported a lovely French bitch co-owned by Linda Weisser and Patricia Princehouse. Their Ch. Catalan Roman was BOB at the 1987 Northwest Specialty.

Ralph, Jan and Susan Gibert of **Montalvo** got their start in the late sixties and have finished many champions. Their breeding program is based primarily on Old California and Karolaska with recent outcrosses to Kaskadian.

Lee and Kim Trowbridge of **Siouxon** are active in the breed and have finished several champions. Dave and Kathy Liles of **Shadee Hill** Kennel have been active for many years. Their Ch. Shadee Hill Scandal was WB and Best BBE at the 1990 National Specialty. Wayne and Mary Ann Feller of **Silver Creek** got their start in Pyrs in the late seventies and have had several champions. The Feller children have been active with the Pyrs in 4-H. Vern and Diane Daarud of **Lazy Acres** founded their breeding program on Marwell and Fran Bennet's Pyr Haven lines in the late seventies.

Steve and Phyllis Hammet of **Quanset** became involved in Pyrs in the late sixties. Thereafter they acquired an English import, a son of Crufts BIS winner Ch. Bergerie Knur. Their Ch. Maleens Kismet was BOS at the National in 1984. Bred to Ch. Quibbletown T.G. of Basquaerie, Kismet produced Ch. Quanset D.G. of Caspyr, BOS at the 1989 Northwest Specialty.

John and Bonnie Ross of **Sunmont** got their start in Pyrs in the late seventies with a pair from Starlaxy. Their Ch. Starlaxy Sunmont Cassandra was WB at the 1982 National Specialty. They have since outcrossed to Euzkotar and have finished numerous champions. Ch. Sunmont Woodstock was WD at the 1983 Canadian National Specialty.

Mr. and Mrs. Gary Mueller of **Winwood** in Iowa bought their first Pyr in 1978 and began showing in 1981. Winwood has used primarily Tip 'n Chip and Karolaska bloodlines. Gary and Marcia's Winwood's New Beginning was Best in Sweeps at the 1989 National Specialty.

Huny Mountain is the prefix of Dwayne and Fay Knox in Arkansas.

Carolyn Coffman with five-week-old puppies. A junior handler, Carolyn is very successful in the breed ring.

Lucy Zorr

Bonbelle Du Comte De Foix, female winner of the 1990 French National Specialty, Best of Opposite Sex at the 1988 Canadian National Specialty. Owners Philip and Arlene Oraby.

Mr. and Mrs. Knox have finished numerous champions since the late seventies. Their foundation male was Ch. Elysee Wufgard of Huny Mountain. His daughter, Ch. Huny Mountain Wuf-O-Will, has been very important to the breeding program. Ch. Summerhill Flora of Huny Mountain HOF is a Hall of Fame producer. The Knoxes also place many Pyrs as livestock guardians.

The **Pyramis** Kennel of Gerard Vandebrug in Nebraska has produced several champions from linebred Quibbletown stock. Jerry writes, "The kennel's goal is to preserve all the good the breed has to offer."

Arizona is home to several kennels. Mickey Chaney of **Pyr-Rab** got her start in Pyrs with her husband, Tom, in 1978 in Ohio. Unfortunately, Tom died prematurely in 1986 and Mickey moved her dogs and horses to Arizona. Pyr-Rab's foundation bitch was Ch. Tip 'n Chip Tadd O' Buff, BOB at the 1986 Ohio Specialty. Mickey has continued with Tip 'n Chip lines with an eye toward, as she puts it, "the highest quality in type, tempyr-ment and pyr-sonality."

Mike and Cindy Thrall of **Stonybrook** purchased their first Pyr in 1977 from Jim and Dee Olsen of **Oeldej**. Since then they have owned seven champions, primarily of Euzkotar breeding. Ch. Sunburst Stonybrook Sonneuse was Best in Sweeps and WB, BOW at the 1985 Arizona Regional Specialty. Ch. Stonybrook Ms. Heaven Can Wait was WB, BOW and BOS at the 1990 Arizona Regional. Cindy writes, "We remain committed to utilizing French lines to maintain the integrity of the breed in the United States." The Thralls also own a Pyrenean Shepherd.

Mary Ann Kenninger's **Sunburst** Kennel has also produced several champions in the eighties. Her Ch. Sunburst's Joanna's Joy was WB at the 1988 National Specialty.

The breed is represented in New York by a variety of bloodlines. Flo Laicher of **Pyr Shire** got her start in Pyrs in the early seventies and has finished several champions and Obedience titles. Her foundation stock came from the last of Frank Koller's Esterhazy bloodlines. Ch. Pyr Shire's Bard O'Esterhazy CD, TDI successfully continues the Esterhazy tradition of great size, wonderful pigmentation and outstanding temperament. Ms. Laicher frequently uses her dogs as therapy dogs in connection with her work with the handicapped and mentally retarded.

Terry and Susan Preston of **Sunshine Acres** purchased their first Pyr in 1981 as a livestock guardian dog. They have since become serious breeders and exhibitors and have finished five American and two Canadian champions. Their Am/Can Ch. Sunshine's Roving Reporter ("Snoopy") was WD at the 1988 Canadian National Specialty under French judge Alain Pecoult. Ch. Abby's Sunshine Boy went WD and BOW at the 1990 Midwest Regional Specialty.

Mr. and Mrs. Phillip Oraby of **Le Bousquet** bought their first Pyr in 1971 from Carolyn Hardy's Balibasque Kennel. She was followed by Ch.

Balibasque Tartouffe and his daughter Ch. Pyr Pasture's Ivy du Bousquet. Mrs. Oraby writes that she "is dedicated to the true type with beautiful heads and expressions." To this end, the Orabys have imported two bitches of top French bloodlines, Urale de Montbernes ("Pompette"), daughter of the famous three-time French National Specialty winner Int/Fr Ch. Nettou du Comte de Foix, and Bombelle du Comte de Foix, daughter of Pompette's brother, French National Specialty winner Fr Ch. Uchan de Montbernes. Bombelle won WB and BOW at the 1988 Canadian National Specialty under French judge Alain Pecoult, and in 1990 went CAC and CACIB (equivalent to WB and BOS) at the French National Specialty. Bombelle had previously returned to the Continent in 1989 to be bred to Fr Ch. Dahir du Rocher de L'Aigle, winner of the 1988 French National. In spite of the voyage, eleven puppies were successfully produced.

Joe and Rhonda Dalton of **Pyragon** in New Jersey are very active in the breed and have finished several champions. Their Ch. Maranatha Pyragon Apollo CD is a Group placer. They also publish a yearly calendar with Pyr photos.

John and Marilyn Thell of **Jonricker** Kennel in Rhode Island became involved in the breed in 1964 with a Quibbletown foundation. Numerous champions and Group placers bear the Jonricker name. Ch. Jonricker Mr. Magoo was a Group winner. Marilyn feels strongly about breeders' responsibilities: "One of the breeder's major jobs is to educate. Be ready to give all the time needed to make sure people will understand. Puppies are like children. They did not ask to come into this world. The breeder is responsible for that dog being here."

Also in Rhode Island is Freda and Marco Troiano's **Pyrport** Kennel. The Troianos have finished several champions in the eighties.

Maureen and Dave Simon of **Whitehope** in Pennsylvania acquired their first Pyr, Ch. Balibasque Sugar Bear Brie, in 1984. As newcomers, they decided that they should, as Maureen says: "Go slow, make friends, listen and learn, accept no compromise on quality, get involved and have fun!" With these guiding principles, they exploded onto the show scene at the 1987 National Specialty, where Brie took WB and Award of Merit under judge C. Seaver Smith, Jr. After finishing her championship Brie has been specialed only twice, once for BOB at the 1990 Pennsylvania Specialty, and once for BOS at the Eastern Regional Specialty. Her daughter, Ch. Whitehope First Impression ("Libby"), has been specialed once, also for a Specialty BOS.

In 1988 the Simons acquired Ch. Euzkotar Whitehope Wizard, son of National Specialty winner Ch. Euzkotar Dire Straits. Wiz was Best in Futurity at the 1989 National Specialty, and has sired the WB at a Regional Specialty. Bred to Libby, he produced Ch. Whitehope Lady of The Lake, RWB at the 1990 National Specialty. The Simons' other male, Ch. Kaskadian Whitehope Timber finished with three five-point majors, his first from the Puppy 6–9 Class at the 1989 Eastern Regional Specialty, and his third at the 1990 National, where he went WD, BOW and Award of Merit. He then took BOB at the 1990 PFNE Regional.

The Simons' goal is to produce dogs of excellent health and temperament, outstanding head and expression, balance, elegance and soundness along with larger size than the current average. Maureen says: "Neither frailty nor any hint of heaviness can be allowed to creep in to this big white hope of ours." Maureen is also deeply involved in Pyrenees rescue work.

The Great Pyrenees is well represented from coast to coast.

10

The Great Pyrenees in Canada

LEGEND TELLS US that the Great Pyrenees once graced the shores of Canada in the sixteenth and seventeenth centuries. Certainly as early as the year 1500, the fisheries off the coast of Newfoundland were operated by French, Portuguese, Basque and other seafarers. Since the mainland abounded in wolves and other wild animals, it was only natural that the Pyrenean should be brought to Greenland and Newfoundland to fulfill a traditional role—that of protector and companion to the early settlers. Why there are not descendants today in Canada remains a mystery, but apparently there are not.

In the early part of this century a French woman, a Mlle. Prevotient, brought back with her from France, to guard her home in Carlisle on the Gaspé Peninsula, five great white dogs from the Pyrenees. This tale was told to Mrs. Francis Crane by a woman who had called and seen the dogs. Unfortunately, she could shed no light as to whether there had been breeding of these dogs or not.

An intrepid Canadian explorer of the early thirties was Basquaerie Marie Blanque, who accompanied her mistress, the wife of Reverend Tom Greenwood, to within thirty miles of the Arctic Circle. Reverend Greenwood had been assigned to an Indian outpost in the Northwest Territories. Here Marie thrived in the cold northern winter, living outdoors and making herself useful (as becomes a Pyrenean) by pulling ice and wood on a sled for her mistress.

CAN/AM Ch. Quibbletown Limberlost Rogue was Canada's Top Pyrenees for 1970 and 1973. Owned by Lois Mackintosh. *Weston*

Can. Ch. Quibbletown Valkyrie. Canada's top producing Pyrenees dam with fourteen Champion offspring. The foundation bitch at the Limberlost Kennels of Lois Mackintosh.

CAN/AM Ch. Quibbletown Val's Heritage HOF, bred and owned by Lois Mackintosh, a multiple BIS winner and the first Great Pyrenees to place in the top ten of the Working Group in Canada.

Great Pyrenees were first exhibited in Canada by Mrs. Crane in 1935. The benching of six Pyreneans at Exhibition Park in Toronto created a sight to stir the admiration of many Canadian visitors.

In 1938 Champion Zayda Van Euskara of Dutch parentage became the first Great Pyrenees to win a Canadian championship. He was owned by Marjorie Butcher.

Then in 1948 came the first Great Pyrenees to win Best in Show in Canada—Basquaerie Edgemere's Rex—scoring at Truro, Nova Scotia, on September 23. In 1952 Cote de Neige Orpheus won a Working Group Third at the famous Canadian National Exhibition, but little more was heard from him in Canada. It is believed he returned to the United States with his owner, where he completed his American title.

A few Canadian kennels flourished briefly in the late thirties and forties. One of these, Combermere, has already been mentioned. The bloodlines were almost exclusively Basquaerie and Cote de Neige. Breeding was frequently limited to the ownership of a single pair.

In the early fifties only a few scattered specimens were exhibited. These included Laurie 2nd of La Colina (Mrs. Warde), Basquaerie Babillard (Timberly Kennels), Minorduke's Grand Duke (M. Cox) and two specimens from Skahaven Kennels in British Columbia (E. Cardinall).

By the end of the decade, entries at the shows for the year had plummeted to one Great Pyrenees. However, the single entry, Xarine de Fontenay, was destined to become the granddam of the first Canadian-bred Best in Show Great Pyrenees.

BLOODLINES IN CANADA

In 1963 the magazine *Dogs in Canada* instituted a new rating system, the Top Three in each breed. Pyrenees who have won this honor more than once are: Can/Am Ch. Quibbletown Minute Man (1963, 1964, 1966), Can/Am Ch. Limberlost Rogue (1970, 1973) and Can/Am Ch. Quibbletown Val's Heritage (1974, 1975). All three of these outstanding winners made an important contribution in the Canadian bloodlines of the late sixties and seventies.

Quibbletown Minute Man was purchased by Mr. and Mrs. Van Osselaar and, along with Quibbletown Misti Maid, produced a number of very nice progeny, including Champion Armil's Miss Muffet, who was the Top Pyr in Canada in 1967. Another important breeding was Ch. Quibbletown Minute Man to Can Ch. Rampart House Arete Panda, a daughter of Xarine de Fontenay and Basquaerie Bali. This mating produced the dog Can Ch. Karlston Snowden Kiter.

"Dominic," as he was known, wins a place on the Canadian honor role by being the first home-bred Champion to go Best in Show at the Progressive Kennel Club show in Ontario, June 7, 1969, under judge Maxwell Riddle. He was bred by Mrs. T. M. Jones and was sold before his win to Mr. and Mrs. O'Dell of Ontario.

The O'Dells continued the bloodlines of **Armil** and **Karlston** under the registered prefix **Nimbus**. A number of very nice dogs were produced from Can Ch. Armil's Amanda and Can Ch. Karlston Kiri of Nimbus. Through their foundation stock the O'Dells brought together the bloodlines of Quibbletown, Basquaerie and de Fontenay. Through additional purchases later, Tip 'n Chip blood was added.

Limberlost is the prefix of Lois McIntosh of Ontario. Ms. McIntosh became seriously interested in Great Pyrenees in 1965 and shortly thereafter acquired her foundation bitch. Ch. Quibbletown Valkyrie, from the Smiths. Val stamped her quality well on her offspring, and is the top producing bitch in Canada with fourteen champions. Two of her best-known sons were Ch. Limberlost Rogue ("Monty"), who was the Number One Pyr in Canada in 1970 and 1973, and Can/Am Ch. Quibbletown Val's Heritage ("Dennis"). Dennis was campaigned in 1974 and 1975 and set a breed record with twenty-six Group placements and a Best in Show. He was the first Great Pyrenees to place among the Top Ten Show Dogs in the Working Group. He was also a Group winner in the States. He sired many champions including Ch. Limberlost Gold O'Chryshaefen, who was Best of Breed at the U.S. Midwest Specialty.

Dennis's most famous son was Can/Am Ch. Le Dauphin of Limberlost ("Mike"). Mike was a real pathfinder for the breed in Canada. He was the first Great Pyrenees to become the Top Show Winner of All Breeds. Owned and handled by Dr. Ellen Brown of Ontario, he finished his championship in just three shows, with three Puppy Bests in Show. He went on to win a total of sixteen Bests in Show, with over 250 Working Group placements. He won BOB at the 1979 GPCC National Specialty under judge Paul Strang and was Top Great Pyrenees in Canada in 1978, 1979 and 1980. In the all-breed rankings, he was fourth in 1978, second in 1979 and first in 1980. In limited showing in the United States, Mike was BOB at Westminster, BOB at the Midwest Regional Specialty, and went Best of Breed from the classes at a Supported Show under Mrs. Francis V. Crane. Dr. Brown described him as: ". . . a placid, calm dog. I knew he was a beautiful, sound dog with the correct head, coat and balance—the epitome of his breed!" Mike sired numerous Canadian and American champions.

Mike's son, Can/Am Ch. Limberlost Kennebecasis Beau ("Spike"), won five all-breed Bests in Show, and a total of forty-eight Working Group placements to make him the Number One Great Pyrenees in Canada in 1987. He was WD, BOW at the U.S. Midwest Specialty in 1987 and WD, BOW and Award of Merit at the U.S. National Specialty in 1987.

Ms. McIntosh breeds for three main things: overall balance, excel-

CAN/AM Ch. Le Dauphin of Limberlost was a real pathfinder for the breed in Canada with owner-handler Dr. Ellen Brown. Winning a total of sixteen BIS, he was the number one dog, all breeds, in Canada in 1980. *Storeham*

CAN/AM Ch. Limberlost Kennebecasis Beau, a multiple BIS winner handled by owner, Carole Baxter.

lence in movement (front and rear) and correct type, because "If a dog doesn't have a correct head and expression, it just isn't a Great Pyrenees!"

Gisela Fischer of **Walburga** became interested in the breed in 1967 and acquired as her foundation female a sister of Champion Limberlost Rogue (Limberlost Vicki). Later she imported the dog Bergerie Neptune, son of the Crufts Best in Show winner Bergerie Knur. A daughter of Neptune, Walburga's Pandora, was Winners Bitch at the Canadian National Specialty in 1974.

Anayobon is the registered prefix of Donna Gleeson. Mrs. Gleeson became interested in Great Pyrenees in 1969 and acquired as her foundation brood matron Nanibijou Teeto O'Limberlost, bred by Ms. McIntosh and Mrs. Fischer. Teeto quickly acquired both a Canadian championship and an Obedience degree. She was bred three times and produced nine Canadian champion offspring, two American champions and three dogs with a CD degree. Two of these dogs, Sir Galahad O'Diro and Lady Guinevere O'Diro, went to Mr. and Mrs. Roy Addie as the foundation pair for the Diro Kennels, of which more will be said later.

Although Anayobon is no longer active as a breeding kennel, it can be counted as the top Obedience kennel in Canada, having four resident Pyrs with CD degrees: Teeto, Can/Am Ch. Anayobon Eet Too Brutus, Can Ch. Anayobon's Canook, and Can Ch. Annie of Anayobon.

Delgada is the registered prefix of Peter and Dawn Lake. This kennel began with the acquisition of Snow Sonnet Wolfsong CD of Tip 'n Chip background. Bred to Ch. Limberlost Marquis de Neige, this female produced Ch. Delgada's All White Pirate. The Lakes have confined their breeding activities to an occasional litter, and recently have shown some promising offspring, including a Group placer, Delgada's Tarascon.

The **Barbann** Kennels of Barbara Hay Belsito began with the purchase of Ch. Delgada's All White Pirate from the Lakes in 1969. Pirate was shown extensively in 1972, twice winning the Canadian Booster Show. Today, Pirate is the family companion and guardian, fulfilling both roles well.

Rum Point is the prefix of Ruth Cram. The Crams first became interested in the breed in 1964 while living in Harvard, Massachusetts. Mrs. Cram writes, "The name of Rum Point originated in 1970 when we moved to an old farm on a point of land jutting out into the back harbor of Lunenburg, Nova Scotia. In the rum-running days it was the practice of local boats to slip out along our shores and rendezvous with the big vessels engaged in the illegal traffic. Neither we nor our dogs have yet found an old cache of the famous liquid, but since the farm is some seventy acres we are still hopeful!"

When the Crams moved to Nova Scotia, the two dogs, Wynken's Ringo Star and Jack Frost, came with them. The Crams' breeding in Canada has so far been confined to this pair. Jack Frost has his Canadian Championship, as does his daughter, Bridget of Rum Point.

Dave and Marty Joos of **Pyradise** Kennels in Nova Scotia are the owners of several Canadian champions, two of which, Ch. Pyradise Zuni and Ch. Quibbletown Moki of Pyradise, have placed in the Groups.

The **Chenil Dauverniac** in Quebec Province is the kennel of Jacques Jumelles. In the words of M. Jumelles, "Born in France, I have known Great Pyrenees as watchdogs and have always admired the nobility of the breed. Twenty years ago I immigrated to Canada and thought the Great Pyrenees would adapt well to our country. I imported my first two Great Pyrenees from De La Franche Pierre Kennels in 1970. Both were tall and powerful dogs, with very typey heads and big bones. From their alliance I kept my present champion, Raton Dauverniac."

Raton was presented for the first time in 1974 and completed his title in two weekends with eighteen points. Raton has been bred to two Canadian bitches and has produced several promising puppies. Through the importations of M. Jumelles, French bloodlines will continue to be seen in Canada for many years.

Henry and Mary Ellen Hanemaayer of **Ventisquero** Kennel got their start in Pyrs in 1971. Their foundation dogs were Ch. Auroja's Mona, which was of Soleil and Armil background, and Skeel's Benkurion, whose career got a promising start but was abruptly ended by an accident.

Benkurion was bred once to Mona in the fall of 1972 and produced three champions. One of these, Ch. Ventisquero Samson The Great, was Winners Dog at the California Regional Specialty. The Hanemaayers purchased other dogs from Soleil and Skeel and, in 1973, imported an outcross bitch, a daughter of Ch. Lisblanc Cristoph, from Mrs. Sheila Ball in England.

The Hanemaayers discontinued their breeding program in the early eighties and passed their kennel name, Ventisquero, on to Gerald Scott and Sandy Glas in Surrey, British Columbia. Mr. Scott had previously produced many winners under the **Pastoure** affix, including the 1983 National Specialty Best of Breed winner, Ch. Feerique Ruisseau de Pastoure ("Sunshine"), and top winners Can/Am Ch. Coldcreek Patou Christopher and his son, Can/Am Ch. Eternal Spirit de Pastoure.

Important in the kennel's success in the eighties have been outcrosses to Euzkotar bloodlines. Ch. Euzkotar El Amor Diablo was Sunshine's father. Can/Am Ch. Euzkotar Natani sired Ch. Ventisquero Gold Dust Woman, who was BOS at the National in 1983, and her brother Ch. Ventisquero Fleetwood Mac, BOS at the 1986 National Specialty, and sire

Can Ch. Ventisquero Fleetwood Mac, a very international dog—born in Canada, sired by an American dog out of a French dam, he was BOS at the 1986 British Columbia Specialty and sired the winner of the 1990 American National Specialty. Owned by Gerald Scott and Linda Weisser.

CAN/AM Ch. Wildrose Cast A Giant Shadow won BOB at the Canadian National Specialty in 1990, handled by owner Julie Mackey. *MikRon*

of the 1990 U.S. National Specialty winner. Another important influence was Am Ch. Quibbletown T.G. of Basquaerie, who sired Can/Am Ch. Ventisquero's Friend of the Devil, Best of Breed at the 1988 National and BOS at the 1986 National under French judge Alain Pecoult. French imports have also played a great role. Ch. Nemausa du Font Buis de La Chenaie was the dam of Sunshine, Gold Dust and Mac. Other imports include Ch. Val Fier du Duche de Savoie who won the French National Specialty in 1986, and Ch. Uxem du Grand Baou who sired the 1986 Canadian National Specialty Winners Dog.

Pyrbliss Kennel of Mr. and Mrs. Richard Mackey was established in 1977. To date they have owned or bred thirty-five champions and numerous others with Obedience titles. Their foundation stud was Can/Am Moorings A'kron Prinz TT, Top Pyr for 1982, Best in Show, multiple Booster and 1982 National Specialty winner. He was the first champion Pyr in Canada to receive a Temperament Tested degree. This set off a trend across Canada to have breeding stock formally temperament tested by the ATT Society. Prinz has many champion descendants that have Group Firsts and placements, Best Puppy in Show, etc. His son, Can/Am Ch. Ebro St. Elmo's Fire, is also a BIS winner. Another son, Can/Am Ch. Pyrbliss Prince Charming TT, was Number One Pyr in 1987. The Mackeys' foundation bitch was Ch. Limberlost Liza.

In 1982 the Mackeys leased Can/Am Ch. Ebro's Afternoon Delyte, a bitch of Soleil breeding, from the Yuricks of **Ebro**. She went on to be Top Bitch in Canada five years running, with four Bests in Show and BOS at the National. Bred to Prinz, she produced the typey, sound pups of good size that the Mackeys were looking for. One of these was Can/Bda Ch. Pyrbliss Ebro's Snow Dancer, a National Specialty winner and multiple Group placing bitch, and the only Canadian-bred Pyr to gain a Bermudian championship. Thus Pyrbliss' current success stems from a combination of Quibbletown and Soleil.

The Mackeys current special, Prinz grandson Can/Am Ch. Wildrose Cast A Giant Shadow ("Chaos"), won the National Specialty in 1990, has won Regionals and Boosters, and is a multiple Group placing dog. Chaos was Number Two Pyr in 1989 and 1990.

Carol Baxter's **Kenneview** Kennel is one of the few registered Great Pyrenees breeding kennels in Atlantic Canada and the only one in New Brunswick. Kenneview was established in 1982 with the acquisition of a pair from Limberlost. Its foundation male was Can/Am Ch. Limberlost Kennebecasis Beau ("Spike") who, as mentioned earlier, won five BIS, eighteen Group Firsts and a total of forty-eight Group placements in Canada. He also had impressive wins in the United States. Spike's son, Ch. Kenneview Premier Performance, has also had several Group placements.

In 1988 a bitch was leased from Wyndsong in Michigan and bred to

Am Ch. Jenstin's Noah's Inspiration, a multiple Specialty winner. This produced the young dog Ch. Kenneview's Tuff Stuff. Tuffy finished his championship at seven months of age and was Number One Pyr Puppy in Canada for 1989 with a Group First, three other Group placements, four Best Puppy in Show wins and thirteen Best Puppy in Working Group wins. He was Best in Sweeps at the Milwaukee Regional Specialty. As an adult, he took his first Best in Show at fifteen months under respected judge Nigel Aubrey-Jones.

Pendouglas, owned by Douglas and Penny Numbers of Ontario, got its start in 1971 when Penny started handling dogs for the Gleesons of Anayobon. They purchased a Pyr of their own in 1972, Ch. Anayobon's Pax of Pendouglas. In 1975 two bitches were obtained from the Stuarts' Skeel kennel. They lost Pax and replaced him with Can/Am Ch. Anayobon's Eet Tu Brutus. Their first litter of seven puppies earned thirteen titles, including Canadian and U.S. championships and CD Obedience titles. Their second litter earned the GPCC's "Snowdrift Award" for the most champions produced from a single litter born in Canada. To date, 80 percent of all Pyrs bred by Pendouglas have been titled.

The Numbers have twice produced the top Obedience Pyr: Ch. Pendouglas Fionn MacCumhail CD in 1984 and Ch. Pendouglas Fabrena Delposita CD in 1987. Ch. Pendouglas Alabastros CD was among the top winners in Canada for five years.

Penny Numbers has now formed a partnership with Mary Milliken of Colorado. They register their co-bred dogs under the prefix **Rip'n'Pen**. The 1990 Canadian National Specialty saw Rip'n'Pen A Jillion Kisses go WB, BOS and Best Puppy at eleven months, and Rip'n'Pen Crunchy Pickles take WD, BOW.

Weskyuwin was established in 1977 when Sharon Armstrong acquired Can/Am Ch. Euzkotar Forever Afternoon Can/Am CD. Bred to Ch. Euzkotar El Amor Diablo, she produced Ch. Weskyuwin Hi Mountain Odyssey TT ("Ody"), Number One Pyr bitch in Canada in 1981. Ody produced some dozen champion and Obedience titled offspring in both Canada and the States, including the 1989 De Fontenay Trophy winner, Can/Am Ch. Weskyuwin Excalibur, co-owned with JoAnn Teems of **Snowmass** (California). Shown as a brace, Ana and Ody had many Best Brace in Show and Best Brace in Group wins. Weskyuwin has utilized Euzkotar, Starlaxy, Pompier and French bloodlines.

In 1985 Weskyuwin relocated from Alberta to British Columbia. There Ch. Weskyuwin Jonson Shadow Bandit became a Group placer. In addition to show dogs, Weskyuwin places many Pyrs as livestock guardians and as active companions in pet-facilitated therapy programs at hospitals, senior care homes and similar facilities. Ch. Weskyuwin Mystic Warrior TT, Am CD has won recognition by both the West Coast Great Pyrenees

Two-year-old Can Ch. Pendouglas Charley's M'Darling (standing), with his fourteen-year-old grandmothers, Ch. Skeel Pendouglas Patrician and CAN/AM Ch. Hidalgo's Nothing Much.

Rip 'N Pen A Jillion Kisses winning Best Puppy, WB and BOS; and Rip 'N Pen Crunchy Pickles Winning WD, BOW at the 1990 Canadian National Specialty. Both are owned by Mary Milliken and Penny Numbers. *MikRon*

167

CAN/AM Ch. Rivergrove's If Looks Could Kill is the top winning Great Pyrenees of all time in Canada with over thirty BIS. Bred by Jean Boyd and Judith Cooper. Owned by Ed and Lise Gravely and Jean Boyd. *Alex Smith*

Association and the Great Pyrenees Club of Canada for his work as a Therapy Dog.

Michael and Patricia Moore have used Weskyuwin dogs to found their **Misthria** Kennel. Ch. Misthria Cypress went BOS at the West Coast Specialty in 1990.

Ed and Lise Graveley of **Pyrcrest** in Quebec have caused a sensation recently with their multiple BIS American import, Can/Am Ch. Rivergroves If Looks Could Kill. Looker was Number One Pyr in 1987, 1988 and 1989, and is currently number one dog all breeds with over twenty Bests in Show.

In addition to the above, there have been many other individuals who have helped establish the breed in Canada. In Nova Scotia, there is **Beaupyr** of Fran Delaney. **Kamay** of Louise Biron and **D'Ory** of Rachael Demarais support the breed in Quebec.

Ontario has the largest population of Pyrs and breeders. Val Toth brought her first dog with her from England and frequently places livestock guardians. Although she has never had an extensive breeding program, she has been involved with Pyrs for over twenty-five years, longer than any other breeder in Canada. Ruth Goodwin of **Aragon** has over twenty years in the breed. Paul and Ann Rivard have been in the breed many years and done extensive winning, especially with their Ch. Limberlost Silver Moon, a National Specialty winner. Several others have joined the Pyr scene more recently, including Marion and Bob Hassebroek of **Moonshine**, Tally Hill of **Taralyall**, Kay Hildreith of **Kayhills**, Judy McPherson of **Whiffletree**, Sue and Graham Clemmons of **Avery Hill**, Dr. Carol Graham, Judy Timpson and Debbie Stroud. Vince Murphy was the proud owner and exhibitor of Cymru, the first Canadian Great Pyrenees to earn a Utility Dog Obedience title. Linda Yelland of **Argeles** has done extensive breeding and showing. Her Can/Am Ch. Tip 'n Chip Pride d'Argeles was a Specialty winner and a Best in Show winner in the United States. Althea Townes of **Wildrose** is very involved in the breed.

In western Canada, the breed is represented in Alberta by Marie Klimek of **Skeenawhip**, Helen and Robin Johnson of **Kaslan**, and Harry and Christine Simoens of **Pola**. In British Columbia, the breed was supported over the years by Karen Gallagher of **Westfjord**, Bud and Edna Vye, Dwight Keller, Chris and Sharon Cooke, and Fred Glasbergen. Presently, Lorna and Doug Hastings are very active.

Diro is the registered prefix of Roy and Diana Addie of Carleton Place, Ontario. In 1970 the Addies acquired the previously mentioned foundation pair from Anayobon, Sir Galahad O'Diro and Lady Guinevere O'Diro. These two puppies were shown together as a brace, and at eight months of age achieved their first of four Best in Show brace wins. Both went on to fine show records and attained Canadian championships. Guinevere was honored as Top Dam for 1974 and 1975.

The mating of Ch. Lady Guinevere to Ch. Quibbletown Bonhomme, owned and shown by Angus Morris of Ontario, established the Diro reputation. Six champions were produced, including the home-owned pair, Can/Am Ch. Diro's Abydos de Pau and Ch. Diro's Arya d'Argeles-Gazost. Abydos, in particular, has had a distinguished career in the show ring, winning the Canadian Booster Show three years in succession (1974, 1975, 1976), the first Great Pyrenees to achieve this distinction. Abydos had four all-breed Bests in Show.

In the second breeding, Lady Guinevere was bred to Am/Can Ch. Espirit Blanc, owned by Patricia J. Alteri, of Michigan. This mating procured five champions, of which one, Ch. Diro's Banquise, was bred back to Sir Galahad and produced a promising litter which is just beginning to be seen in the show ring.

Diro dogs have gone to some fine young kennels as foundation stock. For Great Pyrenees bred under this prefix, as with the breed elsewhere in Canada, prospects are high.

While the breed in Canada owes much to its many breeders, through the years there have been many active owners who have been deeply involved with the breed and the Great Pyrenees Club of Canada. Such individuals possess a simple, genuine love of the breed. Without a doubt, some of the most dedicated people in the breed have been Eileen Bull and her late husband, Bob, and Winston and Donna Cheatley. Lois McIntosh insists that: "Even though they've never bred a litter, Win and Donna have contributed more to the Great Pyrenees in Canada than any other individuals." Such selfless souls serve as an example to all of us.

11

The Modern
Pyrenean Mountain
Dog in France

THE PYRENEAN MOUNTAIN DOG is at an all-time high in popularity in France today and many new fanciers have entered the picture. The ever-increasing competition at the shows is having an effect and some evolutionary changes are inevitably taking place.

When Senac-Lagrange published the 1927 Standard, he wrote: "As to size we find that it has, unfortunately, been decreasing over the last years. Measurements we took about twenty years ago show that this loss of size amounts to at least three centimeters. It is imperative that fanciers strive to overcome this size degeneration."

That both breeders and judges heeded this plea is apparent in the French show ring today for the smaller dogs are now in the decided minority. In fact, for M. C. Douillard, a modern French authority, the pendulum may well be swinging too far. He writes, "I would caution my friends that what we really must have is a well-balanced subject. It is useless to pursue size and weight to the extreme. When an owner tells me his Pyrenees weighs 175 or 180 pounds, I shudder."

Guy J. Mansencal, Secretary of the French Pyr Club, describes Rouky, a winner at recent shows, as about ideal at 32 inches and 140 pounds. He also finds Rouky close to perfect in type as well:

Int/Fr Ch. Ubelle de Chatigny just before her historic BIS win at the 1989 Paris Championship Show. Bred, owned and shown by Dr. Tassy.

Patricia Princehouse

The outstanding head and expression of Vallire du Comte de Foix. Bred and owned by Dr. and Mrs. Giralt.

Courtesy I.G.P.R.

INT/Fr Ch. U'lzoure du Comte de Foix, an all-breed BIS Winning Bitch. Breeder-owner, Mrs. Giralt. Note the emphasis that mountain breeders place on the head.

Alpy. Tarbes, France

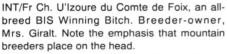

The famous Fr Ch. Moulouk du Comte de Foix pictured at eight years of age.

Dr. Millemann

This dog presents an imposing figure of elegance. He has a good coat and a well-plumed tail, carried low in repose and wheeled over the back when the dog is at attention. Though the rear is a bit straight, the bone structure is strong. He has an excellent temperament. And he is siring excellent puppies.

The excellence of his puppies stems, in part, from the perfection of type found in Rouky's head. The ears are not too large or heavy and they lie close to the skull, almost hidden in the dog's ruff. We should never tolerate big heavy ears set on above the level of the eyes.

Rouky's eyes are rather small, slightly oblique, rimmed with black and they have the true Pyrenean expression. His muzzle is of proper length and proceeds from the forehead without an abrupt stop. Lips are tight and they have full black pigment. We must remember that an abrupt stop, a loose-lipped drooling mouth and lack of pigment are all very serious faults.

Senac-Lagrange also mentioned in 1927 that many of the Pyreneans of that day were "often too straight behind." For the most part French breeders have been able to overcome this, and most of today's winners are sufficiently angulated. But the fact that Mansencal mentions this defect in Rouky points out that it is a problem to which breeders continue to give attention.

Monsieurs Douillard, Mansencal, and such prominent breeders as Delattre (**Pontoise**), Docquin (**Du Grand Baou**), Giralt (**Du Comte de Foix**) and Mme. H. Gimenz (**Du Clos d'Argent**), all attach great importance to what is considered the correct head. In 1907 when the French Pyr Clubs were attempting to draw up a standard, the correct head was one of the primary causes of dissension. Some thought it should be described as "wolflike," with a good length of muzzle. Others violently disagreed, preferring "Mastiff-like," indicating a broadly rounded skull.

Senac-Lagrange solved the problem, temporarily, by declaring that the head approached that of the Pyrenean brown bear, possessing both breadth of skull and a tapering muzzle.

At the Cauterets Pyrenean Speciality in 1938, this writer found that after ten years of experience with the Senac-Lagrange standard most of the mountaineers had come to accept it, though many were unhappy with the description of the head in that no mention had been made regarding what the shepherds believed to be a cardinal point . . . the slight protrusion of the occipital bone at the rear of the skull.

Pierre Houert, breeder of the de Barzet Pyreneans, was most voluble on the point, explaining that his father and grandfather before him had always insisted on the bump. When asked why the bump was so important, he explained it had always been considered a sure sign of a keen nose, a superior intelligence and a tractable disposition.

Pierre's dogs did not win many prizes at the show and I had nearly forgotten his comments, but in 1970, when the new French Standard became official, lo and behold, I found the bump had at last been incorporated into the description of the head. When I asked why, I was told breeding for the breadth of skull called for in the previous description (without the bump) had led, gradually, to a shorter, squarer, untypical muzzle; while the dogs possessing the slightly protruding occipital bone were usually found to possess the correct tapering muzzle.

The wording in the 1970 Standard (which is given in an earlier chapter) is explicit: "*The peak of the occipital bone, being visible, gives the posterior portion of the skull an ogival, vaulted, form.*" And also, incidentally, serves to accentuate the muzzle length.

Pierre Houert, and the other Pyrenean breeders who believed as he did, are at last vindicated, at least as far as the head description is concerned. But still to be determined is whether or not the genetic pattern governing the shape of the skull is also responsible for passing on mental and psychological qualities.

Probably the most visible evidence the writer noted on seeing the French dogs in the show ring at the Paris Exposition in 1974 was that indeed the skull does not fall away abruptly at the back and the ears and muzzles are slightly longer than we see commonly in our own show rings. It should be noted that while the ears are somewhat longer they are not at all thick or heavy, but rather thin and fine-textured.

Formerly most Pyrenees in the kennels of France were first and second generation descendants of stock purchased directly in the mountains. Today this is no longer true and there is a constant interchange of bloodlines between fanciers throughout France that is many generations removed from the mountains. Contact is also maintained with kennels in Switzerland, Holland, England, Belgium, Norway, Sweden, North Africa, Italy and the Middle East. Some dogs have also been imported from the United States.

The modern European show scene is, then, quite active and growing ever stronger. The upstanding French dogs tend to be taller than some of their foreign counterparts with more depth of skull and somewhat less angulation in the rear. And although many of the dogs are now being bred outside of the mountain region, the old mountaineers have been able to write into the Standard a point they consider essential.

Only a few breeders with kennels founded prior to World War II are left. Mlle. Lamazou-Betbeder of **Poeymayou** in the Pyrenees started breeding in the twenties and is still producing winners. Mlle. Leger of **Guerveur** still keeps a few dogs. Unfortunately, Mr. Delattre of **Pontoise** died in 1984. Countless French breeders have based their breeding programs on stock from these fine breeders and others who had the determination to continue in spite of hard times.

Numerous other breeders are active today. M. and Mme. Giralt of **Comte de Foix** came to the fore in the sixties with the incomparable Micoune du Comte de Foix and continue to produce quality dogs. M. and Mme. Docquin of **Grand Baou** produced many champions in the seventies and eighties, as did Mlle. Dinard of **Nardesca**. M. Ducrey of **Duche du Savoie** has produced several champions, National Specialty and BIS win-

Ch. Samy du Domaine de Nardesca, bred in France by Mrs. Caroline Dinard, finished his American Championship at ten months of age. Owned and shown by Joseph, Frances and Patricia Princehouse.

Ashbey

Fr Ch. Vestale de Baccala at home in the Pyrenees. Bred by Anny Lavergne; Owned by M. Gerbeau.
Patricia Princehouse

Five of Comte de Foix's outstanding brood bitches. Bred and owned by Dr. and Mrs. Giralt.

175

ners. Other enthusiastic breeders of top winners include Mme. Niollet of **Val des Champs D'Or**, M. and Mme. Estrampes of **Montbernes**, M. and Mme. Henrio of **Patou des Neiges**, M. Procureur, M. Cockenpot of **Pic du Viscos**, Dr. Millemann of **Vallon des Sauterelles**, Mlle. Lafitte, Mlle. Rigole, and Dr. Tassy of **Chatigny**. There are, of course, many others.

It is relatively rare that a Pyr wins Best in Show at a French show. So it was particularly exciting when, in 1989, the year of the bicentennial anniversary of the French Revolution, at the French Championship show at Longchamps in Paris, a Great Pyrenees, Dr. Tassy's Ch. Ubelle de Chatigny, won BIS over a record entry of some 5,000 dogs.

Nineteen ninety saw another unusual event. Bombelle du Comte de Foix, owned by Americans Phil and Arlene Oraby, went CAC, CACIB (French and International championship certificates) at the French National Specialty. Purchased from the famous Comte de Foix Kennel in France, Bombelle had already won WB at the Canadian National Specialty in 1988 under the respected French judge Alain Pecoult.

FRANCE'S R.A.C.P., THE OLDEST GREAT PYRENEES CLUB IN THE WORLD

La Réunion des Amateurs des Chiens Pyrénéens (R.A.C.P.) has its roots in the work done by fanciers around the turn of the century. The First World War brought added difficulties but the breed was finally officially recognized by the S.C.C. (French Kennel Club) in 1923. As described elsewhere in this book, Bernard Senac-Lagrange was instrumental in preserving the Great Pyrenees and several other breeds.

M. Senac-Lagrange served as president of the R.A.C.P. until 1953, when the presidency passed into the hands of Charles Duconte. M. Duconte died in 1984, making it the better part of a century that the breed club had been under the knowledgeable leadership of just two presidents. The third president, Guy Mansencal, has been involved in the club since 1948 and is dedicated to continuing in the same tradition.

The R.A.C.P. was founded in order to preserve not just the Great Pyrenees but also its herding counterpart, the Pyrenean Shepherd (Berger des Pyrenees). In 1985 the R.A.C.P. also took the two Spanish Pyrenean breeds under its protective banner. These are the Gos d'Atura, a herding dog, and the Mastino de los Pirineos or Pyrenean Mastiff. The Pyrenean Mastiff guarded livestock on the Spanish side of the Pyrenees. This breed is more heavily built than the Great Pyr and is always marked with a full dark mask and body spots.

The Pyrenean Shepherd and Gos d'Atura are both small herding dogs. The Gos, sometimes known as the Catalonian Shepherd, is the larger of the two and is a longhaired fawn or gray dog with floppy ears. There

Rough-faced Pyrenean Shepherd, Ch. Urrugne de L'estaube, twice BOB at the American National Specialty. Bred by Guy Mansencal; owned and handled by Patricia Princehouse.

Patricia Princehouse

Smooth-faced Pyrenean shepherd, Tourmalet Bleu de L'estaube, multiple BIS and French National Specialty winner. Bred by Guy Mansencal; owned by Mr. and Mrs. Claude Person.

Courtesy RACP

Rough-faced Pyrenean Shepherd.   *Paul Redam*

are two varieties of Pyrenean Shepherd, the Rough-Faced and the Smooth-Faced (Face-Rase). The two varieties occur in the same litters, but are shown separately, as with Rough and Smooth Collies.

Though largely unknown outside France, the Pyrenean Shepherd is currently the thirteenth most popular breed in France. However, in recent years clubs have sprung up in Germany, Austria, Switzerland and the United States. In the United States the breed was introduced via several routes in the eighteenth and nineteenth centuries, and it is believed that Smooth-Faced dogs were ancestral to the Australian Shepherd. Mary Crane brought a pair over in the thirties. However, the male died of distemper and, much as she loved her bitch, Soumise, Mrs. Crane did not feel the breed well suited to the vicissitudes of modern American life.

In the 1970s and 1980s, several Pyr Shepherds have been imported and breeding programs started, most notably by Linda Weisser and Patricia Princehouse. The Pyrenean Shepherd Club of America was founded in 1987. There are currently fewer than a hundred Pyr Shepherds in the United States. Thus, the breed is classified as a "rare breed" and is not eligible for competition at AKC events. However, the AKC does maintain a file for the breed complete with PSCA newsletters and the current address of the secretary. It is expected that the breed will be recognized well before the year 2000.

The Pyr Shepherd stands 15 to 20 inches tall and weighs between 15 and 35 pounds. The temperament is typical of most herding dogs: bright, vivacious, always ready for action, devoted and very affectionate with their owners but often distrustful of strangers. Extensive socialization is usually required to achieve an outgoing Pyr Shepherd. They are outstanding workers, not only for herding but also for obedience, agility, tracking, search and rescue, almost anything. They make excellent jogging or hiking companions. However, their attachment to their owners means that the owner must be equally committed. The kenneled or neglected Pyr Shepherd quickly withers from lack of affection.

12

Pyrenean Mountain Dogs in Great Britain

by Joyce Stannard

READERS IN AMERICA will be interested to know that in England and the majority of the countries in the British Commonwealth, the title of Champion is earned by winning three Challenge Certificates under three different judges at shows designated as Championship Shows. There are a number of smaller Open Shows in which dogs may compete for prize money, but not a CC. The number of CCs is strictly limited by the Kennel Club, and is linked to the number of dogs registered during the previous three years. A judge awarding a CC can do so only to Best of Sex, and only if he is clearly of the opinion that the dog or bitch is worthy of the title of Champion. Recently, in England there were twenty pairs of CCs for the Pyrenean Mountain Dog (as the breed is officially known in Britain) and therefore twenty Championship Shows throughout the year and throughout the country. In Britain champions are entered in the Open Class and so compete against each other and the aspiring champions for the Certificates. Therefore, if a dog is to win its championship, it must do so by defeating those that are already established. The top Pyrenees in Great Britain, in any year, is the dog or bitch that has won the most CCs. It is not uncommon for only a handful of Pyrenees to gain their titles in a given year.

The story of the Pyrenean in England must necessarily begin with mention of the Pyrenean owned by Queen Victoria in 1848. This was Cabas, a popular dog at Court, that was honored by having his portrait painted by a famous artist of the day. We understand this painting is still in existence at one of the Royal residences.

In the 1850s two English explorers returned from the Pyrenees Mountains with several dogs that had faithfully served them as pack animals. But apparently they left no progeny.

In the 1880s we find that our breed was listed under the following names: Pyrenean, Pyrenean Wolfhound, Pyrenean Sheepdog, Pyrenean Mastiff and Pyrenean Wolf Dog. A number of these dogs, all registered with the Kennel Club, were being shown annually at the great Crystal Palace show.

The first attempt to truly establish the breed in England must be credited to Lady Sybil Grant. Lady Sybil first learned of the breed through the pictures of Neron and Diane in de Bylandt's Encyclopedia. This triggered her interest in the dogs, and in 1909 she visited the Pyrenees Mountains in search of foundation stock for her **Milanollo** Kennels. It became readily apparent to her that there were certain difficulties to be met with in purchasing really good specimens; but nonetheless one of her selections, Milanollo Patou, took first place at the Kennel Club Show just one week after leaving his quarantine! Thus began what promised to be a distinguished career of the Pyrenean in England. However, serious food shortages during the First World War and the need to convert her estate into a hospital for the wounded forced Lady Sybil to break up her kennels. And it seems that none of her puppies went to people sufficiently able or interested enough to perpetuate the breed.

The next reference to the Pyrenean Mountain Dog is in connection with the French Duke d'Orleans, who took up residence in exile at Wood Norton, Eversham. He brought with him three specimens from France. When he was forced to give up his residence in 1920, the dogs were presented to Lady Milbank of Eaton Place, London; again nothing further is known.

In the 1920s Sir Cato Worsfold of Mitcham tried to introduce the breed again, but unfortunately five of his imports died in quarantine. By January 1933, he apparently had only two dogs left which had been unsuccessful at stud. Apart from one bitch owned by Mr. A. Croxton Smith, one-time Chairman of the Kennel Club, these two were the only Pyreneans in Great Britain—after more than one hundred years!

It was therefore an event of singular importance when Mme. Jeanne Harper Trois-Fontaines opened her distinguished **De Fontenay** Kennels in 1934 with stock imported from France. After several unsuccessful attempts, during which it is said the puppies died in quarantine from sheer loneliness, Madame was able to import a ten-month-old Pyrenean from the de Careil Kennels in Loire. This was Kop de Careil, perhaps the most famous dog

CABAS. From a painting by J. M. Joy, discovered by Mrs. C. R. Prince in the Queen's Collection at Windsor Castle. Photograph taken by appointed photographer.

A.C. Cooper Ltd.

A group study of de Fontenay's first Pyrenean family pictured with Mme. Harper in her garden at Moor Park. Left to right: the dam, Ianette de Boisy; her puppy, Monne de Fontenay at the age of eight months; Rip de Fontenay, a litter brother; and the sire, Kop de Careil.

Thomas Fall, courtesy, Mrs. C. R. Prince

in English Pyrenean lore, and in her words, "He was the best I ever had."

After her initial success with Kop de Careil, Mme. Harper began a program of importation which spanned many years. In 1934 she returned to the Château de Boisy and collected the puppy bitch she had bought the year before—Ianette de Boisy. The first litter at de Fontenay, out of Ianette and Kop de Careil, was born January 4, 1935. Her next import, Iarkotte de Pontoise, was mated in France to the Comtesse de Savigny's famous International Champion Estat d'Argeles and had her litter in quarantine.

Next came Labeda du Mont Picry from Belgium, and l'Nethou de Langladure from France. l'Nethou was later to become the sire of England's first homebred champion, Hubert de Fontenay.

In 1938 the de Fontenay Kennels moved to Hyde Heath, Amersham, Bucks, where they remained to the end of their era.

In 1946 Mme. Harper imported Patou de la Montagne from the du Pic du Jer Kennels of M. Abadie-Toulet at Lac Lourdes. In the following year came Basquaerie Perce Neige II from the United States. Perce Neige became the first American-bred Champion in England, with fifteen CCs to his credit.

By a skillful policy of importation and breeding, Mme. Harper built up an array of bloodlines of such strength that her kennels continued throughout the Second World War. When hostilities ceased, puppies were shipped to Ireland, Scotland, Norway, Switzerland, Canada, the United States, India, South Africa, Australia and New Zealand, where in many cases they played a major role in establishing the bloodlines of these countries.

Over thirty de Fontenay champions are recorded in England, among them the famous Ch. General de Fontenay and Ch. President de Fontenay (son of Madame's Basquaerie import) that was the winner of twenty-five CCs.

In 1936 Mme. Harper founded the Pyrenean Mountain Dog Club of Great Britain and remained its President until her death in 1972.

The story of English bloodlines now takes a new turn. In part, this is the story of the issue of one dog, Ch. Bedat de Monda, whose progeny have had a profound influence on the type shown in Great Britain for the past twenty years.

Bedat de Monda, bred by M. Monda of Argeles-Gazost in the High Pyrenees, was presented to Field Marshal Lord Alanbrooke in 1947 by the people of his birthplace, Bagneres-de-Bigorre. Later, Bedat was acquired by Joan Passini-Birkett of the **Pondtail** prefix. Mrs. Birkett, an untiring worker on behalf of the Pyrenean in England, soon made him up a champion, and to his credits were added a total of nine CCs, numerous Bests of Breed and three Bests in Show at Open Shows.

Under the expert management of Joan Birkett, Bedat de Monda was placed at stud and sired English Champions Pondtail Marechal, Pondtail

Niven, Pondtail Nevina, Commander Kip, Tartuffe of Oloron and Am Ch. Pondtail Rafael.

Another distinguished import of the late forties, also under the direction of Mrs. Birkett, was Basquaerie Louis O'Mont Louis, from the kennels of Mr. and Mrs. Crane. He was shown to his championship and was used at stud, where he was to make an important contribution to the British scene in the years to follow.

Meanwhile, the Second World War had left its aftermath in France. Only a few Pyrenean dogs of quality were to be found in the Pyrenees. For the second time in history the Pyrenees Mountains were combed for the best specimens available, this time by M. Senac-Lagrange and the Doctores Gleises. A jointly owned kennel, the Chenil de Pas de L'Ours, was opened in the early fifties.

This kennel, it seems, was to have a greater influence on British bloodlines than on the French. Lady Celia Morris, who was at that time the owner of Ch. Pondtail Marechal, was a yearly visitor to the Pyrenean Mountains. Having the advantage of being able to communicate with the mountaineers in fluent French, and being a perennial visitor, she was finally accorded the privilege of exporting from the Chenil de Pas de L'Ours a Pyrenean puppy bitch who later became known as Ariane of Oloron.

Breeding under the prefix **Oloron**, Lady Morris mated Ariane to Ch. Bedat de Monda. In 1955 this mating produced the famous Tartuffe of Oloron, a true "dog of the mountains." "Tuffy" quickly followed in his sire's illustrious footsteps and won his championship. In turn, Tuffy sired many famous offspring, including Ch. Bergerie Charlemagne de Bedous, Ch. Bergerie Diable and Ch. Pondtail Zborowski. Lady Morris ceased as a breeder many years ago, but still maintains an avid interest in all aspects of the breed.

The first famous son of Ch. Tartuffe of Oloron was born in 1961 out of Pondtail Laudley Sonata. Owned and bred by Mrs. Birkett, this was Ch. Pondtail Zborowski. "Jason" shattered all previous records held by a Pyrenean in England. He virtually dominated the show scene in the middle sixties, winning a total of twenty-nine Challenge Certificates, fourteen Working Groups and eleven Bests in Show at Open Shows. Of the four annual P.M.D.C. Open Shows he attended, he was Best in Show at three, and Reserve at the other.

Ch. Pondtail Zborowski sired many champions during his illustrious career, including Ch. Lisblanc Christoph, about whom more will be said later.

A second famous son of Ch. Tartuffe of Oloron was born in 1962 out of Ch. Bergerie Deborah. Owned by Mr. and Mrs. F. S. Prince, this was the dog Ch. Bergerie Charlemagne de Bedous, who was destined to become the first Pyrenean ever to win Best in Show at a Championship

Ch. Bedat de Monda, one of England's most influential French imports, pictured here with three of his puppies. Owned by Mrs. Joan Passini-Birkett.

Courtesy Mrs. C. R. Prince

CH. BEDAT de MONDA

	Ch. Pondtail Niven	Princess Ysanne	Ch. Tartuffe of Oleron	Rosalie of Oleron	Am. Ch. Pondtail Rafael of Basquaerie
Ch. Laudley Pretitly Natalie		Ch. Bergerie Charlemagne de Bedous	Ch. Bergerie Diable	Am. Ch. Pondtail Tattoo of Basquaerie	Am. Ch. Soleil Baron
	Ch. Laudley Nevar		Am. Ch. Soleil Rayon	Am. Ch. Soleil Belle Rose	Am. Ch. Soleil Coquette
Ch. Laudley Lanieve Blanche		Ch. Lisblanc Christoph			Am. Ch. Soleil Pierre de Blu-Crest
Ch. Laudley Nito		Ch. Briarghyll Falstaff			

Show. This distinguished win on behalf of the breed was gained at the largest one-day show in the world at that time, the West of England Ladies Kennel Society in 1965.

It was followed in 1968 by another unprecedented victory for **Bergerie** and the Princes—a Reserve Best in Show at Crufts by Ch. Bergerie Diable, the third famous son of Ch. Tartuffe of Oloron.

But the crowning achievement of the Bergerie Kennels, and perhaps the most talked-of win of all time, came in 1970 when Bergerie Knur, from a field of 8,000 at Crufts, was named Supreme Best in Show. His breeding will be mentioned later.

As a lasting achievement of the Crufts victory, Heredities Ltd. commissioned Geoffrey Davien to do a sculpture of Bergerie Knur for a limited edition (350) to be cast in bronze. Three of these rare collector's items were given to Mr. and Mrs. Prince, who in turn donated one to the GPCA as an annual trophy to be presented in America to the winner of the National Specialty.

Mr. and Mrs. F. S. Prince have judged the breed in England, on the Continent and in the United States. Both are officers of the Pyrenean Mountain Dog Club of Great Britain; Mr. Prince being the current President, and Mrs. Prince the Vice-President, positions they have occupied since the death of its founder, Mme. Harper. Mrs. Prince sent us the following:

When my husband and I bred Ch. Bergerie Auguste in our first litter, we thereupon formed a partnership and determined to teach the world how to breed champions in one easy lesson! Foundation stock was obtained, as far as possible, from unrelated sources, and breeding began in blissful ignorance of the many years of problems and disappointment which lay ahead.

We decided to build up a nucleus of both the colored mountain types and the all-white show types which we felt would enable Bergerie to keep great size in the breed.

In practice we found that the accepted techniques of line and inbreeding tended to lose the massive conformation and majestic presence of the Pyrenean Mountain Dog. The continued mating of all-white dogs, although achieving some degree of standardization and improvement in many of the show and breed points, appeared to produce smaller, untypical Pyreneans, and this could ultimately lead to the loss of the Great Dog of the Mountains as we once knew him.

From time to time Show successes were achieved and up to thirty dogs were kept at one time. A few champions were bred and on one occasion at Birmingham National Championship Show, Bergerie dogs won both the Dog and Bitch Challenge Certificates and the Reserve Best Dog.

By the judicious use of good dogs and bitches from all available sources, including those imported by Bergerie from France and America, both show and mountain types continued to be bred. Although the dogs were not, of course, highly standardized, they nevertheless were consistent winners in the show ring and were in demand by new breeders requiring healthy and vigorous foundation stock. This was the breeding background that eventually produced the top Bergerie winners.

Mrs. Prince will long be admired for her work on behalf of the Club's displaced Pyrenean program at Bergerie. Countless Pyreneans have been found new homes, and happy new lives—not without its emotional cost.

Lisblanc, the prefix of Sheila Ball, began showing and breeding Pyrenean dogs in 1948, and although this kennel was to produce a constant supply of winning dogs over the ensuing years, the kennel's supreme achievement is to be found in the success of its home-bred champion, Lisblanc Christoph, born in 1964. His sire was the previously mentioned Ch. Pondtail Zborowski and his dam was Ch. Lisblanc Serena.

In the late sixties, when his sire was at the peak of his career, "Bru" gradually obtained the three CCs required to make him a champion. Then in 1972 he suddenly attained the renown which was to make him the top winning Pyrenees of all time in England.

By the end of the year he had surpassed his sire by winning a total of thirty-three CCs, including a record thirteen in one year alone! Bru finished his career with 120 first prizes, forty-eight Bests of Breed, seven Bests in Show at Open Shows and one Championship Show, and three wins of the Working Group.

Lisblanc continues to produce top winning Pyreneans, including Ch. Briarghyll Falstaff and English/Irish Champion Lisblanc the Maverick. South African Champions are also listed among the kennel's accomplishments.

Among the bitches in England, special mention must be given to Ch. Laudley Prettily Natalie. Mrs. Beryl Lord of the **Laudley** prefix became interested in breeding and showing Pyreneans in 1951. Two years later, Prettily Natalie was born out of Princess Ysanne and Ch. Pondtail Niven.

Prettily Natalie began her show career at 2¼ years of age and quickly obtained her championship. There is little doubt that Natalie dominated the show ring in the late fifties. Her record, which included twenty-three Challenge Certificates, remained unbeaten for ten years. She was BOB at Crufts four years running and was the first Pyrenean to win a Group at a Championship Show. By great misfortune she was struck down at the peak of her career by a mystery virus.

Natalie bred three litters, all by Ch. Basquaerie Louis O'Mont Louis. The first created a record in any breed with four CC winners. The second produced three champions: Laudley Nito, Laudley La Nieve Blanche and Laudley Nevar.

Also during the 1960s came another top winning bitch, who, although not beating the record held by Ch. Laudley Prettily Natalie in the fifties, made her mark indelibly on the show ring. This was Pandora Faymous,

Ch. Carabrae Superdocious, pictured after her famous BOB win at Crufts, in 1973. Owned by Brenda Judson.

Peter Gilbert

Ch. Bergerie Knur, the only Pyrenean ever to go Supreme BIS at Crufts, 1970. Pictured in the Princes' garden.

born in 1964, out of Andora Fay and sired by Cobber de Bedous. She started her show career at six months and won consistently, soon becoming a champion. She received eighteen CCs under eighteen different judges, several Reserve CCs, and was Club Pyrenean of the Year in 1967. She won many Bests of Breed and was Group winner at three Championship Shows. Sadly she was never successfully bred and died at just under ten years of age.

The third of the great winning bitches in England was Ch. Briarghyll Camilla. Her dam, Ch. Briarghyll Fleur-de-Lys, was herself a Best in Show winner with many CCs to her credit.

Camilla began a distinguished career by becoming the first Pyrenean to win a Challenge Certificate as a puppy. In the late sixties she was a consistent winner and in the first two years of the seventies she was proclaimed the top CC winning bitch of the year. Her record to date, which surpasses all other English bitches, is twenty-four CCs, six Bests in Show and multiple Breed wins.

The story of the **Briarghyll** Kennels of Mr. and Mrs. M. Fielden would not be complete without mention of the outstanding achievements of their current show dog, Ch. Briarghyll Falstaff. Sired by Ch. Lisblanc Christoph out of Ch. Briarghyll Fleur-de-Lys, "Taffy" began his show career at 6½ months of age in 1971. By 1975 fanciers in Great Britain were beginning to revise the record book. He had gone Best in Show at three Championship Shows, including the Club Championship Show; Reserve Best in Show at two other Championship Shows, and winner of a Working Group. It was of singular importance in 1975 when Taffy was named the winner of "Dog of the Year" under the Vetzym/Our Dogs System, and Top Dog under the Dog World System—the first dog *in any breed* to win both titles outright in the same year!

During the past thirty years, many other breeders have been making their contribution to the show ring and the breed in general and it is a pity that space is not available to give them all the recognition that is due, but mention can be made of only a few.

First, Peggy Grant-Dalton and her **Moncal** Kennels, established in 1958. In 1967 a litter bred out of Moncal Laudley Yaronola and sired by Bergerie Abila de Fontenay produced Ch. Chazen Oscar and Bergerie Knur, the previously mentioned Supreme Best in Show winner at Crufts in 1970.

Moncal Pyrmont Arabella is the dam of two consistently winning champions: Castlenovary Ambassador and Castlenovary The Crusader. Arabella is the daughter of Bergerie Knur out of Ch. Pyrmont Moncal Charmain.

Moncal Pyreneans have been exported to several countries. Their South African Ch. Moncal Erskin de Chateau is a top CC winner and is proving a valuable stud in that country.

Then there is the **Kipsno** Kennels of Mr. and Mrs. R. Canning. For many years hardly a Championship Show has gone by without a Kipsno being "in the cards." The foundation stock of this kennel came from Beryl Lord at Laudley, being Ch. Laudley Seren Arian, and Ch. Kipsno Laudley Gaillard which was Best of Breed and Reserve in the Working Group at Crufts in 1971. Within a few years three more Kipsno Champions were recorded: Ch. Kipsno Trevanion Clairon, Ch. Kipsno Zarahemia's Deb's Beau and Ch. Kipsno Comet.

Another is the **Carabrae** Kennels of Brenda Judson, located in Sussex. Mrs. Judson bred her first Pyrenean in 1965. During the past ten years she has gradually built up a team of stud dogs of her own breeding that together with their progeny, are regularly winning in the show ring. Mrs. Judson houses more than twenty Pyreneans at Carabrae, where the facilities are also used as a boarding kennel.

Carabrae Pyreneans have been exported to fifteen countries. The pride of this kennel must naturally be Ch. Carabrae Superdocious who was the Best of Breed at Crufts in 1973.

There are many other kennels and many other award-winning dogs all over Great Britain today, but these must necessarily be the subject of another chapter and their turn is to come when they can rightfully be cast in the history of the breed.

British fanciers are very internationally minded. When Frans Dekkers ceased publication of the *International Journal of Pyrenean Dogs* (which was itself a continuation of the *International Great Pyrenees Review* and the *Pyrenees World*), The Pyrenean Mountain Dog Club of Great Britain sponsored a new publication, *The International Magazine of Pyrenean Dogs*. This popular magazine brings fanciers together from around the world. Current editor is Mrs. Joyce Stannard, Sandycot, Darite, Liskeard, Cornwall, PL14 5JS, England.

Ryoko Hayashida with Na-Na, a bitch owned by Dr. and Mrs. Tsuguo Katsumata.

13

The Breed
Around the World

DURING the past three decades, the Great Pyrenees has made noteworthy advances around the world. Specimens from some of the finest bloodlines are to be found in such far-flung places as Belgium, Finland, Holland, India, Italy, Korea, Japan, Mexico and South America, to name but a few. In Ireland, Scotland, Australia, New Zealand and South Africa the breed is fast becoming a well-recognized and popular addition to the world of dogs.

IRELAND

The popularity of the Pyrenean Mountain Dog in Ireland is certainly on the increase if one considers that twenty years ago there were but a dozen Pyreneans in the "Emerald Isle." Today the majority are family pets. Only a few Irish owners are actively engaged in breeding and showing Pyreneans.

Canine activities in Ireland come under two separate authorities. In the North the Kennel Club (England) guides the affairs, whereas in the South the Irish Kennel Club has jurisdiction.

Under Irish K.C. rules, Green Stars are awarded in place of Challenge Certificates. They have different point values according to the number of dogs presented for judging. To become a Champion, a dog must win sixteen points made up of at least one four-pointer or two three-pointers, the balance as they come.

The first Pyrenean known in Ireland was the dog "France," imported by Georgina McMahon in 1898. Vacationing in the High Pyrenees, Mrs. McMahon returned via England with her puppy dog—quite unaware that she was breaking the quarantine. However, the customs officials were said to have "turned a blind eye" (this would never be heard of today) and so she continued merrily to her destination in Dublin. At the age of seven, France was struck by pleurisy.

In 1932 Mr. and Mrs. Brown-Clayton of Carlow purchased two Pyrenees Mountain Dog puppies from Mme. Harper. The Claytons gave up the breed in 1940, possibly because of the difficulties imposed by World War II.

In 1951 the family of Brighid O'hEigeartaigh imported a puppy called Barcelona Brumas. On the death of his master he refused to eat and became so wasted that he had to be put to sleep. Having learned the wonders of owning (or being owned by) a Pyrenean, a new puppy, Xillian de Fontenay, was quickly acquired from Mme. Harper. He lived for twelve happy years as the family companion. On his passing the O'hEigeartaighs came to the aid of displaced Pyreneans and thus, over a twenty-five-year period, they must be ranked as the oldest Pyrenean family in Ireland.

Today's Irish Pyreneans trace their bloodlines to five imports of the late fifties: Yaan of Pondtail, Bergerie Bertha, Mount Louis Shepherdess, Laudley Yanason and Caruso de Fontenay.

Renee Millington of **Perenvay** Kennels is the leading Pyrenean breeder in Ireland. To her Ch. Vanessa of Perenvay goes the honor of being the first Irish-bred champion.

Mrs. Millington's foundation bitch, Ch. Clarissa de Bedous, bred by Mrs. Alcock out of Ch. Laudley La Nieve Blanche and Ch. Tartuffe of Oloron, was the first Pyrenean to win an International Championship. Clarissa's son, Ch. Perenvay Fincarra, sired by Bergerie Kennard, is the top-winning Irish Pyrenean with twenty-three Green Stars to his credit at the last counting. He is also the winner of two Bests in Show, including a Championship Show in 1974.

The top-winning bitch in Ireland is Ch. Perenvay Goolagong, owned by Mr. Michael Coad.

Lisblanc the Maverick, owned by Mr. and Mrs. Tonk and bred by Mrs. Sheila Ball, became the second English/Irish Champion, an honor he attained in 1975.

Other champions to make an impression on the show scene in Ireland include Croftside Centaur, Renean Atgos, Andres of Drumbuoy, Davdier O'Doda, Belinda of Siffin and most recently Pat Brown's Karlina of Perenvay.

SCOTLAND

The first reference to the Pyrenean Mountain Dog in Scotland is given by Robert Leighton, who, in *The New Book of the Dog*, tells of the use of Pyrenean blood to restore quality and strength among several breeds, with special reference to the Scottish Deerhound.

The next Pyrenean "influence" in Scotland must be credited to the activities of Lady Sybil Grant's Pyreneans in the 1920s.

Lady Sybil's family had an estate in Wester Ross. Ena Calvert tells us that to this day there are dogs in this area with many Pyrenean characteristics—obviously part descendants of Lady Sybil's early Pyreneans.

In 1948 Mme. Harper exhibited her dogs at the Championship Shows in Scotland. Miss Lockhart, a member of a well-known family in the linen trade in Kirkcaldy, Fife, owned a Pyrenean that is pictured carrying its mistress' golf clubs over its shoulder.

Little more is heard of the Pyrenean in Scotland until the late fifties. At this time Mr. and Mrs. Calvert started their famous **Braegaul** Kennels with their foundation bitch, Vivienne de Fontenay, purchased from Mme. Harper.

To complicate matters, the day after the Calverts arrived in Scotland, with Vivienne in full season, Mr. Calvert departed once more for England, leaving Mrs. Calvert in a sea of furniture and boxes to mate Vivienne with Ch. Colas of Hi-dene. Two months later Vivienne presented the Calverts with a litter of ten, from which they had their famous Ch. Braegaul Chicot, the first Scottish-bred Pyrenean to attain a championship.

At the Scottish Kennel Club's Championship Show the next year, Vivienne was benched among the Obedience dogs (apparently the organizers didn't quite know what to do with a Pyrenean). All day the Calverts listened to those passing remarks which are so familiar to owners of Pyreneans: "A white Saint Bernard," or "Alsatian" being the favorite speculations. Finally, a Mr. Know-It-All arrived and, with his head cocked quizzically to the side, declared to one and all, "Aye, that one's mother went a bit wrong. There's a fair mixture there." Mr. Calvert had to be forcibly restrained by his better half. Such an insult to his wonderful Pyrenean!

With only a few shows available in Scotland, the formation of a Scottish club was proposed. This actually came about when Margaret Cairns, a very good friend of Pyreneans, suddenly turned to Mrs. Calvert at the Championship Show in Edinburgh and said, "Ena, I will give you a hundred pounds if you can get a Scottish Pyrenean Club started!" The club was formally established in 1970.

Mrs. Calvert writes, "We now have quite a number of breeders, with well-known prefixes, including Mishow, Braegaul, Choucoune, and more recently Chendimer, Zilken, Millchase and Ashley. New blood has been

Irish Ch. Perenvay Fincarra, the top winning Irish Pyrenean, owned by Renee Millington.   *Courtesy I.G.P.R.*

Buckland Decius Brutus, owner, W. D. R. Calvert, Breagaul Kennels, Scotland.

Ch. Elegant Man of the Mountains owned by Ruth Nicholson, Australia, 1954.
                    Courtesy Ranee Van Eck

brought in from selected puppies from well-known bloodlines in England and Ireland, and every effort is made to encourage owners to breed dogs to the requirements of the standard and with excellent dispositions."

There can be little doubt that breeding in Ireland throughout the sixties was dominated by the dogs at Braegaul. Braegaul Zender, winner of a Scottish Challenge Certificate, is hale and hearty at 11½ years of age, sire of 217 Pyreneans at last counting. In addition to Zender, the Braegaul Kennels offer four dogs at stud: Buckland Decius Brutus, son of the renowned Ch. Pondtail Zborowski; Braegaul Gay Stuart, winner of Best in Show; Royal Apollo of Bergerie, a young dog already a leading winner in the show ring; and Braegaul Gaskiogne, also a Best in Show winner. There are thirteen bitches, including stock from Bergerie, Laudley, Millchase and de Fontenay.

The esprit de corps found in today's Scottish Pyrenean Club can be seen in the following passage, sent to us in 1974 by Mrs. Calvert:

> As we had a record number of Scottish dogs qualified for Crufts this year, the Scottish Pyrenean Club hired a private coach to convey our contingent 400 miles to Crufts, taking seats out so that the dogs had plenty of room. So it was a comfortable journey for all concerned. We were amply rewarded as, with the exception of one bitch, all the Scottish dogs were in the prize tickets. Our President had gifted bottles of champagne to be presented to any Scottish winning dogs and these were split in the coach. So it was a very, very happy, cheerful party on the way home!

The Calverts are past officers of the Scottish Pyrenean Club and the authors of an attractive booklet on the breed. Success of the breed in Scotland has been the result of a lot of hard work, not to mention the constant encouragement of new members to show and breed to a standard of perfection. Although both Mr. and Mrs. Calvert have, as they say, "reached their allotted span of three score years and ten," they still hope to keep Braegaul to the fore for many years to come.

AUSTRALIA

Pyrenean Mountain Dogs were first brought to Australia by an Irishman, Samuel Pratt Winter, who landed them at Portland, Victoria, on Monday, October 30, 1843. The dogs were shipped to Australia in the care of Winter's servant, Paddy Hickey. Little is known about these dogs other than they were named after rivers in the south of France and that Hickey "never could understand why His Honour called a dog 'a door' (Adour)." In Victoria, during the early 1850s, Winter used his Pyreneans in their traditional role, as Fetherstonhaugh related in his book *After Many Days*: "Winter told me that when the diggings broke out in 1851 and labour was not to be had, he put all his sheep into two flocks, and two magnificent [Pyrenean Mountain] dogs used to take the sheep out all day and look after them and keep them apart, and then at night these grand dogs used to sleep between the two flocks and guard them." In 1883 one of Winter's nephews visited Carrick, Tasmania, to inquire about a stone memorial erected by his uncle "in memory of a fine dog he had brought from the Pyrenees" but was informed that the only remaining piece of the memorial was in use as a hearthstone!

It was 1939 before the next Pyreneans were brought to Australia. Mrs. Gatehouse obtained her dogs Costaud de Fontenay and Comtesse de Fontenay from the then-leading kennel in England belonging to Mme. J. Harper Trois-Fontaines.

An important prefix in postwar years was **Chateau** belonging to Mr. and Mrs. K. Nicholson, who in the mid-fifties bred litters from Walwood, Magnolia and their own Chateau bitches using their striking dog Ch. L'Admiral de Fontenay (imported from Britain) and Mrs. K. A. Hart's Alamars Ambassador (imported from New Zealand). The late fifties saw a decline in Pyrenean numbers and throughout the sixties the occasional litter from the **Dunnellan** (Mr. and Mrs. H. J. Fullwood) and **Nidaros** (R. D. and E. G. Williams) kennels using imported dogs just managed to keep the breed extant in Victoria.

A resurgence of interest in the breed began in 1968 when the first of many litters with the **Andorra** prefix was whelped by Ranee Van Eck's Ch. Nidaros Pastourie. Subsequently the **Brean** prefix of Mrs. B. Luck, the **Sanitae** Kennels of Mr. E. Bright, and **Barreges** of Mrs. V. James were founded.

In the following years several other Pyrenean enthusiasts began breeding in Victoria and the breed was firmly established. The Van Ecks' U.K. imports, Ch. Briarghyll Kelso and Ch. Pyrillon Achernar of Briarghyll, a bitch, both became BIS winners. Many other BIS and Group winning Pyrs have followed.

Since the early seventies interest in the breed has spread to other areas of the country due to the efforts of Mr. and Mrs. R. J. Crago, Barbara Sharland, Mrs. J. Werner, Mr. and Mrs. R. Courtenay, Mr. and Mrs. Doughan, Mrs. Cartledge and many, many other devoted Pyrenean fanciers.

SWITZERLAND

The Great Pyrenees has long been known in Switzerland. Currently the major breeders are in the French-speaking areas and maintain close contact with French breeders. Mme. Fatio of **Chalethumbert** founded her line on Poeymayou and Comte de Foix. Mme. Chabloz of **Rocher de l'Aigle** obtained her foundation bitch from Mme. Fatio and has continued emphasizing Comte de Foix in her breeding program. She has produced two French National Specialty winners. Mme. Philipp of **Bois d'Ore** has also

Switzerland's leading sire Int/Fr/Swiss Ch. Atchoum du Rocher de l'Aigle, BOB at the 1987 French National Specialty, breeder-owner Michele Chabloz.

Patricia Princehouse

JAP/CAN Ch. Val-Fier du Duche de Savoie, owned by Mrs. Sakuramoto, shown winning BOB at the 1986 French National Specialty from the Young class, handled by breeder, Raymond Ducrey. After a brief sojourn in Canada, he continued on to Japan where he was BOB at the 1989 Japanese National Specialty.

Patricia Princehouse

One of the most recent imports of Tsutomu Wada.

had a great deal of success with her dogs, including taking the breed at the French Championship show in 1990.

BELGIUM

The breed was established in Belgium prior to the turn of the century and a number of Mrs. Crane's and Mme. Harper's early imports came from fine Belgian kennels. Today quality continues to be very high in Belgium. Henri Remy's **Griffe d'Ours** bloodline, based on Comte de Foix and Pontoise, is very prominent. Several of his dogs have taken top honors at French, Belgian and other European National Specialties and all-breed shows. Mr. Remy has exported breeding stock to numerous countries including the United States, Britain and Canada. The **Mas de Beauvoisin** Kennel of M. and Mme. Detollenaere is also very active in breeding and showing. M. and Mme. Perree of Pic de l'Astazou have had many winners and are working closely with Dr. and Mme. Giralt of Comte de Foix.

JAPAN

The Great Pyrenees is very popular in Japan. Much of its popularity is due to Ryoko Hayashida, Mrs. Sakuramoto, and Mr. and Mrs. Mochizuki. Primarily through the efforts of Mrs. Hayashida, the Great Pyrenees Club of Japan was founded in 1977.

At that time there were fewer than one thousand Great Pyrenees registered with the Japanese Kennel Club. By 1990 the total had reached nearly ten thousand. It is estimated that the number will continue to increase by approximately 10 percent a year.

Mrs. Hayashida has put in a great deal of hard work. The first step was to edit a club bulletin. Quickly realizing she needed more background information, she joined the breed clubs in France, Britain and the United States. Through a network of correspondents, she proceeded to assemble a library. Diligently combing the catalogs of in- and out-of-print books, she located de Bylandt's Encyclopedia, Senac-Lagrange's original monograph on the breed, the books of Mrs. Crane and Mme. Harper, and many others.

In 1981 the Japanese TV series "Jolie," based on the books of French writer Cecile Aubrey dealing with the adventures of a young boy, Sebastian, and his Pyrenees, Belle, provoked a public outcry for more information. In 1984 Mrs. Hayashida authored the first book in Japanese on the Great Pyrenees. It was an instant best-seller.

In 1986 Mrs. Hayashida journeyed to France and England and returned with a four-part video of the trip including shows, kennels, interviews with breeders and over one thousand color photographs. To say that

Ryoko knows the Pyrenees world is putting it mildly! When asked if she thought Japan would produce a national "type" as has happened in England and the United States, she responded: "We are enchanted more with the internal integrity of the breed rather than with its external beauty."

Great Pyrenees in Japan fall into five groups:

1. English imports from 1960 to 1970. These are generally big, strong, rather heavy dogs, often a bit weak in the rear.
2. Old California bloodlines imported in the late sixties. Not quite as large as the English dogs, sometimes lacking in pigment and elegance.
3. Karolaska dogs, 1970 to the present day, by far the largest group. Many are AKC champions. Rather small but usually sound and with the head, expression and gait we look for in a show dog. This writer saw Ch. Karolaska Bristol Bay in 1988 in Nagoya and found him undoubtedly one of the best in Japan at that time.
4. Dogs from other U.S. kennels: VilleVieux, Rivergrove, etc. Again, often U.S. champions. Ch. Rivergrove's Adored took Best Bitch at the 1989 National.
5. French imports. Mrs. Sakuramoto and other breeders have gone back to the source for their breeding stock. These French dogs usually excel in size, head and expression but often do not have the reach and drive one would like. French-bred Ch. Val-Fier du Duche de Savoie took Best of Breed at the 1988 National.

Considering the accomplishments of the past few years, it would appear the Japanese breeders have total success almost within their grasp. Perhaps a three-way combo: R-F-K Rivergrove-French-Karolaska?

NEW ZEALAND

Credit for the revitalization of the breed in New Zealand must be given almost exclusively to Mrs. Lynlie Watson of Tauranga and her **Del Aprisco** Kennels. As her first step, Mrs. Watson went to England and personally selected a promising daughter of Ch. Pondtail Zborowski as foundation matron for her kennel. This female, Cherryglen Elizabeth, quickly fulfilled her expectations by becoming New Zealand's first Pyrenean Champion.

In 1971 Cherryglen Elizabeth was bred to Carlos de Bellaire and gave the country its first pair of home-bred Pyrenees champions: Michelle and Candida del Aprisco.

In July 1972 Mrs. Watson added still another dimension to the New Zealand scene by importing from Mrs. M. Fielden the English dog Briarghyll Excelsior. Excelsior, sired by Ch. Pondtail Zborowski out of Ch. Briarghyll Lisblanc Fleur-de-Lys, won his championship in short order.

Ch. Freddy de Fontenay, the first South African import, with his grandson, in 1973. Owner, Denise Tudhope, Aylward Kennels.

The First Open South African Pyrenean Specialty, 1976. Pictured left to right: Sancho de La Neige bred by Ivan and Marie Cooper and owned and handled by Mrs. P. Robbins, BOS; judge Paul Strang; and Princesse Sur La Montagne, bred by M. Shana and owned and handled by Mr. Fuller-Peterson, BOB.

Doubling up on the Zborowski line, Mrs. Watson bred Ch. Excelsior to Ch. Cherryglen Elizabeth. This mating gave Mrs. Watson three more Champions: Benedict, Bastien and Bonita del Aprisco.

A number of recent imports to New Zealand include Andorra el Dorado, a de Fontenay-sired male owned by Karen Harrison; Notsuch Cassiopeia, a bitch obtained by Ms. D. Harris from Brenda Judson; Shiloonas Joanna and her little brother, Ronan (offspring of Ch. Lisblanc Christoph), owned by Betty Foster; and Briarghyll Paragon, a son of Meredydd-y-Myndd sent from England by Mrs. Fielden to Ann Downing.

The Pyrenean Mountain Dog Club of New Zealand was formed in 1972. Its aims are to popularize the breed, improve the standard of breeding and ensure the general welfare of the country's Pyrenean dogs.

SOUTH AFRICA

Denise Tudhope's successful introduction of the breed to South Africa, and her generous and unstinting devotion to its well-being, parallel to a striking degree the accomplishments of Mrs. Crane in America and Mme. Harper in England.

Mrs. Tudhope was born in France but emigrated to Africa before World War II to become a schoolteacher. Her posts were deep in the rugged interior of the veldt, where the ranchers required semiprivate instruction for their children. As a result she developed the extraordinary self-reliance that characterizes her personality today. Her school-teaching days are vividly portrayed in Eileen Bigland's novel *The Lake of the Royal Crocodiles* in which Denise is the Mademoiselle.

After marrying a South African and rearing a fine family of five children she was widowed and subsequently became involved with dogs.

Her first breeds were Saint Bernards and Bernese Mountain Dogs. One of her Saints became the leading show winner in South Africa. But always in the back of her mind was an early love affair with a Pyrenean bitch named Cora, her childhood playmate.

And so in 1967 Mrs. Tudhope made contact with Mme. Harper and imported her first pair of puppies, Freddy and Fidelia de Fontenay. The media had been alerted for this intriguing event and as a result press photographers and reporters gave the arrival of the puppies unprecedented coverage. Pictures and stories about the great white dogs appeared in dozens of South African newspapers and magazines. The Pyreneans had achieved instant fame, but a lot of hard work remained to be done.

As no Pyreneans had ever been shown in South Africa it took two years of constant effort. Dogs were shown all over the country; others were encouraged to show their puppies from Mrs. Tudhopes' **Aylward** Kennels; more dogs were imported for new owners; a Pyrenean Mountain

Dog Club was formed in April 1969. The breed was finally recognized and became eligible for the award of Championship Certificates.

Although Freddy de Fontenay had throughout this time collected nine CCs and nine Bests of Breed, they all counted for nothing. Mrs. Tudhope had to start again from scratch in order to make him the first Champion Pyrenean dog in Southern Africa.

As President of the Eastern Transvaal Pyrenean Mountain Dog Club, Mrs. Tudhope was a tireless correspondent, keeping in touch with overseas clubs and journals as well as leading breeders in England, France and America. She contacted isolated owners from Cape Town on the Indian Ocean to Salisbury in Rhodesia. More puppies and dogs were imported for interested fanciers from the kennels of Mme. Harper, Mrs. Pledge, Graham Alcock, Mrs. Prince Captain Grant Dalton and Sheila Ball in England; Ena Calvert in Scotland; and André Delattre in France. These imports, coupled with the puppies raised by South African breeders, led to a rapid increase in the country's numbers. The population grew from the two original imports in 1967 to 1,500 dogs in 1976. Mrs. Tudhope died in 1982, happy in the knowledge that she was leaving the breed in many capable hands.

Mr. and Mrs. G. Elliott of **Roy de Blicquy** imported their first breeding pair, Fidele and Fleur de Fontenay, from Mme. Harper in 1967, just a few months after Mrs. Tudhope's original pair came to South Africa. However, this pair had puppies first, making the Elliotts the breeders of the first litter born in South Africa.

Inge Briechle's **Du Chateau** kennel was founded in 1969 with a bitch from Mrs. Tudhope and a male imported from André Delattre of Pontoise in France. Always seeking to improve her bloodline, Mrs. Briechle has imported seven more Pyreneans from France, Britain, Germany and the United States. Her American import, Ch. Balibasque Teddy Bear du Chateau, bred by Bruce and Carolyn Hardy, proved himself an excellent producer as well as a top winner in his own right. Teddy Bear's son, Ch. Du Chateau Medici won the breed at the Goldfields Championship show in 1978 over an entry of ninety-two under American judge Mrs. Francis V. Crane. BOS went to Ch. Du Chateau Elvira, daughter of Inge's French import Souky de Pontoise du Chateau. Mrs. Briechle's famous Ch. Lisblanc The Xebed du Chateau, an English import bred by Mrs. Sheila Ball, had a stellar career with five BIS, eight Group Firsts, thirty BOB's and thirty-one CCs. Mrs. Briechle's two newest imports embody largely French Comte de Foix pedigrees. The newest champion, Ch. Du Chateau Reagan de Pomobali, a truly large dog standing 32 inches at the shoulder, is beginning to make a name for himself at the shows.

Peter and Joan Wilkins of **Pendragon** Kennels bought their foundation stud, Ch. Pendragon's Fairbanks of Aylward from Mrs. Tudhope in 1969. Over the years, Pendragon dogs have been an important influence on the breed in South Africa. Their current star is Ch. Pendragon Fingal.

Mrs. Gisele Zilberman emigrated to South Africa from France in the mid-seventies. She brought with her numerous Pyrenean Shepherds and also the magnificent Pyrenean Mountain Dog Lancelot du Comte de Foix. Lancelot sired several outstanding litters and is the grandfather of the lovely Ch. Castillo Jean-Marc, owned by Warren and Carol Trew of Johannesburg.

Ronnie Morrison's **Pardessus** Kennels made an impact on the breed throughout the eighties. Numerous Pardessus dogs have finished their championships, including the Best in Show winner, Ch. Pardessus Astre, who won the breed at the Natal Specialty in 1982 under judge Paul Strang. Ronnie's tireless pursuit of knowledge of the breed led her on a journey to the breed's homeland, France, in 1987. She was very proud to acquire her French-import stud dog, Ales du Duche de Savoie. Mrs. Morrison's tragic death in 1989 was a real loss to the breed in South Africa.

Bokara Kennel was established in 1976 by Geoff Jamieson and Mike Twoco of Johannesburg. They are enthusiastic supporters of the breed. Their Ch. Du Chateau Leonardo de Pomobali won the breed at the Transvaal championship show in 1984 under judge Mr. O. Honda of Japan.

De La Neige of Ivan and Marie Cooper was founded with the acquisition of Ch. Ramos de Pontoise from Mrs. Tudhope, who had imported him from M. Delattre. Their foundation bitches were Ch. Goya de Fontenay, and Blanche, a bitch imported from England by Mr. E. Von Gericke. Numerous champions have been produced including Sancho de La Neige, who won the breed at the first South African open Pyrenean Specialty under judge Paul Strang. De La Neige dogs have served as foundation stock for other breeders.

The **Basque** Kennels of Robin and Kathleen De Kock obtained Ch. Noble Seigneur de La Neige from the Coopers. This dog became the first South African-bred champion. He was sired by Ch. Freddy de Fontenay out of Ch. Goya de Fontenay, and proved himself a good producer for the De Kocks.

Elizabeth Raubenheimer's **Van Amstel** Kennel in Cape Town is well established. She has bred several champions including Ch. Royalton Mafuttah of Van Amstel, winner of thirteen CCs and twelve BOB's. Other notable kennels include **Craig Dune** of Mr. John Matthews, also in the Cape Town area; Mr. and Mrs. Douglas Pitchford's **High-Ercall** Kennels; **Cauterets** of Mr. and Mrs. J. Smith; and Ronnie Watts' **Montrachet** Kennel.

Mention must also be made of Ch. Larando, bred by W. C. K. Viljoen and owned and handled by J. J. Human. Larando is the first dual-champion Pyrenean—conformation and obedience—in the history of South Africa.

From the foregoing quick glance at the South African kennels we see that the best bloodlines of France, England and the United States are represented. Most of the dogs are big. Males average about 30 inches at the shoulder and bitches around 28. Type is generally excellent and the heads and expression reflect the true attributes of the breed. South Africa actively promotes x-raying to guard against hip dysplasia. More than 500 South African Pyreneans have been certified free of hip dysplasia.

14

Proper Care of the Great Pyrenees

EVERYONE WANTS a healthy, well-behaved Great Pyrenees which will live well into its teens. The well-behaved, healthy, long-lived Pyr is not simply a matter of good luck. There is much the owner can do to help.

For example, one of the easiest ways of preventing cancer is to spay or neuter at six months of age. The GPCA health information committee survey indicates that cancer is the leading cause of death among elderly Great Pyrenees, and cancer of the reproductive organs is the most common form. Spaying and neutering removes these organs, making it impossible for them to become cancerous later in life. If a pup is not a top breeding or show prospect, it should be neutered. Contrary to old wives' tales, spaying and neutering produce no effect on a dog's personality and will not make a dog fat. Overeating causes obesity, pure and simple.

Spaying and neutering also prevent accidental breedings which lead to unwanted puppies. Over 15 million unwanted dogs and puppies are euthanized every year at shelters across the country. Most are the result of accidental breedings. Most are first- and second-generation offspring of purebreds. Some 20 percent are themselves purebred, the products of "puppy mills," pet shops and kindhearted but ill-informed "backyard breeders."

CHOOSING A PUPPY

Pyrenees puppies are charming, disarming, adorable little teddy bears covered in white fluff. Impossible to resist. It is difficult to imagine the fifteen-pound fluff ball of seven weeks growing to one hundred pounds by seven months. But, be assured, it does happen. Choosing a puppy carefully is the best way of assuring that it's still going to be happy and healthy ten or more years later. Before buying, the reader is strongly urged to read the outstanding book *How to Raise a Puppy You Can Live With* by Neil and Rutherford (Alpine). This book explains all about the psychological stages in a puppy's life, how to choose and rear a well-adjusted pup, and how to avoid behavior problems before they happen. The best advice to the prospective puppy buyer is: Never, ever, buy a puppy on impulse. Do not buy the first pup you see. Do not even consider buying a pup at a pet shop.

Virtually all pet-shop puppies come from filthy, flea-ridden puppy farms where puppies are bred as a cash crop and receive no veterinary attention and no love or affection. Many well-intentioned souls will purchase a puppy from a pet shop in an effort to save the poor thing from its fate. Unfortunately, any sale at any price only encourages the pet shops and puppy millers to continue. In saving one, five others of the breed are condemned to endure the same miserable existence since the shop owners perceive a market for the breed and order additional pups, which prompts the breeding of additional litters. Also, pet shops almost always charge at least twice the price a reputable hobby breeder charges, and the pet-shop pup is usually of very poor quality.

One of the best ways to go about finding a healthy Great Pyrenees pup with a good temperament is to contact the American Kennel Club, 51 Madison Avenue, New York, NY 10010, and request the address of the current secretary of the Great Pyrenees Club of America. The secretary can provide you with a list of hobby breeders in your area and across the country. Such breeders are bound by the GPCA Code of Ethics, which requires that all breeding stock be x-rayed for hip dysplasia and that any genetic problems known to occur in the line be disclosed to the potential buyer prior to the sale, also that the buyer has two weeks to return the puppy for a full refund if any health problem or defect is found. The puppies must have been vaccinated and the buyer must be supplied with a four-generation pedigree. The spirit of the Code is that all puppies produced by all GPCA members must be healthy, physically and temperamentally sound, and honestly represented—preferably with a guarantee. Unfortunately, the Code is sometimes subject to "interpretation" or ignored altogether. Thus, while there is definitely a greatly increased likelihood of obtaining a good dog from a GPCA member, this is not a certainty. Therefore, the puppy purchaser must be forearmed with a list of questions to ask the breeder. If the answers do not check out, or sound odd or contradictory, DO NOT BUY THE PUPPY. There is no shortage of Pyr pups in this country. With a little patience a good, healthy pup can be found.

Ask about the pedigree. A good breeder knows the pedigree of his litter backward and forward because a great deal of planning has gone into producing the litter. He should be planning on keeping one of the pups as a show and breeding prospect. Both parents, and preferably the grandparents and great-grandparents as well, should be certified free of hip dysplasia (a crippling disease) by the Orthopedic Foundation for Animals (OFA) or a similar organization. At least one parent or grandparent should have an AKC championship or obedience title. The breeder should freely discuss with you issues such as longevity and temperament and problems such as dysplasia, subluxating patellas, PRA, OCD, epilepsy, bad bites, cancer, allergies, etc., and what he is doing to minimize or avoid them in his line. Beware the breeder who quickly assures you, "Oh, we don't have any health problems in this line." He is lying. All lines of all breeds have genetic health problems just as all human families have inherited health problems of one kind or another, be it cystic fibrosis or a tendency to arthritis. Some breeders discuss genetically based defects and do their best to avoid them. Breeders who refuse to admit they exist are usually ignoring them rather than avoiding them. Ask what steps have been taken to socialize the pups. Also ask for references—dogs this breeder has placed in your area. If the breeder lives far away, go visit some of these dogs. Speak with their owners to find out if they are happy and what difficulties they have had.

If you locate a good breeder in your area who has or is expecting puppies, make an appointment to visit well before the pups are old enough to take home. Meet the puppies' parents, at least the mother. Make sure she has the sort of temperament you want your Pyr to have. A litter of pups, no matter how young, is no excuse for the dam to be aggressive or unapproachable. She may not want you to touch the pups, but she should not show any aggression or fear just because you are in the room. The kennel should be clean and all other dogs there (presumably relatives) should look healthy and have good temperaments.

No puppy should leave its litter before seven weeks of age, otherwise it may not develop the proper body language necessary for communicating with other dogs. Similarly, if a pup remains with the litter past ten weeks, it may become too dog-oriented and have a harder time adjusting to its new household. If you are buying a pet puppy, the breeder may require you to sign a spay/neuter or nonbreeding agreement. This is normal. The price of a pet pup with such an agreement is usually around $300 to $500. Show pups should cost more, $600 and up. Whether you are buying a pet or a show prospect, the pup should be friendly and outgoing, and have bright eyes and a clean, healthy coat. Never buy a shy or droopy puppy.

If you are buying a show pup, be sure that the eyes are almond-shaped, the lips are tight, the bite is correct and that the pigmentation is completely filled in on the nose, lips and eyerims, and that rear double dewclaws are present. If it is a male, both testicles should be fully descended into the scrotum. Beyond these few measures, it takes considerable experience to discern how promising a pup is for the show ring. An honest breeder will point out the virtues and faults of each prospect. This is one of many reasons why choosing the right breeder is more important than trying to choose the best pup on your own.

CARE AND TRAINING

At the outset a few ground rules must be understood. A successful relationship between a Pyr and an owner is based on consistency. The owner must not allow a liberty one day and refuse it the next. If the 130-pound, shedding, muddy adult Pyr will not be allowed on the couch, then the ten-week-old adorable teddy bear must not be allowed on the couch either. Consistency leads to trust. A Great Pyrenees must never be struck— not with the hand, a newspaper, a stick, not with anything. The breed is very sensitive and independent. Harsh treatment will only alienate a Pyr, eventually making it impossible to train. Usually a few words are all that is needed to correct a Pyr for misbehavior. Severe correction should be given as a firm shake by the scruff of the neck or by rolling the dog over onto its back and staring it in the eye until it looks away, or by a jerk on the choke collar. Similarly, never, ever call a Pyr to you in order to punish it. This only succeeds in teaching the dog *not* to come. The Pyr is not a natural retriever. It has very little instinct to come when called. Coming must be reinforced with vast amounts of praise and petting and a frequent tidbit. If you feel that a dog must come when called because you are the master and it is the dog, then do not buy a Great Pyrenees. A Pyr will never learn to see the situation in that manner. A fence is absolutely necessary. The Pyr was bred to work over hundreds of acres. It will consider a backyard or even a fifty-acre estate to be quite small. However, most Pyrs are willing to accept a fence as a boundary, as long as they are not left there long enough to become bored.

Before the new puppy arrives, the owners should make every attempt to find a reputable trainer in the area who offers a socialization or "Kindergarten Puppy" class. Such a class allows the pup to continue to develop normal relations with other dogs through play sessions and introduces basic obedience commands in a positive, controlled setting. A good trainer can advise the owner on how to nip potential problems in the bud before they become serious. Remember, the puppy is learning constantly. If you aren't teaching it proper behavior, you're teaching it improper behavior whether you mean to or not. If a socialization class cannot be found, a conformation class for show dogs is a good idea. Even if you are not going to show the dog, the socialization and contact with knowledgeable dog owners is very

A promising youngster at five months. Note the excellent position of the ear, the root being set at the level of the eye. The "Shepherd's Crook" is also apparent.

Beautiful testimony to the results of good care and a loving home, Ch. Sunshine of Karolaska HOF/HOF, at eleven years of age with his BIS days behind him, all dressed up for Tracey Rappaport's wedding as a distinguished member of the wedding party.

beneficial. A regular obedience class is a possibility if intelligently instructed.

Before the puppy or adult Pyr comes home, the owner should acquire a number of useful items. A good pin or slicker brush and toenail clippers are essential. All Pyrs should be brushed and have their toenails trimmed, especially the dewclaws, once a week. Yes, that's once a week for the rest of its life. This is particularly important with puppies. If they acquire the habit of being groomed when small, no nail-cutting battles will ensue when the dog grows up. A thorough brushing and nail-trimming should take no more than half an hour. It promotes good behavior and familiarizes the owner with the dog's normal state. Problems such as ear infections, skin problems or lumps are much more likely to be noticed when the owner follows a routine of weekly brushing.

When the dog is healthy and regularly brushed, baths become largely unnecessary. A good bath every six months is all that is needed for most Pyrs. Be on the lookout for fleas, especially around the base of the tail. At the first sign, dip the dog and any other dogs and cats in the household in flea dip and fog the entire house. The dip and foggers should be obtained from the vet, not the grocery store.

Of course, always make sure your Pyr is up to date on its vaccinations and during the summer, maintain a program of heartworm preventative pills such as Ivermectin. Daily toothbrushing is highly recommended. The veterinarian can clean his teeth every few years but this does not help the way regular brushing does. Feeding a quality food bought from the vet or at the feed store or pet shop, rather than the grocery store brands, is very important to good health. Per pound, puppies eat several times more than adult Pyrs and need lots of fresh water. It is very important that the adult Pyr remain slim. Its metabolism makes it a very light eater for its size. Do not overfeed. Feeding a quality food in the right amount can add years to a Pyr's life.

Another essential item is a dog crate, to be used as a bed at night and when a puppy cannot be closely monitored. As descendants of wolves, dogs like a den they can call their own. The crate is made of metal or durable plastic (airline crate). When properly used it is an enormous aid in housebreaking. A puppy will not soil its bed. So the pup learns patience and self-control in a positive setting. It is always praised when put into the crate. The crate must never be used as punishment. When removed from the crate the pup is carried outside to relieve itself. Accidents are not given a chance to happen. Gradually the pup learns the rules of the house. With the proper use of a crate, a Pyr pup can be successfully housebroken with one to three accidents.

Similar to the idea of a playpen, the crate is used to keep the pup out of trouble when no one has time to watch it. This keeps the Pyr from acquiring the habit of chewing its owner's belongings. The owner can leave the house without fear of returning to the shredded remains of what was once the couch or an expensive pair of shoes. Pyrs quickly learn that they can go to their crates when they want to take a nap or have a moment to themselves, away from boisterous children or other pets. Taking the crate when traveling means the dog always has its own usual bed. This is enormously comforting to a Pyr. Many hotels will accept dogs only with crates. More detailed instructions on the use of crates and on obedience training can be found in the earlier mentioned book by Neil and Rutherford, and in *Mother Knows Best: The Natural Way to Train Your Dog* by Carol Benjamin (Howell), and *Dog Training Made Easy* by Michael Tucker (Howell).

It is best to give the Pyr toys of its own—dog toys, not old shoes. The dog cannot tell old shoes from new and will not understand when it is encouraged to chew up one shoe, then punished for chewing up another. Never play tug-of-war with a Pyr. This encourages aggression and one-on-one competition with humans—very undesirable traits in a giant dog.

A puppy needs to learn to walk properly on a lead. To accomplish this a buckle collar should be placed on its neck whenever it is out of its crate. Collars should never be left on a crated dog as they can become caught on something and choke the dog. The pup will scratch at the collar for a while, from a few minutes to a few days, depending on the pup.

When it feels totally comfortable with the collar, a light lead, four to six feet long, can be attached to the collar. This is best started in the house or garage where there are fewer distractions than outdoors. Do not pull on the lead; the Pyr's reaction will be to pull in the opposite direction. Instead, use praise, toys and tidbits (professionally referred to as "bait") to encourage the pup to walk with you. Continue this for several days.

Eventually you can give small tugs on the lead to let the pup know it is attached. Never attempt to pull the pup along. Dragging will get you nowhere. When you have succeeded in teaching the pup that good things happen when the lead is on and it follows you, you can introduce changes in direction. Turn to the right or left and if the pup doesn't turn with you, let it get almost to the end of the lead and give a gentle but extremely quick tug and immediately release. This should get its attention. Immediately praise and call the pup to you. Two or three sessions a day of no more than five minutes each should result in the pup being reliably lead broken within a week or two. This method is slower than dragging the puppy around but results in better control and a more confident pup that is much more likely to be receptive to further training.

The puppy's personality is formed during the first six months of its life. It is essential that it be exposed to as many friendly people and new situations as possible throughout that first six months. This socialization is necessary so that it will learn what sort of behavior to expect from normal, everyday people. As a natural guard dog, the Pyr regards unusual behavior as suspicious. Thus, it is important that it have a good idea what normal behavior consists of, that it can better discern someone who is up to no good. A well-socialized pup becomes a trustworthy, sensitive and self-confident adult.

OLD AGE

After seven the Pyr slowly starts to show its age. It may have a bit of arthritis. It may enjoy long afternoon naps. However, it will still enjoy a good, long walk. The more you can walk it, the healthier it will be. It is not just the exercise but the camaraderie that it will appreciate.

The aging Pyr will need less food and its diet should be no more than 5 percent fat. High-quality brands of dog food usually have a line of less active, diet or senior food. This can be canned or dry. If the elderly Pyr has trouble digesting or seems to have stomach trouble, canned food usually helps. Rawhide and other chewables which it relished in its youth may become difficult or impossible for its old teeth to manage and are best left off the shopping list.

The Great Pyrenees is among the longest-lived of the giant breeds. Many make it well past ten, some into their teens. One Pyr is reported to have lived over eighteen years. However, heartbeaking as it is, eventually the time does comes. Then we look back through the years and remember the happy moments we shared with our wonderful friend.

SOME DO'S AND DON'TS

DO find a reliable veterinarian and take your Pyr in for regular checkups. Don't hesitate to call your vet if your Pyr seems under the weather. Pyrs are very stoic and don't usually show signs of distress until seriously ill. Worm only at the direction of your vet with products supplied by him/her. Keep all vaccinations current. Maintain a regimen of heartworm prevention under the direction of your vet.

DO register your dog with AKC. Have an identifying tattoo administered, usually your social security number. These measures will prevent any disagreement about ownership and will help ensure its safe return if lost.

DO take your Pyr to obedience class. It is an excellent outing for the dog and you might just learn something yourself.

DO teach your children to respect the puppy. This is excellent training for children, as well as necessary for the dog's peace of mind.

DO provide plenty of fresh water at all times.

DO give plenty of daily exercise. This assures its good health and can add years to its life.

DON'T force your Pyr to take strenuous exercise in hot weather. This can lead to heat stroke.

DON'T clip your Pyr's coat in the summer. This ruins the coat and exposes the skin to sunburn.

DON'T chain or tie the dog. This leads to barking, digging, destructive behavior, aggression, poor health and poor physical development. Either put up a fence or don't buy a Great Pyrenees.

DON'T remove the dewclaws, especially if you want to show.

DON'T leave a choke collar on your Pyr.

A well-behaved Great Pyrenees is a source of pride and joy, a tremendous asset to any family and a notable deterrent to any would-be thief or vandal. It instinctively feels that its home and family are the center of the universe and that it is duly-bound to guard and protect them against all trespassers. All the hard work, kindness and affection which you show to your puppy will return to you measure for measure, with love and devotion, in the years that follow.

Ch. Rivergrove's For Your Eyes Only, obviously enjoying good health. *Lucy Zorr*

15

Health Problems

by Robert Brown, D.V.M.

and Patricia Princehouse

AN IDIOSYNCRASY in the Great Pyrenees breed is a rolling cephalic vein on the front legs. This fact is important since these veins are the usual site for intravascular injections. Intravenous anesthesia, one type of antiparasitical and arsenic for treatment of heartworm infection, are among the preparations given through this vein. Many preparations will cause a severe tissue reaction if inadvertently injected outside the vein. The cephalic vein must be trapped and held until a needle can be inserted well into its lumen.

The Great Pyrenees has a lower metabolic rate than many other breeds. Adult nutritional requirements are considerably less than one would estimate on the weight of the dog alone. The body temperature may be 100° instead of the usual 101.5°. The lower metabolic rate is reflected in a typically easygoing manner.

Generally, the Great Pyrenees will require a surprisingly small amount of sedative and anesthetic. This phenomenon may be due, in part, to the fact that Pyr weight is often "guestimated." A second factor is their lower metabolic rate which requires less drug to achieve the same end. As a rule of thumb, I figure half of the usual dosage as determined for the weight of a dog, and then if the desired plane of anesthesia has not been achieved, more anesthesia can be given to effect.

Many veterinarians do not have a scale that can accurately weigh a dog over one hundred pounds and will ask you what your dog weighs. I find that Great Pyrenees owners usually overestimate the weight of their dogs by about thirty-five pounds. Make it a practice to take your Pyr to a freight scale or a farm elevator that has a high-capacity scale and weigh him accurately. It may save the dog's life.

Heartworms are becoming an increasing source of morbidity among dogs in the United States. The Pyrenees is no exception, being as susceptible as other breeds. In some communities, 30 percent of the dog population is infected. Heartworms are found in all states in the southern zone and as far north as Minnesota and Maine. In areas where the disease may be endemic, routine blood studies should be made twice yearly to identify Pyrs harboring the disease.

Heartworm preventives (Ivermectin, Caracide, Sterid-Caracide) are 100 percent effective when used as directed. They should be started before the mosquito season and continued beyond the first frost. In southern climates, the preventive should be given year-round. The dosage is given according to the weight of the dog. These compounds may safely be given to older puppies.

Great Pyrenees are very susceptible to heat stroke. This almost always occurs because someone has forgotten the animal and left it enclosed in a car parked directly in the sun. In summer, a Pyrenees should always be transported in open wire crates so that the windows of the car can be rolled down completely. Always park in the shade and return often to check on the dog and be sure the car remains shaded.

A Pyrenees' food intake should be reduced in hot weather and it should be given plenty of fresh water at all times. This breed requires more water than do most others. A Pyrenees should never be forced to take vigorous exercise during the heat of the day.

THE LAME DOG

A Pyrenees that suddenly begins to favor one of its legs may be suffering from a minor sprain, a pulled muscle or a tendonitis. Such minor injuries are not uncommon in the active dog. Usually, with moderate rest and restriction, the dog will recover.

On the other hand, a serious limp in a Great Pyrenees, especially one which appears during the first year of its life and doesn't clear spontaneously, may be due to one of several conditions of a more serious nature. In the differential diagnosis, one would need to consider whether the limp involves one or more extremities, and whether it involves the front or the rear.

Front limps may be due to osteochondritis dessicans, elbow dysplasia, or panosteitis. Rear-end limps are commonly due to canine hip dysplasia, the hyperextension syndrome (popping hocks), osteochondritis dessicans and panosteitis. If, after a careful veterinary examination, one of these conditions is found to be the cause, the animal should be considered unacceptable for stud work or breeding. With the possible exception of popping hocks, all of these conditions have a hereditary basis and affected animals can pass them along to their offspring.

Canine Hip Dysplasia is the most important of these conditions because there is no satisfactory treatment for the badly crippled animal. In addition, the disease is not uncommon in the breed, with certain bloodlines showing a high incidence of clinical and radiological involvement. Currently, 15 percent of Pyrenees' x-rays sent to the Orthopedic Foundation of America are read as showing various grades of dysplasia. This does not reflect the true incidence, since the x-rays are screened by local veterinarians before they are submitted.

Hip dysplasia is moderately heritable. It depends upon a combination of genes. Although afflicted dogs do not always throw dysplastic puppies, the disease, once established in the bloodline, reappears often enough to warrant strong measures to see that it is eliminated completely.

The problem resides in the structure of the hip joint. The head of the femur should sit solidly in the cup *(acetabulum)* of the pelvis. Loose ligaments allow the head to work loose, or begin to "subluxate." A shallow acetabulum also predisposes to joint laxity. Finally, the mass or tone of the musculature around the joint socket is an important determinant.

Tight ligaments, a broad pelvis with a well-cupped acetabulum and a good ratio of muscle mass to size of bone, are all factors which predispose to good hips. The reverse is true of animals who are likely to develop the disease. Environmental factors, including the weight of the puppy, and joint stress, all figure into the final outcome.

The first signs usually appear during a period of rapid growth (four to nine months), during which time the Pyrenees puppy may show pain in the hip, walk with a limp or swaying gait, bunnyhop when it runs and show difficulty getting up on its hind legs. Once established, the disease usually progresses. Radiographically, hip joints grow worse with time.

Properly taken x-rays are essential to the diagnosis. Usually this is done under sedation or general anesthesia. The OFA currently certifies dogs who are twenty-four months of age, or older.

Some veterinarians claim to be able to tell whether a puppy is going to be dysplastic by palpation, which is an attempt to subluxate the hip joints of the anesthetized animal. This would appear to correlate mainly with joint laxity; and it must be remembered that by no means do all Pyrenees with joint laxity become dysplastic.

The incidence of canine hip dysplasia can be controlled by carefully selecting and using only breeding stock known to be free of the problem. It is to the advantage of the buyer to investigate the records of the bloodlines in question and to come to an understanding with the breeder about any warranties covering dysplasia. This should be done before the puppy is purchased.

Elbow Dysplasia, or ununited anconeal process, is uncommon. This process normally fuses with the ulna bone by four months of age. If it doesn't, the result is lameness in the front leg, a characteristic deviation, and instability of the joint by palpation. Surgical removal of the ununited process alleviates the lameness.

Osteochondritis Dessicans (O.D.) is more common in the shoulder joint but may be found in the stifle joint also. Ordinarily, young males are the ones affected. The condition is due to an injury to the cartilage overlying the head of one of the long bones. A puppy that jumps off a high perch might sustain such an injury. The tendency for cartilage to be easily damaged is based on hereditary factors. The condition can be treated by total cage rest, or if not successful, by surgical removal of the damaged cartilage.

Eosinophilic Panosteitis ("growing pains," "wandering lameness") is a rare condition which has recently been found to affect Great Pyrenees. Various degrees of lameness appear in one leg and can, from time to time, shift from one leg to another. Males over six months of age are the ones usually affected. The disease is accompanied by fever, joint inflammation, muscle wasting and unthriftiness. Anti-inflammatory drugs are usually prescribed. The etiology is unknown but there may be a tendency for the disease to run in some bloodlines.

Popping Hocks ("slipping hocks," the hyperextension syndrome) is a condition which is accompanied by laxity of the supporting structures around the hock joints. The result is that the hock "slips out of place," either forward or to the side, when the joint is extended. Pyr pups who are repeatedly allowed to jump up on their hind legs, with their front feet on people or a fence, could potentially stretch the ligaments and tendons which stabilize the hock joint. An underlying weakness of these structures may be a contributing cause also. It is usually observed in pups from four weeks to six months of age, and is more common among animals with very straight rear-end angulation. Proper early immobilization may possibly reverse the condition in young pups.

BONE CANCER

Osteogenic sarcoma is the most common form of cancer in Great Pyrenees. It ordinarily affects the long bones. While it can strike at any age, it is usually a disease of the middle years. Unfortunately, by the time the Pyr exhibits lameness or swelling in the area of the cancer, it is too late to treat. This form of cancer spreads early and to the lungs.

SKIN DISORDERS

Beneath his heavy coat, the Great Pyrenees actually has a sensitive skin. A few guidelines will help to keep it as healthy as possible.

Do not clip or shave a Pyrenees in the summer as it will easily sunburn.

Since our breed possesses a double coat, when the soft woolly undercoat dies and starts to loosen, it should be removed. A dead undercoat is irritating to the skin and can start a bad case of acute moist dermatitis ("hot spots"). Hot spots are always indicative of some underlying problem. Other causes are fleas, and ear and anal gland infections.

White-coated breeds are somewhat more disposed to develop skin allergies. Various soaps and chemicals applied to the coat, as well as food allergens, may cause an atopic dermatitis. The use of allergy testing may be necessary to determine the cause. Pyrenees should be bathed only with appropriate dog shampoos—*never* shampoos used on people.

A Pyrenees that scratches itself for any reason may abrade its skin and convert a hot spot or skin allergy into a secondarily infected bacterial dermatitis. This can be a serious problem. Medical consultation should be sought rather than treating such a disorder with patent preparations.

Being a long-coated breed does not necessarily protect the Great Pyrenees from demodectic mange. This can be diagnosed by skin scrapings and treated accordingly.

EYE PROBLEMS

Some strains of Great Pyrenees exhibit a condition in which the eyelashes of one or both lids turn inward and scratch the cornea *(entropion)*. If the irritation is severe, the dog will tear excessively, as indicated by a reddish-brown discoloration at the inner corner of its eye. Tearing, of course, can also be due to mild forms of allergic conjunctivitis and contagious infections.

A Pyrenees with excessively loose lids will exhibit the opposite condition *(ectropion)*. This is characteristic of Pyrs with coarse heads and heavy flews which pull the lower lids away from the globes.

If either condition is found to run in bloodlines (it is hereditary) the animal should not be used for breeding. Cosmetic surgery will correct both disorders. Of course, this eliminates the dog from dog show competition.

THE BITE

A number of undesirable dental problems can appear in the Pyrenean. The *overshot mouth* (parrot jaw) appears in very young puppies. An animal with an overshot bite has a great deal of difficulty in grasping food with its incisors since they don't line up in correct apposition. An overshot bite may improve as the animal grows; but if it hasn't done so by eight months of age, it's unlikely it ever will.

The *undershot mouth* is a more severe malocclusion problem since the teeth wear abnormally, especially the canines. A pup may have a normal bite until it is three months old, and then could begin to "go under." If proper preventative measures are started at the earliest sign of deviation (at twelve weeks), the condition can be corrected. While the overshot mouth in an adult is definitely hereditary, the undershot mouth *may* be hereditary, or it may be due to the breeding of two strains of Pyrenees with different muzzle lengths.

The *wry mouth* is the worst of the malocclusion problems. In this situation the teeth on one side of the mouth are in a different plane from the same teeth on the other side. In simple terms, the jaw is crooked. A bitch with this condition has a hard time severing umbilical cords properly, and subsequently licking newborns in the usual aftercare. Great Pyrenees with this condition will be severely penalized in the show ring.

All Pyrenees with dental malocclusion problems should be eliminated from breeding programs.

Pyrenees cut their baby teeth more rapidly than smaller breeds. In the majority of cases, the replacement of teeth occurs quite naturally and never comes to the owner's notice. Occasionally, a milk tooth does not fall out. This can deflect a permanent tooth or even cause a double row of teeth. It should be watched closely. If it exists at four months of age, an extraction may become necessary.

THE ANAL GLANDS

These are two secretory sacs, analogous to the scent glands of the skunk, which are located on each side of the anus. They are normally emptied by activity, or during a bowel movement. However, on occasion these glands may become impacted. Usually, a Pyrenees that rubs its bottom on the ground, or that scoots, is having an anal gland problem. Chewing at the base of its tail may be a sign of infection. If impaction of secretion is suspected, the anal sacs should be examined. It is a good idea to check these each time the dog is groomed or bathed.

GPCA HEALTH INFORMATION COMMITTEE

The Great Pyrenees is a hardy breed. Pyrs are generally healthier and longer-lived than most other giant breeds. However, all dogs, mixed-breed or purebred, are subject to genetic defects and other health problems. One advantage of owning a purebred dog is that individual breeds have groups of people who care about and study the health problems which most frequently affect that breed. Thus, in communication with other people who care about the breed, one can better predict what sort of problems an individual Great Pyrenees may have, spot warning signs earlier and quickly obtain information on how best to handle the problem.

The Great Pyrenees Club of America maintains a standing committee called the Health Information Committee. The purpose of this committee is to discern the most important health problems affecting the Great Pyrenees and educate club members, breeders and the rest of the Pyr-owning public about the nature of these problems and how best to avoid and/or treat them.

The committee frequently conducts surveys of Great Pyrenees owners and breeders concerning the strengths and weaknesses of their dogs' health. A major survey is currently under way. The results of this survey will be analyzed, both statistically and with common sense, to reveal the most important health problems found in the Great Pyrenees breed. The GPCA will then grant funding to veterinary researchers familiar with these problems to study them as they relate specifically to Great Pyrenees. All information obtained in the survey is kept strictly confidential. Access to names and pedigrees is restricted to the owner and breeder of the dog concerned.

Preliminary survey results are very encouraging about the state of the breed's health. Sixty percent of owners have reported their dogs' health to be excellent. Another 31 percent were good or average. Only 6 percent of the dogs were reported as having poor health. Most owners reported that their Pyrs died of "old age." The average Pyr lived more than ten years. The oldest reported Pyr was sixteen when it died.

So far, the surveys reveal that the leading cause of death in Great Pyrenees is cancer. Fourteen percent of Pyrs are reported to have had cancer. By far the most common types of cancer were (1) cancer of the reproductive organs and (2) bone cancer. A fifth of all cancers are those of the reproductive organs (uterus, mammary glands, testes). It is important to realize that these cancers would have been prevented by spaying or neutering early in life. Forty percent of Pyrs are reported to have chronic health problems. About 90 percent of these chronic problems were ear infections, skin problems and allergies.

Several health problems which have been known to affect Great Pyrenees are discussed by Dr. Brown earlier in this chapter. These include anesthesia sensitivity, heat stroke, osteochondritis dessicans, hip dysplasia, elbow dysplasia, panosteitis, popping hocks, cancer, skin allergies, demodectic mange, entropion, ectropion, bad bites and anal gland problems. In addition to these, Health Information Committee surveys have reported cases of bloat (gastric torsion), subluxating patellae (chronic dislocation of the kneecaps), achondroplastic dwarfism (and possibly other kinds of dwarfism), thyroid deficiencies, allergies and other immune system problems, idiopathic epilepsy, heart malformations, liver and kidney failure, stroke, chronic arthritis, pancreatitis, chronic urinary infections, benign tumors and cysts, and other disorders.

This list is not printed here to frighten anyone. It is here merely to encourage open communication about these problems. Some are quite rare in the breed. The hope is to keep them rare. Others are more common than one would like (indeed, a single case is more than one would like). The hope is to reduce or eliminate them.

Prospective Great Pyrenees buyers are encouraged to discuss potential health defects when speaking with breeders. The GPCA Code of Ethics requires breeders to inform buyers about known hereditary defects in their bloodlines. The Code also requires breeders to x-ray their breeding stock for hip dysplasia and make the results known to buyers.

Some breeders offer health guarantees of various sorts. The value of such documents is highly variable, ranging from excellent to "not worth the paper they are written on." Their worth is directly related to the integrity of the breeder. These agreements usually spell out what problems are covered and what sort of compensation the breeder will offer the buyer if a health problem occurs. The GPCA Code of Ethics recommends:

> . . . written contractual proof of sales and guarantees. No promise shall be made orally which is not later put into writing. . . . It is the ethical obligation of member-breeders to guarantee pups produced and sold by them to be as represented. Any replacement or refund arrangement agreed to by breeder and buyer, and just to the interests of both parties shall be considered satisfactory. It is understood, however, that any dog that dies or must be destroyed before the age of 15 months due to physical or temperamental conditions which are hereditary, shall be replaced one for one, or if this is not possible, the full purchase price shall be refunded.

Do remember, however, that buying a dog from a caring, responsible breeder does not absolutely guarantee that the dog will not have any health problems. Breeders are not infallible. Ideally, all they can do is educate themselves, try their best and hope for good results. When a problem arises, it should be dealt with honestly by both breeder and owner. The GPCA Health Information Committee seeks, through education, to help Great Pyrenees breeders and owners raise the healthiest Pyrs they can.

16

Showing Your Great Pyrenees

by Mary W. A. Crane

LET ME SAY right at the outset that showing is *hard work*. If you are not prepared to take the time to train your dog, right from the start, in good manners, etiquette and behavior in the ring; if you are not willing to spend the hours on the grooming; if you are of a disposition that cannot stand *disappointment* when you lose (and *no dog* will ever win all the time); and if you are too sensitive to take fault-finding and gossip—then, but only then, *Don't think of showing your dog.* For unfortunately, all these things are bound to happen to you, first or last, in the dog-show game.

Competition can be harsh. Feelings can rise to the surface and words or looks can seem to convey disapproval, criticism and even ill-will among competitors. A loss today for the same dog that won only yesterday calls for a broad philosophical outlook, as well as faith and devotion to the dog, and an optimistic hope for the future! This observation is true with *all* breeds—it is not meant as a criticism of Great Pyrenees' owners alone, of course.

Now that we have eliminated the weak at heart, let us proceed with the positive, brave souls who have the great desire to show their dog. We shall assume, therefore, that you have trained it from puppyhood to *walk* freely on a leash; to let people handle it and feel it all over; and to learn not to shy away from or fear the presence of other dogs nearby.

Before you consider taking the fatal step, I earnestly suggest that you

AM/CAN Ch. Poco Pyrs King Crusher HOF/HOF, outstanding sire and showdog. Breeder: Vic and Sue Capone. Owner: Jean Boyd.

William Gilbert

Ch. Quibbletown Cavalier HOF/HOF, outstanding sire and showdog. Breeder: Mr. and Mrs. C. Seaver Smith, Jr. Owner: Mr. and Mrs. Charles McConnell.

Ch. Quibbletown Jim Dandy HOF/HOF, outstanding sire and showdog. Breeder-owner Mr. and Mrs. C. Seaver Smith, Jr.

Ch. Soleil Pierre de Blu Crest HOF/HOF, outstanding sire and showdog. Breeder: Mr. and Mrs. Jack Magoffin. Owner: Vic and Sue Capone.

Sonya Larsen

attend at least one dog show to observe the procedure and see how it appeals to you. If, having been subjected to it, you have caught the bug, I then suggest that you take your puppy to a *match show* in your vicinity. These are often called *sanctioned matches*. They are informal and instructive, often being more in the nature of picnic get-togethers. One can usually find side classes for all sorts of humorous points from costumes to "the most endearing puppy," to cart pulling, and others. While held under Kennel Club rules, they remain informal in every respect and do not count for championship points.

At these matches you will have the opportunity to meet other "doggy people," although not necessarily in the Great Pyrenees breed. They, in turn, can advise you how and where to write the show superintendents for listings and entry blanks, Notice particularly the closing date for entries. They close well in advance of the actual day of the show. You alone are responsible for getting your entry in on time. This is step number one. Now you are ready to enter a championship show.

If your dog is a puppy (under one year of age), enter in the *Puppy Class*. If it is over one year, but purely a novice and born and bred in the United States, I would suggest the *American-Bred Class. Open* is usually considered the class for older and more experienced dogs.

Assuming that your dog is now entered, proceed to step number two. This is to groom well, so that when you appear in the ring you will have a dog of which you can be justifiably proud. A dog clean and white, well brushed, with whiskers and eyebrows trimmed and with the excess hair around the dewclaws and back of the leg from hock to pad, as well as around the perimeter of the foot, trimmed to a neat line. (This is purely in the interest of tidiness.)

I might add that your own appearance should be one of neatness, good grooming and conservatism in dress. In this you will complement your dog to the fullest!

Step number three is to have your entry on a suitable leash attached to a loose choke collar. The collar should be applied so that the weight of the chain slackens the loop when the lead is held loosely. One keeps the dog alert, and attentive to one's commands, through gentle but firm tugs on the leash, and under control at all times. Do *not* "string" your dog up too tight under the chin as this forces its ears too high and alters its expression. Always move the dog in the ring on a loose leash.

Having your dog thus prepared for its ring debut, be sure that you are at ringside well before the designated time to enter the ring. This is wholly the responsibility of the exhibitor. You will be given an armband by the ring steward which is your designated number for this show and is so recorded in the judge's book. The judge is not allowed to see a show catalogue before judging, so neither you nor your dog is known in advance.

Now is the time for you to collect yourself, for when your class and number are called you must walk into the ring. Always remember that the

Ch. Tip 'N Chip Sonny's L'Air HOF/HOF, outstanding dam and showdog. Breeder: Paul Turner. Owner: Jean Boyd.

Booth

Ch. Tip 'N Chip Sonny's Reflection HOF/HOF, outstanding sire and showdog. Breeder-owner Judith Bankus-Cooper.

Ch. Elysee Eve HOF, outstanding dam. Breeder: Dr. and Mrs. James Giffin. Owner: Dr. and Mrs. Robert Brown.

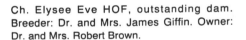

Ch. Tip 'N Chip Sonny's Side Up HOF/HOF, outstanding sire and showdog. Breeder: Judith Cooper. Owner: Merry Hauff. *Schley*

Ch. Karolaska Captivator HOF/HOF, outstanding sire and showdog. Breeder: Carol Kentopp. Owner: Mr. and Mrs. Joseph Gentzel.

Ch. Karolaska Puffin HOF, outstanding dam. Breeder: Carol Kentopp. Owner: Carol Kentopp and Elli Pasicznyk.

Roberts

Ch. Karolaska Glacier HOF, outstanding sire. Breeder: Carol Kentopp. Owner: Edith Smith.   *Gilbert*

best help you can give your dog is assurance of your faith in it. Convey this confidence to it by a kindly pat. But if your hand is shaking and you are continually fussing over it, resetting its legs, etc., you are only going to make it react nervously as well. This is also annoying to the judge who, wherever he may be, is always conscious of movement in the ring.

Now a word about "baiting" your dog to get an alert expression. Even professional handlers, on occasion, can overdo this gesture. It consists of holding a tempting morsel, a bit of cooked liver, in front of the dog's nose just out of its reach. A handler knows when to lower or remove it for the judge to examine the dog's expression. In a Pyrenees, *expression is very important*. It consists of a tight-lipped mouth with an even bite, a strong, rather lengthy and adequate muzzle, slanted oblique eyes, a medium ear set on a level with the eyes, and a broad flat skull. All too frequently the novice exhibitor does not know when to remove the bait, thus keeping the dog off balance and continually stretching out to grab the morsel. This can prevent the judge from properly appraising the animal's head.

Ring procedure is usually pretty stylized. The entries are first moved around the ring, counterclockwise, one behind the other. As they line up, the judge looks them over in a general way and then goes over each dog individually for conformation points (and this is a detailed examination from the mouth to the tail and dewclaws). Each exhibitor is then asked to move the dog up and down in a straight line on a loose lead, often both at a trot and a *walk*. Nothing shows up gait—its action and faults—more quickly than a walk. As the dog approaches the judge it is asked to stop and stand just as it is for the judge's inspection. After these examinations have been completed, the dogs are posed again, one behind the other, while the judge picks the winners down to fourth place (if the class is large enough to boast that many entries).

WHAT THE JUDGE IS LOOKING FOR

Since there has been considerable interest in the matter of what constitutes a good gait, a few words from the judge's viewpoint may be timely. As the entries move about the ring, the judge is watching the reach of the legs, both fore and aft, to see that they are of good length and stride, looking at the topline, especially at the withers, to see if it bobs up or down, or remains smooth and level as it should. When the dog moves straight away and back on a loose leash, it is to see if the dog travels straight and true in front, or whether the dog is "out at the shoulder," is throwing its legs or feet inward or outward instead of straight ahead, or raising them in a hackney gait. From the rear the judge looks to see if the legs and feet toe-out (implying cow hocks), inward (bowed legs), move too narrowly or too widely (faulty structure), or whether the stride is true and straight ahead at a walk while converging toward the center line as speed increases. When a dog is told to stand naturally its leg structure shows immediately. The front legs should be straight. The stance behind should be well angulated and wide with feet pointing straight ahead, the weight evenly distributed. Movement and stance, as described, often reveal the presence of hip dysplasia, certainly when of a severe nature, and other anatomical faults as well.

The judge will prefer the well-balanced dog, whose height at the withers is as long as its body, that is well proportioned, sound in gait and *true* to *type*.

When all the individual classes have been judged and the winners of each selected, the first-place contestants in each sex enter the ring for the judging of Winners Dog followed by Winners Bitch. The second best is designated Reserve Winners. Eligible for this competition is the entry that was second in the same class as the winners, that thus competes against the remaining winners of all the classes in each sex, for the Reserve titles.

The final breed competition then moves into the ring. It includes Winners Dog, Winners Bitch and those Champions in the breed, irrespective of sex, that have been entered as Specials. It is from this final array that Best of Breed is chosen, as well as Best of Opposite Sex to Best of Breed, and Best of Winners (competition between Winners Dog and Winners Bitch). Later, the Best of Breed will be called to enter the Working Group, which, in turn, is composed of the Best of Breed winners in the breeds found in this Group.

The final progression is the judging for Best in Show, which brings together the winners of the seven Groups: Sporting, Hound, Working, Terrier, Toy and Non-Sporting.

In closing, let me again emphasize five pertinent facts:

1. The judge is looking at *your dog*, not you—so don't be self-conscious.
2. The perfect dog has yet to be born! So the ultimate selection comes down to each judge's personal appraisal of the merits of the dogs under him on that day.
3. A win depends upon the competition present. A dog that wins one day may not win the next under another judge, or against different competition. Dogs vary in their actions from day to day. After all, we all have our good days and our bad—and so do our dogs. It always helps to have a dog that exudes personality and is animated in the ring. You can usually depend upon it to do its best at all times. Shyness, timidity and viciousness are always severely penalized and condemned.
4. Try to watch the techniques of the professional handlers. You can learn many valuable and helpful points by watching how they

Showing is not all fun and games! Wayne Boyd sloshes through the mud carrying Ch. Rivergrove's Run For The Roses HOF/HOF in an attempt to keep him clean for the judging. It worked! "TR" went on to become the top winning Great Pyrenees in the history of the breed. Owned by Jean Boyd and Judith Cooper.

Lucy Zorr

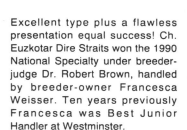

Excellent type plus a flawless presentation equal success! Ch. Euzkotar Dire Straits won the 1990 National Specialty under breeder-judge Dr. Robert Brown, handled by breeder-owner Francesca Weisser. Ten years previously Francesca was Best Junior Handler at Westminster.

present their dogs, for their expertise brings out the *best points* in any dog they handle. If they seem to win much of the time (and this is something the perennial "kicker" is apt to complain about), look again and you will see how well their dogs are "put down" (groomed), how well the dogs are moved and posed. These all help the judge to form an opinion of the dog.

5. And last, remember always that the dog you come out of the ring with is the one you took in. If you loved it then, love it now! Enjoy the show—it should not be a chore. Above all, *always be a good sport*—win, lose or draw. Congratulate your opponent and don't argue with the judge!

Ch. Euzkotar Devil May Care HOF, outstanding dam. Breeder-owner Francesca Weisser.

Ch. Rivergrove's Designer Genes HOF, outstanding dam. Breeder: Jean Boyd. Owner: Jean Boyd and Judith Cooper. *Gilbert*

17

Breeding the
Great Pyrenees

IT IS IMPORTANT to begin with a mental grasp of what it is you are trying to accomplish before deciding on specific breedings. The object of any breeding program is to preserve the essential qualities and physical characteristics of the breed. Put aside any thoughts of "doing your own thing" insofar as trying to improve on basic type and conformation. The French judge M. Douillard recently wrote in a French canine review, "It is both ignorant and presumptuous to try to improve the Pyrenean Mountain Dog. One only succeeds in making the dog ugly." To this we can only add a fervent "Amen!"

A thorough understanding of the breed Standard is a basic requirement for anyone planning to breed dogs. Beyond the Standard, however, there is an illusive something extra: a certain almost extrasensory perception that gives to those who have it a kind of success which others, perhaps more knowledgeable but less wise, never seem quite able to grasp.

A successful breeder is one who knows what he likes and is willing to stick by it. Knowledge of this sort does not come spontaneously. An eye for a good dog is something you can be born with, but an eye without a mind behind it is just an eye. You need to learn everything you can about the breed, and especially the bloodlines from which you plan to choose your stock. Visit as many kennels as you can, talk to the owners, see the tried-and-true producers, the retired dogs and the up-and-coming ones.

Attend dog shows and make mental notes on the different types you find in the ring. Read McDowell Lyon's *The Dog in Action*, the "bible" on balance and gait. Study pedigrees for at least three generations.

A successful breeder is one who sees the faults in his own dogs as readily as he sees those in his rival's. Perhaps that little "extra" is the good sense to breed with the *whole* dog in mind, and not to put emphasis on any one single attribute at the expense of the overall dog.

Keep these thoughts at the front: The Great Pyrenees is a large and powerful working dog, his *soundness* arising out of his correct proportions and well-knit morphology. *Type* is in the head. *Beauty* is a combination of type, coat and bearing. And most important, a *sound disposition* in a Pyrenees leads to a spirited, intelligent, self-confident, outgoing and dependable companion and protector.

Pedigrees are important because they are the means to study the bloodlines and learn the relationships between the various dogs. They are of greatest value when the dogs are known, or have actually been seen.

Champions do indicate merit and do give some indication of quality. However, they are not always completely informative as to the overall superiority of the individuals listed. Some championships are won through the accident of less than normal quality in the competition. And the opposite is also true—some dogs do not win their medals simply because of lack of exposure.

Count the championships, but also study the patterns of inheritance. Look for qualities which have endured from generation to generation. Familiarize yourself with the individual dogs. This will give you a sound perspective on the assets of the bloodlines in question.

In any plan for mating there must be a positive and systematic approach. Broadly speaking, any litter which has the same Great Pyrenees on each side of the pedigree is an *inbred* one. However, this term is usually applied only to those matings which are in the order of parent to offspring or brother to sister. Interbreeding among common dogs further removed is *linebreeding*.

When one breeds two dogs with a common ancestry, their litter inherits some of the same genes from each side of the pedigree. This allows for the statistical possibility that genes will "double up" at the same locus. The result is twofold: the expression of all traits is more uniform, but recessive genes may come to the surface, thereby giving rise to serious or lethal problems.

Linebreeding is the safest and best method to preserve type and conformation, provided that the foundation dogs are well chosen and one has the judgment and experience to pick the best puppies.

Inbreeding, on the other hand, requires a genetically clean stock, a knowledge of the faults and virtues of all the common dogs for at least three generations, and the willingness to cull ruthlessly when it becomes necessary.

Most breeders prefer to avoid frank inbreeding. Instead, they keep the overall relationship to common dogs rather high by using them several times farther back in the pedigree. After having linebred for three or four generations, most breeders have found from experience that it is wise to bring in new blood. The use of a stud from a totally different bloodline may be considered. This produces an *outcrossed* litter and "reshuffles" the genes that have tended to become fixed, in a more or less predictable manner, through previous linebreeding. Many times, particularly with an overly refined bitch, an outcross will give surprisingly good results. An improvement in the health and vigor of the resulting pups is apparent from the time they are born. The process is known as nicking. While the litter will sometimes lack uniformity, nevertheless some really good Pyrenees show dogs have been produced in this manner.

When two strains have nicked successfully, other crosses between them may work as well. Pups from such matings are usually bred back into one of the two strains, thereby providing a basis for a new line.

One final method is to breed a dog and a bitch who are both of mixed ancestry. Neither has a linebred background. When using this approach, it is essential that one have a definite goal in mind.

One dog may carry an attribute or quality totally lacking in the other. Or it may be a matter of breeding a good sound bitch to the best stud dog available. But if the mating is a "backyard" one, chosen only because the two dogs are readily at hand for breeding, then in most cases the pups will be no better than their parents.

TEMPERAMENT AND DISPOSITION

In striving to breed dogs of superior type, one simply cannot overlook the importance of character. When you consider that guarding is ingrained, it is somewhat remarkable that viciousness and aggression have never been a problem in our breed. In part, this is due to the fact that the breed has not achieved instant popularity. And in part because those who maintained the bloodlines of the past appear to have understood the supreme importance of using only dogs of sound disposition for breeding.

Aggression in dogs is not always due to inheritance. But at times a dog, like a person, may be born with an unstable personality. In a powerful guard dog, this would be a frank disaster. A Pyrenees, if it has once attacked and injured anyone, for whatever reason, would have to be classified as a potentially dangerous animal. You simply cannot adjust your life to live with a nervous, aggressive or unstable giant dog. In most cases the only acceptable solution would be to put the dog down.

The "soft" or shy dog is another serious behavioral problem which also shows a high rate of inheritance. A Pyrenees that panics at the approach of a stranger could be dangerous and should be kept under observation until some solution can be arranged. A shy dog is not de-

Ch. Karolaska Aleutia Neigerie HOF, outstanding dam. Breeder: Carol
Kentopp. Owner: Michael Patrick.   *Alverson*

Ch. Almac Mountain Mist CD HOF, outstanding dam. Breeder-owner
Kathleen McCue.   .

pendable and cannot be relied upon to overcome it under all circumstances.

Do not confuse fear with aloofness. Some Pyrenees retain a stand-offish attitude toward strangers, but do not display any sign of fear when approached. They are aloof but remain steadfast.

Close linebreeding is said to be responsible for causing high-strung, nervous and aggressive dogs. In point of fact, the statement is a false one, relying as it does on the unfounded assumption that just because two individuals are closely related their offspring are going to be shy or aggressive. Obviously, it is the genetic potential in the background of the pair which determines the outcome. A fundamentally sound strain remains fundamentally sound, and one which uses a mentally unstable dog as a pillar of its program is eventually going to produce nervous and aggressive animals.

Therefore the prime consideration, when breeding the Great Pyrenees—or any guarding breed for that matter—is to select only the most self-assured, intelligent and discriminating individuals to carry on the bloodline.

MARKINGS AND PIGMENTATION

The coloring matter found in the coat and skin of mammals is due to a pigment called melanin. Melanin, in the Great Pyrenees, acts to turn the skin black in those areas where pigmentation is required (eyelids, eyerims, lips, nose and palate), and to impart the necessary color to the coat patches as well. For a more detailed discussion of pigment inheritance, the reader is advised to consult Little's *Inheritance of Coat Color in Dogs*.

There is unquestionably a correlation, although a general one, between a well-marked blaireau Great Pyrenees and one which also carries black pigmentation. Therefore, the value of the blaireau dog is, in the mind of a breeder, further enhanced by his reputation for producing well-pigmented offspring.

When all-white dogs are mated to all-white bitches, there is a grave danger that pigmentation will break down. If this is carried for several generations, missing pigment is almost a certainty. In addition, one approaches the problem of albinism, including deafness and impaired vision. Accordingly, only the most knowledgeable breeder who is familiar with the markings and pigmentation of all the dogs on both sides of the pedigree for at least three generations will attempt to breed two pure-white Pyrenees.

Pedigrees, unfortunately, do not provide information on markings and pigmentation. But most breeders will be happy to provide this information. It is extremely useful.

Breeding an all-white to a blaireau is the safest and best method to use for the typical mating. About half the puppies will be blaireau and the others white. The marked pups will usually have even patches of color on the head, often a patch at the base of the tail and perhaps an occasional spot on the body.

Mating two blaireau dogs will often produce very strong pigmentation, but sometimes a number of color patches on the coat. Nevertheless, some beautifully marked puppies sometimes result from such matings.

The late Marjorie Butcher, addressing a dinner gathering in 1971, observed that in her experience it was the dog with asymmetrical markings, those with a half mask on the head and ear of one side only, which gave the first indication of pigment breakdown. "What I really preferred were those perfectly lovely puppies with badger markings—nice even ones which fade into just a light shading. This is what will give you the good pigmentation. So you don't have to look for the heavily marked dog."

When picking a stud dog, choosing a brood bitch or simply buying a puppy, go over the individual carefully for evidence of strong pigment. Rarely, you may find that heavy markings on the coat are still accompanied by weak pigment, or yellow eyes. So don't rely upon the fact that the dog is known to be blaireau. Look for yourself. A black palate is a better indication of genetically sound pigment than heavy coat markings. And some Pyrenees carry black nails, which is another prized finding. Finally, part the hair on the undersurface of the belly. If you find patches of dark skin, you have a well-pigmented dog.

Finally, in choosing your stud dog and brood bitch, never make the mistake of assuming that extra-strong pigment in one of your producers will automatically overcome poor pigment in the other. Too often it is the one with the poor pigment that dominates the litter.

THE BROOD BITCH

Before you decide to breed your Great Pyrenees bitch, give careful thought to the effort and expense that go into producing a litter of healthy and active puppies. It can be both time-consuming and expensive. A Pyrenees litter can seldom be sold locally. This means added cost in advertising and added work in finding the right sort of home in which to place them. In all, there is no profit to be made from breeding the Pyrenees.

Many people are inclined to believe that a Pyrenees bitch needs to have a litter to be psychologically fulfilled. This is another of those "old wives' tales." A spayed female makes an outstanding house pet!

There are certain special qualities to look for in a female that is likely to be a good breeding prospect. They are:

- *Type* is of paramount importance. The head and the true Pyrenean expression stamp this breed apart from all others. We cannot expect

238

a bitch with a poor head to whelp puppies that will be an asset to the breed.

- *Balance* and *Soundness*. Size and strength are also necessary, but in a bitch we should give greatest consideration to correct proportions. Overrefinement must be avoided, but most breeders agree that a very feminine bitch makes the best brood matron.
- A bitch must have *character*. The calm, intelligent self-assurance that is part and parcel of the breed. A nervous, harebrained or otherwise unreliable female can easily pass these undesirable traits on to her offspring.
- Look for *the imperfections*. No bitch is perfect and even the best have some imperfection, however slight. Whatever the fault may be, remember the cardinal dictum: NEVER BREED A FAULT TO A FAULT. Specifically, if your bitch has long, flat feet and after examining on the spot all the possible choices for a stud dog you choose, in the end, a dog that also has flat feet, the chances are that you will produce a litter of long, flat-footed puppies.

Most breeders prefer to wait until the second or third season before breeding a bitch, at which time she is emotionally mature and well able to adjust to the role of a brood matron. But one should not wait until the bitch is three or four years old before mating her for the first time. Her pelvic ligaments are no longer elastic and this could give her trouble whelping.

It goes without saying that a prospective brood matron should be kept in top physical condition. An overweight bitch, lacking in exercise tolerance, is difficult to mate and many times will not come into season regularly.

Her physical checkup should be as complete as possible and should include a test for heartworms. A maiden bitch should be examined by the vet to be sure that her vaginal orifice is of normal size. There should be no constricting ring which would prevent normal entry. A heavy membrane, or hymen, is common in our breed. This can be removed by simple surgery well in advance of breeding—not during the heat season when you plan to mate her.

Due to the increase in the incidence of brucellosis in dogs in the United States, a serum agglutination test should always be done on both the bitch and stud dog before mating. This test is now available in veterinarian clinics and can be run from a blood sample in a few minutes.

Absence of clinical symptoms is no guarantee that the animal does not harbor a subclinical infection. Once the disease is contracted, it quickly passes by oral or genital contact throughout an entire kennel. There is no satisfactory cure and all infected animals must be eliminated. The stud's owner should therefore request a vet's certificate showing that the visiting bitch has been tested for and found free of brucellosis.

Chronic vaginal or uterine infection is a common problem in the Great Pyrenees, as it is in many of the large breeds. During estrus, the vulva of a Pyrenees female becomes quite enlarged. At the same time, the protective plug of mucus is discharged from the cervix, opening the path for ascending bacterial infection. The result may well be a subclinical metritis. Unsuspected metritis may be the underlying problem when a bitch refuses to accept the male, is bred at the right time but fails to conceive, or delivers stillborn pups or pups which sicken and die during the first few days.

Because of this, many breeders routinely culture the vaginal secretions of every bitch early in the heat cycle. If the culture is positive, the vet will recommend a course of antibiotics.

Before you mate your Pyrenees bitch, have the vet x-ray her pelvis. This should be done after one year of age. If the x-ray indicates actual bone changes of hip dysplasia, *do not breed her*. By the same token, the bitch should be bred only to a stud with excellent hips. Certification by the O.F.A. or other highly reliable authority is most desirable.

Also prior to breeding, the bitch and the stud should be checked for worms. Roundworms are difficult to avoid in puppies, but their number can be greatly reduced by having the bitch wormed before breeding. Any other parasites, if found, should be vigorously treated.

A Great Pyrenees bitch is usually at her best as a brood matron from eighteen months to five or six years. Generally, she should not be bred more often than once a year. However, a strong bitch that has raised only two or three pups and that has lost no condition can safely be bred from on her next season.

In Pyreneans, it would appear that at about six or seven years of age the breeding capacity of bitches is in decline. The possibility of complications increases and one must be prepared to take the risks involved.

THE STUD DOG

If your bitch came from a breeding kennel, it is clearly a good idea to talk to your breeder before making a final decision on the right stud dog. Your breeder is thoroughly familiar with the strengths and weaknesses which lie behind your bitch. This knowledge can be vitally important in choosing a compatible stud.

Some breeding kennels also offer stud service. If you have an outstanding bitch from that bloodline, you might want to give serious thought to using a stud from that same strain to reinforce the best qualities in your bitch. If your breeder does not offer this service, he or she will be able to tell you where to find a suitable mate for your female.

The special qualities to look for in a Pyrenean male that is likely to be an outstanding stud prospect are:

Ch. Rivergrove's For Your Eyes Only HOF, outstanding sire.
Breeder-owner Jean Boyd and Judith Cooper. *Kernan*

New technology has opened the doors to possibilities unavailable to past generations of breeders: Ch. Ville Viuex Ingenue, the first champion from the breed's first litter produced using frozen semen. Her sire, Ch. Ville Vieux Gentil Ours Blanc, was deceased when the litter was bred. *Phoebe*

- *Overall size, bone, and a rugged constitution* tell us that the male is a sound and purposeful working dog. Being a Great Pyrenees, he must be a virile animal with an air of masculinity and a bold temperament. He should be well-knit without appearing too refined, and yet he should possess in good measure all the essential points required by the Standard. Moreover, he should be strong in the qualities lacking in the bitch.
- His *manner* should be open, assured and self-confident; his eyes bright, clear and expressive; his bearing alert and friendly. Should the male appear timid, you would be well-advised to look elsewhere. Overall, he should give the impression of being a dog you would want to own yourself, and one you would trust implicitly. An Obedience title would demonstrate a dog's willingness to accept and execute the wishes and commands of his master. A championship plus an Obedience degree is an added bonus. Beauty and brains are always a good combination.
- *His production record.* If a Pyrenean sire has had a career as a producer, his record becomes a matter of considerable importance. If he has sired the type of Pyrenees you like, particularly if several different bitches were used, you have strong evidence. The number of champions produced is not always as meaningful as you may think. There is usually a lapse of several years between a mating and a championship. The top Pyrenean producers are often recognized well after they have stopped producing. But their offspring may also retain their sire's prepotency.

The show record of a prospective stud dog may include a championship, multiple Breed wins, Group placings or even a Best in Show. Unfortunately, not all great show dogs are outstanding producers. By the same token, some of the top producers have not been particularly distinguished in the ring.

If you have to choose between production and wins, choose production.

Part of the breeding preparation is to see that the stud dog has been chosen well in advance. It is the responsibility of the breeder (who is the owner of the bitch) to come to a clear understanding with the owner of the stud dog concerning the breeding terms.

Usually a stud fee is paid in cash at the time of the mating. Often the stud's owner will agree to take, instead, "pick of the litter," which is a puppy of his own choosing. The age of the puppy should be agreed upon. If the bitch does not conceive, the stud's owner may offer a return service at no extra charge. But this is not obligatory in any way. Terms vary with the circumstances and the policies of the kennel. If these are in writing, there will be no misunderstandings at a later date.

A male offered at stud should at all times be kept in top physical condition with regular exercise, routine health checkups and a sound diet. Excess weight is a severe handicap to a stud dog. A fat dog is apathetic. He could even be so heavy as to lack the stamina to mount a bitch. A poorly kept or rundown dog is obviously unsatisfactory.

Before a Great Pyrenees is offered at stud to the public, a pelvic x-ray should be made and, if the results are less than perfect, the degree of imperfection should be taken into consideration before deciding whether to use him. If actual bone changes of hip dysplasia are diagnosed, he *should not*, in all good conscience, be offered at stud.

A Pyrenean male should ordinarily be used at stud for the first time at about one to two years of age. If an older dog is not a known producer, a sperm count, as well as a culture of the prostatic secretions (if the count is low), should be done. A chronic infection can severely depress sperm formation, or even render the dog sterile. This can often be improved with corrective measures.

A sound and healthy Great Pyrenees male remains fertile for at least eight or nine years. Many are able to sire litters throughout their entire life. This depends to some extent on how often the dog is used and how well he is cared for in his older age. In many cases, however, a Pyrenees older than nine years must be considered on the decline.

Breeding a Great Pyrenees does not make him aggressive, or inclined to fight other dogs. One drawback, however, to keeping a stud dog in the house is that his territorial "marking" instinct *may* become uninhibited. This could be a problem, especially if the dog were previously housebroken. If there are top stud dogs available, one might consider not owning a stud dog at all. The temptation is always there to use him, whether he suits your bitch's bloodlines or not.

Finally, we should not forget that years ago, in the Pyrenees Mountains, our dogs led a very different life. Their days, as well as nights, were filled with action, excitement and challenge. The terrain was rough and it toughened their muscles. Purpose and resolve built character. As working dogs, our Great Pyrenees used to get more exercise in a week than many, today, get in a month. Weaklings fell by the wayside. Only the strong and fit were left to perpetuate the race.

So in choosing the ideal stud dog or brood bitch to carry on the tradition, we should be concerned not only with bloodlines, pedigrees and show wins, but also with past history. And, even more importantly, with a vision of what lies ahead. Our litters will be, hopefully, of show quality. But they must also possess, to a marked degree, the strength and the vitality that will guarantee us future titans of the breed.

MATING

Once the foregoing considerations have been met—that is, the bitch is found worthy to be bred and the right stud dog has been chosen—the only barrier to a successful breeding is the mating itself.

This should provide a few difficulties given that both animals are healthy, keen and receptive. A mating will usually take place very quickly and conception will result.

Much has been written about the mating cycle in bitches. The important thing to remember is that a female, of any species, is unpredictable.

As a generality, estrus, the season of heat, lasts twenty-one days. The onset is signaled by a bloody discharge. The vulva begins to swell. By ten days it is two to three times normal size. When the color changes to straw or watermelon, the bitch is ovulating. This is usually seen from the tenth to the fourteenth day. This is the textbook time to breed.

After that, the discharge becomes creamy due to the presence of white cells. This signals the end of ovulation. The bitch will now refuse to stand for the male.

There are recorded instances of a Great Pyrenees bitch being bred as early as the fourth day and as late as the twenty-first day—and yet conceiving a litter! So practically speaking, a certain amount of trial and error is necessary. The best time to breed a female is any time she will accept the stud.

If the bitch flirts and plays coyly, if she switches her tail, "flags" and stands firm—these are all good signs that she is ovulating and ready to be bred.

An experienced stud will make his own investigations. Some have become so knowledgeable that they actually ignore the bitch until they "know" she is ready. Young ones, however, are inclined to act foolishly and cannot be relied upon at all.

When the bitch is due in season (six months after her last one) she should be watched carefully. As soon as she shows color, the owner of the stud dog should be notified. He will probably want the bitch at once. This has the advantage of letting her settle into the new routine after a nerve-wracking trip. And the owner of the stud is less likely to miss her ovulatory period.

Neither animal should be fed for several hours before the mating. Avoid the heat of day. In summer, bring both dogs into the house, or the kennel room, where it is relatively cool. Otherwise, the bitch should be taken to the enclosure of the dog as the male is often more confident and assertive in his own surroundings.

Keep the number of people to a minimum. The fewer the distractions, the better.

If the female has a heavy or matted coat, it is a good idea to trim the pants away to expose the vulva.

Both dogs are introduced to each other on leads. Once it is seen that the bitch is friendly and receptive, the dogs may be let off lead to romp for a short period. This must be kept to a minimum because it is taxing on the male and reduces his stamina.

A good Pyrenees stud seldom needs or welcomes assistance. Some prefer to have the bitch held; others do not.

If the mating does not proceed within a few minutes, i.e., either the stud is uninterested or the female flies at the male, it usually means that the bitch hasn't begun to ovulate. Separate the dogs and try again in forty-eight hours.

Specifically, *do not* insist that the male attempt to breed an unwilling bitch. This will almost never "put off" a vigorous male, but it does confuse and frighten the female, thereby making future attempts more difficult if not impossible.

A slightly nervous bitch, or one who would rather frolic than get down to the business at hand, may have to be held.

Infrequently one encounters the bitch that, despite all efforts to get her to breed willingly, becomes frantic and throws herself to the ground. This bitch has to be classified as totally unmanageable. If a bitch of sound disposition consistently refuses to receive a stud, it is a good idea to have her examined for hormonal imbalance, vaginal abnormalities and chronic metritis.

When the bitch is ready to be mated she will switch her tail and stand quietly for the dog while he mounts. As the male penetrates he begins to tread up and down rather than thrusting forward. The knot at the base of the penis swells and is clasped by the vulva. This produces the "tie." The dogs are joined and will remain so for ten to thirty minutes. During this time it is wise to have someone posted at the head of the bitch to steady her. If she attempts to jerk away, the male may be injured.

After the tie is accomplished, the male unclasps his forelegs and places both on the ground on the same side of the bitch. He may lift his hind leg over the back of the bitch, and the two dogs will stand back to back.

A court of law will accept "no tie" as proof of no impregnation. Laws are governed by practicality and not exceptions. In rare cases there can be a pregnancy without a tie. But only an actual pregnancy can prove this.

For practical purposes, a bitch will accept a male only during the period when she is fertile. One good tie is therefore usually sufficient. Some breeders, however, prefer to breed twice during the receptive period. This should be done with a forty-eight hour interval in between.

A mating between a tall dog and a short bitch can present a mechanical problem. The answer is to stand the male in a ditch (or breed on a slope), to equalize the difference.

Finally nervous or apprehensive owners will almost always communicate this to the dogs. A calm, collected approach is the best. If one of the dogs is a house pet, or if for any other reason the mating is difficult for the owners, the entire matter should be put in the hands of a capable vet.

18

Spinning The Pyrenees Hair

by Zatha Hockridge and

Constance Kousman

Zatha M. Hockridge and Constance B. Kousman are among the very few spinners who devoted themselves full-time to working with dog hair. These two ladies spun the hair of Afghans, Lhasa Apsos, Old English Sheepdogs, Newfoundlands, Huskies, Shelties, Irish Wolfhounds and many others. But they maintained that nothing could match the lovely white hair of the Great Pyrenees.

THE LUXURIOUS COAT of the Great Pyrenees has been for centuries a practical and economical source of extraordinarily warm, exceptionally beautiful clothing.

Proof against the severe climatic conditions of its mountainous home-land, the Great Pyrenees' long heavy coat provides an abundant supply of raw materials for the handspinner who recognizes its potential quality and elegance.

As Pyr combings include comparatively little of the long, straight, relatively coarse outercoat, it is the dense woolly undercoat, shed at regular intervals, upon which the spinner must primarily depend. Shorter and finer in texture, snow white or delicately shaded with lemon, gray or tan, these combings are softer and lovelier than many of the finest wools. The resulting products are lightweight with exceptional insulating properties and, in our opinion, unsurpassed for warmth.

FROM PYR HAIR TO KNITWEAR

When collecting Pyr hair for spinning, a few points kept in mind will prevent lost time and effort. Hair containing mats, burrs or skin flakes should be discarded. Also reject clippings and unusually short hair. A small quantity of tail hair mixed in while carding ordinarily is not objectionable. However, because of its coarseness, some people prefer to omit it if the yarn is to be used for a delicate garment.

Spinning involves three basic steps: (1) carding or arranging the fibers; (2) drawing out the fibers; (3) twisting the fibers. Sheep's wool, having rough, crimped fibers that tend to cling together, is most easily spun. Therefore, until proper techniques are learned, this should be the starting point for beginners. When the craft is mastered, the smoother fibers of Pyr hair become less difficult to control—and a joy to spin!

Combings from a relatively clean dog need not be washed before spinning—a saving in time and handleability. When excessive dirt makes prewashing necessary, it must be done by hand in very small quantities to prevent felting. It may also need teasing, or pulling apart, to separate the fibers before carding.

Thorough carding, which disentangles and arranges the fibers, is most important as it increases the ability to maintain a smooth continuous draw. When the hair is well brushed, it is rolled off the card in the shape of a hollow tube or curl called a rolag. The efficient spinner will make at least enough rolags to fill a bobbin to minimize interruptions.

Combings from short-haired breeds may be spun by mixing with the longer stable of wool. Pyr hair, however, is of sufficient length to be spun unadulterated into a strong yarn suitable for most projects.

Although yarn can be spun on the simple, primitive drop spindle, most handspinners today recognize the spinning wheel as the faster, more efficient method.

Whether spinning wool or Pyr hair, the fundamentals are essentially the same. As the rolag is fed into the orifice, the fibers are drawn out, twisted and wound onto the bobbin simultaneously. Speed, rhythm, co-ordination, tension and other variables determine the quality and nature of the yarn. Thickness or size is a matter of individual preference—depending upon how the yarn will be used.

Plying, or twisting together two or more single strands of yarn, is also done on the wheel, using a counterclockwise spin and a bobbin rack called a lazy kate. When spinning dog combings, a 2-ply yarn is most commonly used.

Skeining can be done on a simple "niddy noddy" or the more efficient "wrap wheel." In lieu of either, a board wrapped with paper to protect the yarn from any possible roughness may be used. After tying loosely in at least two places, the skein is ready to be washed in warm, gentle suds. We recommend Ivory or Lux, carefully handling one skein at a time to avoid tangles.

We always give each skein at least two sudsings and rinse until the water is clear. We then add a few drops of baby oil to the last rinse water to replace any natural oils lost.

After gently squeezing, the skein is blotted by rolling in bath towels. Then, supported by strips of soft cloth, it is hung on a clothesline or rack to dry. When thoroughly air-dried, the skein is wound into a ball. This should be done loosely to prevent stretching.

It should be mentioned that Pyr hair yarn can be dyed in the skein. However, we doubt that any color can surpass the beautiful natural shadings provided by the Great Pyrenees itself.

Now! This is the moment the spinner has been working patiently and diligently toward—the final adventure in the transformation from Pyr hair to sweaters, skirts, scarves, mittens, afghans, blankets or an infinite variety of projects which are limited only by the imagination and skill of the craftsman. Pyr hair yarn is strong, knits easily and can be raveled, becoming more fluffy as it is handled. Therefore, we recommend rather large knitting needles in order to best display its soft, natural beauty. As individual knitting and spinning techniques vary, it is better to plan on a little more yarn than the pattern calls for; and advisable that all yarn for a specific project be spun by the same person.

Garments made from Pyr hair are easily handwashed. Just follow the instructions given for yarn in the skein. Add four or five drops of oil to the last rinse water, blot, block and dry flat. When thoroughly dry, additional fluff can be gained by tossing it in the dryer for two or three minutes. With reasonable care, the garment should last for years—becoming softer and fluffier with each wash.

Spinning is an ancient art which has been revitalized by the current focus on crafts. For obvious reasons, wool has been emphasized, and this subject has been thoroughly covered in a number of good books.

Although yarn spun from dog combings can be used for knitting, crocheting, hooking, weaving and crewel work, it has received little attention. Yet viewed in proper perspective, its value should not be overlooked. From sentimental, economical and practical viewpoints, the rewards are many. And they are available to each and every Pyr owner.

Ch. Rivergrove's Run For The Roses HOF/HOF, the top winning Pyr in the breed's history. Outstanding sire and showdog. Breeder: Jean Boyd. Owner: Jean Boyd and Judith Cooper.

Lucy Zorr

19

The Great Pyrenees Club of America

THE GREAT PYRENEES CLUB of America was founded on December 2, 1934, as the result of the efforts of Mr. and Mrs. Francis V. Crane. The first President was Professor Will Monroe.

It was through Professor Monroe's untiring researches in the libraries of London and Paris that much of the historical background of our breed was originally uncovered. His is also the honor of having owned the first-born pup of the first litter of Great Pyrenees registered by the American Kennel Club: Basque of Basquaerie (Ch. Urdos de Soum-Blanchette).

From among the early members of the GPCA, only Paul Strang remains active. Mrs. Crane was its first secretary and held this post for nearly twenty years. Her death in 1982 was a great loss to the Pyrenees community. To the end she remained active in the affairs of the club.

The first Club Handbook was published in 1936 (200 copies). It was expanded and revised in 1941, and again in 1949. For many years, a copy of the latest edition was made available to new Club members. Today, the possession of any one of these books is a valuable addition to the library of any student of the Great Pyrenees.

The GPCA held its first Specialty Show in 1935 at the Morris and Essex Kennel Club. The Annual Meeting was held for many years in conjunction with the Westminster Kennel Club Show in New York. Later, it was held in conjunction with the annual GPCA National Specialty, which in the sixties was held at the Trenton Kennel Club show.

Ch. Shadowrun Chance HOF, showdog. Breeder-owner Dorothy Sisco. *Rich Bergman*

Ch. Tip 'N Chip's Pride d'Argeles HOF, showdog. Breeder: Judith Cooper and Nan Hall Hamilton. Owner: Linda Yelland, Judith Cooper and Nan Hall Hamilton. *Olson*

Ch. Pyrson's K'laska of Summerhill HOF/HOF, outstanding sire and showdog. Breeder: Joan Pearson and Carol Kentopp. Owner: Jan Brown.

Ch. Pyr Haven Tonto Indian Summer HOF, showdog. Breeder-owner Mary Lu Vandenavond. *Booth-Phoeb*

252

During the seventies, with the emerging importance of the breed across the country, the GPCA began a policy of moving the National Specialty and the Annual Meeting during successive years from the East Coast to the Midwest to California and then back to the East Coast. Later, four regions were outlined so that the succession became East Coast to Plains/Rockies/Southwest to Midwest to West Coast, and then back to the East Coast. In addition to the National Specialty, the GPCA sponsors several Regional Specialties throughout the year under the direction of regional clubs.

The current activities of the GPCA include the publication of a bi-monthly *Bulletin*, containing a Breeder's Directory and articles of interest to owners and fanciers. An important ongoing project is publication of *The Great Pyrenees Titleholders*. This is a pictorial and pedigree record of all Great Pyrenees to gain a championship or Obedience title in the year of publication. The *Titleholders* is being backdated to 1949, to coincide with the complete records of Mrs. Crane. Together, these will provide a record of every Pyrenees to ever win a championship in America.

The GPCA maintains numerous committees specializing in different aspects of the breed. For example, the Health Information Committee collects and disseminates information on the general health and hardiness of the Great Pyrenees and specific health problems present in the breed. The Livestock Guardian Dog Committee collects information on the Pyr as a working dog, and the best methods of raising and maintaining a working livestock guardian. The Service Dog Committee researches and honors Pyrs which have performed some outstanding service such as saving a life or serving as a therapy dog. The Rescue Committee works hard throughout the country to rescue abused and abandoned Pyrs and place them in loving homes.

The GPCA has adopted a Code of Ethics to which members are expected to adhere. This document concerns the proper treatment, breeding and selling of Great Pyrenees. Copies of this and many other informative pamphlets are available from the GPCA secretary.

In 1982 the GPCA instituted the Hall of Fame to honor great show dogs, Obedience dogs, sires and dams. To qualify as an outstanding sire, a dog must have sired at least ten champions over the course of his lifetime. Dams must have produced six champions. Obedience dogs must have attained a title beyond the CD. Outstanding show dogs must achieve a total of twenty-five points awarded as follows: ten points for BIS, five points for a Group First or BOB at a National Specialty, three points for a Group 2 or BOS at a National Specialty, two points for a Group 3 or BOB at a Regional Specialty, one point for a Group 4 or BOS at a Regional Specialty. The following pages illustrate a few of the over three hundred Pyrs currently honored in the Hall of Fame. Unfortunately photos were not available of them all.

Ch. VilleVieux Yankee Sunshine HOF, showdog. Breeder-owner: Anne and Alan Rappaport. *Booth*

Ch. VilleVieux Le Roi HOF, showdog. Breeder: Renate Craig. Owner: Anne Rappaport. *Olson*

AM/CAN Ch. Euzkotar Hell Or High Water HOF/HOF, outstanding sire and showdog. Breeder: Francesca Weisser. Owner: Francesca Weisser and Jean Cave
Carl

Ch. Rivergrove's Levi Genes HOF/HOF, outstanding sire and showdog. Breeder: Jean Boyd. Owner: Elli Pasicznyk and Jean Boyd.
Kernan

255

Membership in the GPCA is open to any interested fancier in good standing with the American Kennel Club.

The regional clubs active at the present time:

Region 1:
Pyrenean Fanciers of the Northeast
National Capitol Area Great Pyrenees Club
Penn-Dutch Great Pyrenees Club
Great Pyrenees Club of Greater Pittsburgh

Region 2:
Heart of Ohio Great Pyrenees Club
Great Pyrenees Club of Metro-Detroit
Great Pyrenees Club of Greater Chicago
Great Pyrenees Club of Metro-Milwaukee

Region 3:
Central Iowa Great Pyrenees Club
Mile Hi Great Pyrenees Club
Alamo Area Great Pyrenees Club
Grand Canyon State Great Pyrenees Club

Region 4:
Great Pyrenees Club of Puget Sound
Columbia Cascade Great Pyrenees Club
Great Pyrenees Club of California
Great Pyrenees Association of Southern California
Orange Coast Great Pyrenees Fanciers

Should the reader be interested in obtaining further information, the name and address of the current secretary of the GPCA or any of the regional clubs can be obtained from the American Kennel Club, 51 Madison Avenue, New York, NY 10010.

ISBN 0-87605-188-3

00188>

0 21898 02500 5